The Genetics of Mood Disorders

**The Johns Hopkins Series in
Contemporary Medicine and Public Health**

Consulting Editors:

Martin D. Abeloff, M.D.
Samuel H. Boyer IV, M.D.
Gareth M. Green, M.D.
Richard T. Johnson, M.D.
Paul R. McHugh, M.D.
Edmond A. Murphy, M.D.
Edyth H. Schoenrich, M.D., M.P.H.
Jerry L. Spivak, M.D.
Barbara H. Starfield, M.D., M.P.H.

Also of Interest in This Series:

*Family Management of Schizophrenia: A Study of Clinical, Social,
    Family, and Economic Benefits*, Ian R. H. Falloon, M.D., and
    others

Huntington's Disease: A Disorder of Families, Susan E. Folstein, M.D.

The Perspectives of Psychiatry, Paul R. McHugh, M.D., and Phillip R.
    Slavney, M.D.

Psychiatric Polarities: Methodology and Practice, Phillip R. Slavney,
    M.D., and Paul R. McHugh, M.D.

The Genetics of Mood Disorders

Ming T. Tsuang, M.D., Ph.D., D.Sc.

Professor of Psychiatry and Director of Psychiatric
Epidemiology, Harvard Schools of Medicine and Public
Health
Chief of Psychiatric Epidemiology and Genetics,
Harvard Department of Psychiatry, Massachusetts Mental
Health Center
Chief of Psychiatry, Brockton-West Roxbury VA Medical
Center

and

Stephen V. Faraone, Ph.D.

Assistant Professor, Harvard Department of Psychiatry,
Massachusetts Mental Health Center
Director of Family Studies, Section of Psychiatric
Epidemiology and Genetics, Brockton-West Roxbury VA
Medical Center

The Johns Hopkins University Press
Baltimore and London

The Johns Hopkins University Press
701 West 40th Street
Baltimore, Maryland 21211
The Johns Hopkins Press Ltd., London

The paper used in this publication meets the minimum requirements of American National Standard for Information Sciences—Permanence of Paper for Printed Library Materials, ANSI Z39.48-1984.

Figures 2.1 and 2.2 are from S. V. Faraone, M. J. Lyons, and M. T. Tsuang, "Sex differences in affective disorder: Genetic transmission," *Genetic Epidemiology* 4 (1987): 331–43. Reprinted courtesy of Alan R. Liss, Inc.

Figure 8.1 is from M. T. Tsuang, M. J. Lyons, and S. V. Faraone, "Problems of diagnoses in family studies," *Journal of Psychiatric Research* 21 (1987): 391–99. Reprinted courtesy of Pergamon Press.

Library of Congress Cataloging-in-Publication Data

Tsuang, Ming T., 1931–
    The genetics of mood disorders / Ming T. Tsuang, Stephen
V. Faraone.
      p.   cm.—(The Johns Hopkins series in contemporary medicine
and public health)
    Includes bibliographical references.
    ISBN 0-8018-3891-6 (alk. paper)
    1. Affective disorders—Genetic aspects.   I. Faraone, Stephen V.
II. Title.   III. Series.
    [DNLM: 1. Affective Disorders—genetics. WM 171 T882g]
RC537.T78   1990
616.85'27—dc20
DNLM/DLC
for Library of Congress   89-43485
                                                 CIP

Contents

Figures and Tables

Figures

Tables

The Genetics of Mood Disorders

Chapter One

Diagnostic and Methodological Issues

Progress in psychiatric genetics is often hampered by difficulties in clearly specifying the diagnoses of interest. The associated difficulties and disagreements produce a complex set of results not easily understood without reference to relevant nosologic issues. The mood disorders are no exception to this trend in psychiatric genetics. Despite decades of research, there is no universally agreed upon means of defining and classifying mood disorders. This chapter discusses the classification issues and diagnostic practices that form the foundation of genetic studies reviewed in later chapters.

CLASSIFICATION ISSUES

Disorders that are primarily characterized by disturbances in mood range from an extreme state of elation, known as mania, to a severe state of dysphoria, known as depression. In addition to a deviant mood state, these disorders are associated with a variety of signs and symptoms such as weight change, sleep disturbance, and suicidal ideation. The goal of nosologic research has been to isolate the homogeneous subtypes of mood disorder that correspond to different clusterings of these signs and symptoms. Ideally, such subtypes would be clearly delimited from other disorders based on laboratory, family, and follow-up studies (Robins and Guze, 1970). Although no single subtyping system unambiguously achieves these criteria, several nosologic distinctions have received substantial validational support. A comprehensive review of these distinctions is beyond the scope of this volume. The following discussion provides major landmarks of the nosologic map with representative supporting data.

Unipolar versus Bipolar Mood Disorders

Mood disorders are most commonly classified according to the type of mood disturbance experienced by the patient. Unipolar dis-

1

order is diagnosed when the patient experiences only depressive episodes. Diagnosis of bipolar disorder is warranted when the patient experiences both manic and depressive episodes. The bipolar group can be further subdivided into three categories based upon the severity of the manic episode: bipolar I patients have had at least one episode of mania, bipolar II patients have experienced manic symptoms but have never had enough of these to qualify for a manic diagnosis (Dunner et al., 1976), and bipolar III patients have experienced only depressive episodes but have a family history of mania (Depue and Monroe, 1978). Patients who have experienced only manic episodes are usually classified as having bipolar disorder. These "unipolar manic" patients are not frequently observed, and most go on to experience a depressive episode. Although there is some controversy about the diagnostic status of unipolar manic patients, the weight of the evidence suggests they should be classified with bipolar disorder. Abrams and Taylor (1974) compared 14 unipolar manic patients with 36 bipolar patients. The two groups did not differ on psychopathology, demographic characteristics, or response to treatment. Bipolar patients had a younger age of onset. Abrams and Taylor (1974) compared 29 unipolar manic patients who had had two or more manic attacks with 48 bipolar patients. The two groups were similar in terms of psychopathology, response to treatment, demographic variables, severity of illness, presence of abnormal EEG, history of substance abuse, childhood hyperactivity, and history of neurologic insult. Nurnberger et al. (1979) compared 39 unipolar manic patients with 203 bipolar patients. There were no group differences in sex, age, or age of onset. Bipolar patients were more likely to have had four or more episodes of mood disturbance per year and were more likely to have had a history of suicide attempts. Response to lithium treatment did not discriminate unipolar manic from bipolar patients.

Pfohl, Vasquez, and Nasarallah (1981) developed a mathematical model to test the hypothesis that the observation of unipolar mania can be accounted for by individuals who have not yet had a chance to experience a depressive episode. Their results indicate that the observed frequency of unipolar mania in four studies can be explained by assuming that such patients are really bipolar depressives who have not yet experienced a depressive episode. In contrast, the frequency of unipolar depression in these studies could not be explained by the hypothesis that unipolar depressives are actually bipolar depressives who have not yet experienced a manic episode. Although this mathematical analysis is not definitive, it is consistent with the empirical data indicating unipolar mania to be homogeneous with bipolar disorder.

The validity of the unipolar-bipolar distinction has been assessed by examining demographic variables, psychopathology, clinical course, response to medication, and biochemical variables. Bipolar patients tend to have an earlier age of onset than do unipolar patients (Winokur, Clayton, and Reich, 1969). Bipolar disorder is equally common among males and females, but unipolar disorder is approximately twice as prevalent among females in comparison to males (Robins et al., 1984). Depressive episodes of bipolar and unipolar patients manifest some consistent differences. Unipolar depression is associated with higher levels of psychomotor agitation in comparison to the increased psychomotor retardation observed in bipolar depressive patients (Beigel and Murphy, 1971; Bunney and Murphy, 1973; Kupfer et al., 1974). Unipolar patients are more likely to complain of somatic problems and to express anger than are bipolar patients (Ablon, Carlson, and Goodwin, 1974; Beigel and Murphy, 1971). Differences in sleep disturbances are particularly notable with bipolar depressive patients experiencing hypersomnia and unipolar depressives complaining of insomnia (Detre et al., 1972; Kupfer et al., 1972).

Studies of clinical course indicate that bipolar patients experience more episodes but these tend to be of shorter duration than those experienced by unipolar patients (Angst et al., 1973; Perris, 1982). Some studies indicate no prognostic differences between the two disorders (Abrams and Taylor, 1980); others find a greater likelihood of divorce, alcohol abuse, attempted suicide, completed suicide, and increased mortality among bipolar patients (Brody and Leff, 1971; Dunner, Gershon, and Goodwin, 1976; Perris, 1966; Reich, Davies, and Himmelhoch, 1974). However, Taylor and Abrams (1980b) reported no unipolar-bipolar differences in severity of illness at hospital admission, duration of hospital admission, and improvement of symptoms at discharge. Furthermore, in a 30-40 year follow-up of 100 bipolar and 225 unipolar patients, Tsuang, Woolson, and Fleming (1979) found no differences in outcome between the two groups on marital status, residential status, occupational status, and psychiatric status, suggesting similar prognosis for the two disorders.

Studies of pharmacologic response have not consistently supported the unipolar-bipolar distinction. Lithium carbonate, which has therapeutic and prophylactic effects in the treatment of mania, is also an effective treatment for depression. Although several studies indicate that bipolar depression responds better to lithium than does unipolar depression, the difference between the two subgroups is not great and the positive response rate for unipolar depression is substantial (Baron et al., 1975; Goodwin, Murphy, and Bunney, 1969; Goodwin et al., 1972; Mendels, 1976; Noyes et al., 1974). Furthermore, antidepressant medication has been shown to be effective in preventing depressive episodes for both bipolar and unipolar patients (Prien, Caffey, and Klett, 1974; Prien, Klett, and Caffey, 1973). Similarly, although some biochemical differences between unipolar and bipolar patients have been demonstrated, consistent differences that reliably discriminate the two disorders have not been reported (Taylor and Abrams, 1980b).

A failure to find consistent differences between unipolar and bipolar patients on all dimensions does not necessarily vitiate the hypothesis that the two disorders are unique. Robust differences between the two may be obscured by methodologic difficulties. Most important, unipolar samples may be contaminated by patients who are truly bipolar but have not yet had manic episodes. Furthermore, it is conceivable that two phenotypically similar disorders may be genotypically distinct. Likewise, observed similarities in pathophysiology may be due to distinct etiologic substrates.

Endogenous versus Reactive Depression

The most common subdivision of unipolar disorder distinguishes "endogenous" depressive episodes seemingly unrelated to environmental events from "reactive" depressions characterized by a chronic course of less severe, stress-related episodes. This dichotomy has also been referred to as the psychotic-neurotic distinction in depression.

The most consistent difference between the two subgroups has been found in their clinical phenomenology. A comprehensive review by Mendels and Cochrane (1968) indicated endogenous depression to be characterized by early morning waking, psychomotor retardation, severely depressed mood, feelings of guilt, remorse, and worthlessness, difficulty concentrating, loss of interest, and weight change. In contrast, reactive depressions were characterized by late-night insomnia, and feelings of self-pity and anxiety. Similar conclusions were drawn from a more recent review of factor-analytic, cluster-analytic, discriminant function, symptom-frequency, and treatment-response studies (Nelson and Charney, 1981). The symptoms most strongly associated with endogenous depression were psychomotor retardation, lack of reactivity to the environment, severe depressed mood, depressive delusions, self-reproach, and loss of interest. Symptoms more weakly associated with endogenous depression were decreased concentration, symptoms worse in the morning, early morning insomnia, midnight insomnia, weight loss, and suicidal attempts or thoughts. The ability of these signs and symptoms to discriminate between endogenous and nonendogenous depressions has been good. For example, Feinberg and Carroll (1982) used a discriminant function derived on a sample of endogenous and nonendogenous depressive patients to classify depressives in another sample. This cross-validation correctly classified 91 percent of the endogenous depressive patients and 88 percent of the nonendogenous depressives.

How patients respond to treatment has also been used to compare endogenous and reactive depressions. The most consistent finding is that, in comparison to nonendogenous depressive patients, endogenous depressives have a better response to tricyclic antidepressant medication and a worse response to psychotherapy (Liebowitz et al., 1984; Overall et al., 1966; Paykel, 1972; Prusoff et al., 1980). Endogenous depressive patients are more likely to receive electroconvulsive therapy and are more likely to benefit from such therapy (Copeland, 1983). Furthermore, sleep researchers have found that sleep deprivation is more likely to be therapeutic for endogenous depressives. This latter finding is consistent with reports of more pronounced sleep disturbances among the endogenous subgroup. Studies of rapid eye movement (REM) indicate that endogenous depressives have more REM per minute of REM sleep and that they enter REM sleep earlier in the sleep cycle (Gillin et al., 1984). Endogenous depressives are also more likely to manifest disinhibition of the hypothalamic-pituitary-adrenal axis as manifested by abnormalities in basal cortisol secretion, circadian rhythms of cortisol, and cortisol response to dexamethasone suppression (Brown and Shuey, 1980; Pepper and Krieger, 1984).

Primary versus Secondary Mood Disorders

Depressive syndromes are known to occur in the context of many other psychiatric conditions. For example, a postpsychotic depression is commonly seen among schizophrenic patients (McGlashan and Carpenter, 1976b; Steinberg, Green, and Durell, 1967). Patients with alcoholism, hysteria, and anxiety disorders have also been observed to manifest depressive syndromes (Guze, Woodruff, and Clayton, 1971). Depressive episodes preceded by another psychiatric condition were labeled secondary depression by Woodruff,

Murphy, and Herjanic (1967). Although secondary depressive patients did not differ from primary depressives in their clinical phenomenology, Woodruff, Murphy, and Herjanic suggested that the course and outcome of secondary cases would be determined by the nature of the concomitant disorder. Differences in course were observed by Brim et al. (1984), who found significantly greater symptom persistence among secondary depressive patients than among primary depressives. In another study, secondary depressive patients were more likely to have been divorced or separated, more likely to have dropped out of high school, and less likely to have held steady employment. They were also more likely to have engaged in suicidal thoughts or behavior and were more likely to have had drinking problems (Wood et al., 1977). Reveley and Reveley (1981) reported that secondary depressive patients had more prior suicide attempts and a lesser degree of recovery than did primary depressives. They attributed the poor recovery of secondary depressives to continued impairment from the primary disorder.

The primary-secondary distinction, although usually applied to depression, is also applicable to the classification of mania (Krauthammer and Klerman, 1978). This is especially true when the group of secondary affective disorders is extended to include depression and mania in the context of physical disease. Mania has been associated with viral infection, surgical procedures, cerebral tumors, multiple sclerosis, and head injuries (Jamieson and Wells, 1979; Krauthammer and Klerman, 1978). Cummings and Mendez (1984) reviewed 24 studies showing an association between mania and known neurologic disorders. They concluded that most of the focal lesions associated with secondary mania involved the diencephalic region of the brain and that the majority of lateralized lesions were on the right side of the brain.

Frequently, depression is due to the biological sequelae of physical disease. Kathol and Petty (1981) reviewed relevant research and concluded that the prevalence of depressive syndromes in medically ill patients was approximately 18 percent for the severely medically ill. Whitlock (1982) estimated that, among patients with severe depression, 20-30 percent of the cases can be attributed to physical conditions such as presenile dementia, infections, cerebral tumors, epilepsy, cancer, and immunologic diseases.

The distinction between primary and secondary mood disorders is useful for ensuring homogeneous samples in research protocols. This is especially true for mood disorders secondary to physical disease, since these are likely to be cases that mimic a genetic disorder without having the corresponding genes. The presence of such cases in a genetic study is likely to obscure the familial nature of a disorder. The etiology of mood disorders secondary to other psychiatric disorders is less clear. There is some debate on whether the co-occurrence of psychiatric disorders is a rule rather than an exception. Boyd et al. (1984) concluded from an epidemiologic study of more than 11,000 people that the presence of any psychiatric disorder increases the odds of having other disorders. For example, someone experiencing a major depressive episode has about 19 times the odds of having panic disorder of someone who is not experiencing such an episode. Other disorders found to co-occur with major depression were agoraphobia, simple phobia, obsessive compulsive disorder, schizophrenia, somatization disorder, antisocial personality, and substance abuse or dependence. The causes of psychiatric comorbidity remain to be elucidated. Genetic studies are useful in this regard to determine whether common genetic factors can account for this phenomenon.

Psychotic versus Nonpsychotic Depression

Depressed patients can be categorized according to the presence or absence of delusions or hallucinations indicative of psychosis. Several studies suggest that psychotic depressive patients have a more severe clinical presentation (Abrams and Taylor, 1983; Coryell, Tsuang, and McDaniel, 1982; Glassman, Kantor, and Shostak, 1975; Glassman and Roose, 1981; Nelson, Khan, and Orr, 1984). They tend to have a poorer prognosis (Coryell, Tsuang, and McDaniel, 1982) and are differentiated by drug response. Although there are some conflicting data (Howarth and Grace, 1985), most studies suggest that nonpsychotic depressive patients do better on tricyclic antidepressants (Davidson et al., 1977; Glassman, Kantor, and Shostak, 1975; Glassman et al., 1977; Quitkin, Rifkin, and Klein, 1978), whereas psychotic depressive patients have a better therapeutic response when tricyclics are combined with neuroleptics (Charney and Nelson, 1981; Nelson and Bowers, 1978). There is also some suggestion that electroconvulsive therapy in combination with tricyclics may be more appropriate for psychotic depressives (Perry et al., 1982).

Biological differences between the two groups have been reported by a variety of investigators. Neurochemical differences related to catecholamine metabolism have been reported by Sweeney et al. (1978). They found decreased 3-methoxy, 4-hydroxyphenylglycol (MHPG) and increased homovanillic acid (HVA) among psychotic depressive patients but not among nonpsychotic depressive patients. Decreased levels of dopamine-beta-hydroxylase (DBH) associated with delusions among depressives have also been reported (Meltzer, Cho, and Carroll, 1976). These results are all consistent with the hypothesis of excessive dopaminergic activity in psychotic depression. Neuroendocrine studies have reported a higher frequency of overreactivity of the hypothalamic-pituitary-adrenal axis as indicated by increased dexamethasone nonsuppression among psychotic depressive patients (Carroll et al., 1980). Although the effect is not easily replicated (Nelson, Khan, and Orr, 1984), a tabulation of eight studies, each comparing at least 10 psychotically depressed patients with nonpsychotic depressed patients, indicates a consistent trend toward higher rates of nonsuppression among the former group (Coryell, Pfohl, and Zimmerman, 1984).

A possible link between bipolar disorder and psychotic depression is suggested by the work of Strober and Carlson (1982). They found that bipolar patients were more likely to appear psychotically depressed at outcome than were unipolar depressed patients. Coryell, Pfohl, and Zimmerman (1984) found that psychotic depressives were more likely to have bipolar disorder than were nonpsychotic depressives. Lithium, a common treatment for bipolar disorders, has also been shown to have therapeutic effects for psychotic depression (Price, Conwell, and Nelson, 1983). Thus, although there are replicable differences between psychotic and nonpsychotic depressives, the exact nosologic status of the distinction is unclear. The presence of psychosis may indicate a more severe unipolar depressive condition or an alternative manifestation of bipolar disorder. In addition, a relationship between schizophrenia and psychotic depression is suggested by a five-year blind follow-up study reporting a schizophrenic outcome in 12 percent of psychotic unipolar depressives as compared with only 1 percent of nonpsychotic unipolar depressives (Coryell, Tsuang, and McDaniel, 1982). Thus, the relationship between psychotic depression and other disorders remains ambiguous and is likely to be clarified by genetic studies.

Schizoaffective Disorder

Current nosologic thinking in psychiatry separates mood disorders from schizophrenia, a heterogeneous condition characterized by hallucinations, delusions, disordered thinking, and poor social adjustment. Nevertheless, a substantial number of psychotic patients do not fit neatly into either category. These patients are called schizoaffective because they experience the perceptual and cognitive abnormalities of the schizophrenic patient along with disorders of mood and associated characteristics of mood disorders. The noso-logic status of such patients is currently controversial (Levitt and Tsuang, 1988). Are they exhibiting a variant form of schizophrenia or of mood disorder? Are such cases a distinct diagnostic entity or do they indicate the presence of a continuum of psychosis? Although a great deal of research has been devoted to this topic, these questions have not yet been fully answered (Marneros and Tsuang, 1986). Nevertheless, the literature has produced some consistent results that provide useful guidance to the interpretation of genetic studies.

There is general agreement that the clinical picture of the schizoaffective patient is a mixture of schizophrenic and mood-disordered symptomatology. This was impressively demonstrated by the International Pilot Study of Schizophrenia (IPSS) (World Health Organization, 1973). The researchers of the IPSS (World Health Organization, 1973) used cluster analysis to examine symptom scores on 32 dimensions of psychopathology from 177 patients with mood disorder, 107 schizoaffectives, and 704 schizophrenics. The results indicated that there was not a complete correspondence between diagnosis and cluster membership. However, patients from particular diagnostic groups tended to fall within certain clusters. Nevertheless, the empirical clusters manifested substantial within-cluster variability. For example, 24 percent of the manics in the sample clustered together with 35 percent of the schizophrenics. Most of the remaining schizophrenics were spread more or less evenly among seven of the remaining nine clusters, with between 5 and 13 percent of the entire group within each cluster. There was no predominantly schizoaffective cluster; 22 percent of the schizoaffective patients clustered together with 35 percent of the schizophrenics, while 23 percent clustered together with 23 percent of the depressed groups. The clustering results of Everitt, Gourlay, and Kendall (1971) are consistent with the IPSS results but they found a more clear-cut manic cluster that in one sample contained 79 percent of all manics, 33 percent of all schizoaffectives, and only 1 percent of all schizophrenics. A cluster labeled paranoid schizophrenia was similarly homogeneous, but the clusters for chronic schizophrenia and psychotic depression were less well defined. They also found that no predominantly schizoaffective cluster emerged.

A discriminant analysis was performed by the International Follow-up Study of Schizophrenia (IFSS) (World Health Organization, 1979) to discriminate schizophrenics from depressives and schizophrenics from manics on the basis of 129 symptoms. In this analysis the schizoaffective patients were included in the schizophrenic sample. Both distributions were bimodal, supporting the contention that schizophrenia and affective disorder are discontinuous entities. A separate schizoaffective mode did not emerge. Kendall and Gourlay (1970) reported conflicting results. Their study used discriminant analysis to discriminate 146 schizophrenics from 146 cases of affective disorder on the basis of 38 items. Their solution achieved a misclassification rate of only 9 percent but the distribution along the discriminating dimension was trimodal. However, this study is confounded because 25 of the discriminating variables were dichotomous (see Hope, 1969, for details) and their groups were more heterogeneous than those in the IPSS study (e.g., their schizophrenic group included cases of paranoia and involutional paraphrenia and their mood-disordered group included cases of involutional melancholia and unspecified psychotic mood disorders). This latter criticism is supported by their report that the patients falling in the middle of the distribution formed a heterogeneous group having fewer symptoms typical of both schizophrenia and mood disorder. When Brockington et al. (1979) applied discriminant analysis to the Kendall and Gourlay sample after a 6.5-year follow-up, they produced a bimodal distribution. The misclassification rate was 4 percent; the probability that the distribution as a whole was unimodal was 0.003. Overall, the weight of evidence and argument appears to favor the finding of bimodality, suggesting that schizoaffectives do not form a bridge linking a psychopathological continuum including schizophrenic and mood disorders.

A comparison of the courses of schizophrenia, mood disorders, and schizoaffective disorder was made by the IFSS (World Health Organization, 1979). An examination of the length of the psychotic episode that brought patients to the attention of the project indicated no marked difference between diagnostic groups. However, there was a trend in the data indicating that the average episode length was greatest for schizophrenia, least for mood disorders, and in between for schizoaffective disorder. A similar ordering was obtained from the percentage of the two-year follow-up period spent in psychotic episodes and for the pattern of course. The data on schizoaffective disorder for each of these measures did not diverge greatly from the data on either the schizophrenic or mood disorder, suggesting that schizoaffective disorder is related to the two major psychoses and is found throughout the entire range of course severity.

A stronger conclusion was reached in the follow-up study conducted by Welner et al. (1977). They examined a group of 204 schizoaffective patients and were able to obtain follow-up information on 114 of them after an average of six years had elapsed. Ten percent of this latter group had an episodic course, 19 percent had an undetermined course, and 71 percent had a chronic course. On the basis of the large number of chronic cases they concluded that schizoaffective disorder was a form of schizophrenia. The three-year follow-up study of Clark and Mallet (1963) is consistent with the World Health Organization data (World Health Organization, 1979). They found that the severity of the course for schizoaffectives was, on the average, less severe than that of the schizophrenics but more severe than that of their depressed patients.

A course variable that clarifies the longitudinal relationship between schizophrenia and mood disorders is the type of subsequent episode a patient is likely to experience. The results of the IFSS pertaining only to patients who had another psychotic episode indicate that while only 3 percent of the manics and none of the depressives had a definitely schizophrenic episode, 16 percent of the schizophrenics had a subsequent mood disorder episode. In addition, 13 percent of the manics and 7 percent of the depressives had probable schizophrenic episodes. Nunn's (1979) study, which found 29 percent of bipolar patients to experience one or more schizophrenic episodes, is consistent with these findings. Sheldrick et al. (1977) presented some thought-provoking data consistent with the above patterns of results. They presented the 30-year course history of 12 patients who had had a history of short schizophrenic episodes requiring brief durations of hospital treatment. In most cases, the recorded prognoses of these patients were poor. The 30-year course of each patient in terms of type of episode indicated that after each patient had had an episode of mood disorder he or she ceased having schizophrenic episodes. A related phenomenon is the postpsychotic depressive syndrome, which is defined as the occurrence of depressive symptomatology in the wake of a psychotic episode (McGlashan and Carpenter, 1976b; Roth, 1970; Steinberg, Green, and Durrell, 1967; Stern, Pillsbury, and Sonnenberg, 1976). Estimates of the frequency of this syndrome in remitted schizophrenics range from 25 percent (McGlashan and Carpenter, 1976b) to 50 percent (Bowers and Astrachan, 1967).

Outcome studies have found that the outcome of schizoaffective disorder is more benign than that of schizophrenia but less benign than that of mood disorders. For example, Clark and Mallet (1963) reported that after a three-year follow-up, 11, 18, and 34 percent of schizophrenics, schizoaffectives, and depressed patients, respectively, were symptom free. Similar results were reported by Tsuang, Dempsey, and Rauscher (1976), who found that 8, 44, and 58 percent of schizophrenics, atypical schizophrenics, and patients with primary mood disorders, respectively, had recovered from their illness at follow-up. Their definition of atypical schizophrenia overlaps to a large degree with the definition of schizoaffective disorder. In accord with the above pattern of results is the study of Tsuang et al. (1977) that reported that 46.2 percent of 52 schizoaffectives, 7.7 percent of 183 schizophrenics, and 52.8 percent of 289 mood disordered patients recovered from their illnesses.

In one report (Carpenter and Stephens, 1979) the Elgin prognostic scores of schizoaffective and schizophrenic patients were 36.5 and 45.5, respectively. This paper also reported that of 36 schizoaffectives at follow-up, 42 percent were recovered, 50 percent were impaired, and 8 percent unimproved. The corresponding figures for schizophrenics were 21, 49, and 30. These results are consistent with those of Harrow et al. (1978), who found that schizoaffectives and acute schizophrenics tend to have better outcomes than do chronic and paranoid schizophrenics. Furthermore, Clayton, Rodin, and Winokur's (1968) one- to two-year follow-up of 33 schizoaffective patients found that 61 percent were well, 29 percent were ill but not schizophrenic, and 15 percent were schizophrenic. They concluded that schizophrenic deterioration is not the usual outcome of a schizoaffective disorder.

The IFSS two-year follow-up placed each patient in one of five outcome groups on the basis of clearly defined criteria. The pattern of results at extreme outcomes was consistent with the ubiquitous finding that, relative to mood and schizophrenic disorders, the outcome of schizoaffective disorder is of intermediate severity. Although schizoaffective patients were found at all levels of outcome, they were more likely to have had a relatively good outcome than a poor one. Taken together, these studies of outcome lead to conclusions that parallel those drawn from the examination of course. The schizoaffectives have an outcome that is intermediate to the patterns of outcome seen in schizophrenia and mood disorders. Schizoaffectives are found throughout the entire range of outcome severity but are more likely to have relatively favorable outcomes.

If schizoaffective disorder did not respond to those treatments that are effective in treating schizophrenia and affective disorders, a strong argument could be made for considering it to be an independent disorder. However, this is not the case. The effectiveness of electroconvulsive therapy (ECT) and antidepressants was examined by Winokur (1978). He reported that ECT resulted in marked improvement for 51 percent of unipolar depressions, 42 percent of bipolar depressions, and 45 percent of schizoaffective depressions. The respective figures for control groups receiving no treatment were 25, 20, and 17 percent. The improvement rates for antidepressants

(22, 20, and 17 percent, respectively) were all close to the no-treatment baseline.

The most researched treatment for schizoaffectives has been lithium carbonate. Procci's (1976) review distilled the following figures. The combined results of 22 studies were that 87 percent of 149 manic patients and 77 percent of 94 schizoaffective patients manifest improvement with the administration of lithium. Studies following Procci's review supported his conclusion that lithium is effective in treating schizoaffective disorder (e.g., Reiser and Brock, 1976) but also demonstrated that the drug may be an effective treatment for uncomplicated schizophrenia. For example, Small et al.'s (1975) double-blind, placebo-alternation study found that six of 15 Washington University–defined schizophrenics and four of seven schizoaffective patients responded positively enough to lithium to be continued on the drug after the experiment was completed. Growe et al. (1979) found similar results when they studied four schizophrenics and two schizoaffectives. Lithium reduced psychotic excitement and retardation in all of their patients but had no effects on behavior that they considered to be specifically symptomatic of schizophrenia, such as paranoid and psychotic disorganization.

Taken as a whole, relevant research strongly supports the claim that schizoaffective disorder is related to both schizophrenia and mood disorders. This conclusion is motivated by the converging support of the following empirical generalizations. (1) Schizoaffective symptomatology is a mix of mood and schizophrenic disorder symptoms. (2) The schizoaffective pattern of course does not differ greatly from those of schizophrenic and mood disorders. (3) On average, the outcome of schizoaffective disorder is intermediate in severity relative to the other psychoses. (4) The treatment regime for schizoaffective disorder consists of treatments used for schizophrenic and mood disorders.

CURRENT NOMENCLATURE

Three diagnostic systems are frequently used in psychiatric research: the Washington University (WU) Criteria (Feighner et al., 1972), the Research Diagnostic Criteria (RDC) (Spitzer, Endicott, and Robins, 1977), and the third edition of the *Diagnostic and Statistical Manual, Revised (DSM III-R)* (American Psychiatric Association, 1987). These diagnostic systems share a structured approach to classification; diagnoses are based on observable signs and symptoms, not theoretical considerations about etiology or pathophysiology. The introduction of structured diagnosis to the field of psy-

Table 1.1.   Washington University Diagnostic Criteria

Primary Mania	Primary Depression
Must have A, B, and C:	Must have A, B, and C:

A. Both of the following:
  1. Euphoria or irritability
  2. A psychiatric disorder lasting at least two weeks
	A. Both of the following:
	  1. Dysphoric mood
	  2. A psychiatric disorder lasting at least one month

B. At least three of the following:
  1. Hyperactivity
  2. Push of speech
  3. Flight of ideas
  4. Grandiosity
  5. Decreased sleep
  6. Distractability
	B. At least five of the following:
	  1. Poor appetite or weight loss
	  2. Insomnia or hypersomnia
	  3. Loss of energy
	  4. Agitation or retardation
	  5. Loss of interest in usual activities or decrease in sex drive
	  6. Feelings of self-reproach or guilt
	  7. Complaints of or actually diminished ability to think or concentrate
	  8. Recurrent thoughts of death or suicide

C. None of the following:
  1. Preexisting psychiatric condition
  2. Massive or peculiar alteration of perception and thinking as a major manifestation
	C. None of the following:
	  1. Preexisting psychiatric condition
	  2. Massive or peculiar alteration of perception and thinking as a major manifestation
	  3. Life-threatening or incapacitating medical illness preceding and paralleling the depression

Source: Feighner et al., 1972; Tsuang and Bray, 1975.

chiatry has increased the reliability of diagnosis and enhanced the comparability of samples across research studies.

The WU system includes three mood disorder diagnoses: primary mania, primary depression, and secondary depression. The criteria for mania (see table 1.1) require a period of euphoria or irritability in the context of a psychiatric disorder lasting at least two weeks. In addition, the patient must exhibit at least three of six manic symptoms and may be excluded from the diagnosis by evidence of preexisting psychiatric conditions or a prominence of schizophrenic-like psychotic symptoms. The criteria for primary depression (see table 1.1) require an episode of dysphoric mood in the context of a psychiatric disorder lasting at least one month. Five of eight depressive symptoms must be present and, in addition to the manic exclusion criteria, the diagnosis is excluded if the depressive syndrome is preceded by a serious medical illness. The WU diagnosis of secondary depression selects patients with preexisting nonmood psychiatric disorder or serious medical illness who meet the nonexclusionary criteria for primary depression. The WU system provides no criteria for mild mood disorders or mood-related personality disorders.

The RDC criteria cover a wider spectrum of mood disorders than do the WU criteria. These are manic disorder, major depressive disorder, bipolar I disorder, bipolar II disorder, hypomanic disorder, minor depressive disorder, intermittent depressive disorder, and cyclothymic personality. RDC criteria for mania (see table 1.2) are very similar to WU criteria except for four notable differences. RDC requires only one week (instead of two weeks) of symptoms and includes poor judgment as a manic symptom. The severity of disturbance required (criterion C) in RDC is not required by WU criteria, and the former does not exclude patients with preexisting psychiatric disorders other than schizophrenia.

The RDC diagnosis of major depressive disorder (table 1.2) is similarly different from WU primary depression. RDC requires only two weeks (instead of one month) of symptoms and includes a severity of disturbance requirement (criterion D). Unlike the WU system, RDC does not exclude patients with preexisting psychiatric disturbances other than schizophrenia. Criteria for 10 subtypes of major depressive disorder are provided by RDC. Primary major depressive disorder is diagnosed if the disorder was not preceded by schizophrenia, schizoaffective disorder, panic disorder, phobic disorder, obsessive compulsive disorder, Briquet's disorder (somatization disorder), antisocial personality, alcoholism, drug use disorder, or preferential homosexuality. Secondary major depressive disorder is diagnosed if the depressive syndrome was preceded by any of these disorders. Recurrent unipolar major depressive disorder requires two or more episodes of major depressive disorder and no previous episodes of manic disorder or hypomanic disorder. Psychotic major depressive disorder is diagnosed if delusions or hallucinations are present and the patient does not meet the criteria for schizophrenia or schizoaffective disorder. A diagnosis of incapacitating major depressive disorder is made if the patient is unable to carry out any relatively complex goal-directed activity, such as work, taking care of the house, or sustaining attention and participation in social or recreational activities. Endogenous major depressive dis-

Table 1.2.   Research Diagnostic Criteria

Manic Disorder	Major Depressive Disorder
Must have A through E:	Must have A through F:
A. One or more periods of persistent elevated, expansive, or irritable mood not due to substance use	A. One or more periods of persistent dysphoric/irritable mood or pervasive loss of interest or pleasure
B. At least three of the following if mood is elevated or expansive, at least four if only irritable:	B. At least five of the following:
1. More active than usual	1. Poor appetite/weight loss or increased appetite/weight gain
2. More talkative than usual	2. Insomnia or hypersomnia
3. Flight of ideas or racing thoughts	3. Loss of energy
4. Grandiosity	4. Psychomotor agitation or retardation
5. Decreased need for sleep	5. Loss of interest or pleasure in usual activities
6. Distractibility	6. Feelings of self-reproach or inappropriate guilt
7. Poor judgment (e.g., buying sprees, foolish investments)	7. Diminished ability to think or concentrate
	8. Recurrent thoughts of death or suicide

C. At least one of the following:
  1. Meaningful conversation is possible
  2. Serious social or occupational impairment
  3. Hospitalization
	C. Duration of dysphoric features at least one week

D. Duration of manic features at least one week (or any duration if hospitalized)	D. Sought or was referred for help, took medication, or had impaired functioning
E. No psychotic symptoms suggestive of schizophrenia	E. No psychotic symptoms suggestive of schizophrenia
	F. Does not meet criteria for schizophrenia, residual subtype

order is diagnosed if the patient exhibits six of 10 possible endogenous symptoms (e.g., lack of reactivity to environmental changes, worse in the morning, weight loss). Agitated major depressive disorder is diagnosed if two of the following are present for several days during the depressive episode: pacing, handwringing, inability to sit still, pulling on or rubbing hair, skin, clothing, or other objects, outbursts of complaining or shouting, and excessive talking. If two of the following symptoms are present, retarded major depressive disorder is diagnosed: slowed speech, increased pauses before answering, low or monotonous speech, mute or markedly decreased speech, and slowed body movements. Situational major depressive episode is diagnosed if the depressive episode follows an event or situation that appears to have been a likely contributor to the episode. Simple major depressive disorder is diagnosed when the patient has shown no signs of psychiatric disturbance in the year before the depressive episode excluding depressive or manic symptoms.

The remaining RDC mood disorder diagnoses deal with combinations of manic and depressive symptoms, schizoaffective disorders, and syndromes of lesser severity. Bipolar I disorder requires a history of manic disorder and major depressive disorder, minor depressive disorder, or intermittent depressive disorder. Bipolar II disorder requires a history positive for both hypomanic disorder and major, minor, or intermittent depressive disorder. Hypomanic disorder is a mild version of manic disorder, having similar criteria except that only two manic symptoms under criterion B (table 1.2) are required (three if mood is only irritable) and the duration of the mood disturbance is only two days. Minor depressive disorder is similar to major depressive disorder, but requires the presence of only two depressive symptoms from a larger symptom list including relatively mild experiences such as pessimistic attitude and self-pity. Minor depression does not require impairment in functioning or referral for psychiatric services. Intermittent depressive disorder is diagnosed when there are no clear-cut episodes of a sustained depressive mood but the patient has been bothered periodically by depressed mood for at least two years. The category of cyclothymic personality is reserved for patients who experience recurrent periods of depression lasting at least several days alternating with periods of notably good mood characterized by at least two of the symptoms seen in hypomanic disorder. The periods of mood change must have been present since the early twenties and must be too numerous to count (i.e., the patient is rarely in a normal mood).

The *DSM III-R* criteria for mood disorders are used both in clinical practice and in research settings. These official diagnostic criteria of the American Psychiatric Association have their historical roots in the WU and RDC systems. The *DSM III-R* criteria for a manic episode are essentially identical to those for RDC manic disorder, with the exception that RDC criterion D is excluded. The *DSM III-R* and RDC criteria for major depression are also nearly identical, the only difference being that *DSM III-R* excludes RDC criterion D. Like RDC, *DSM III-R* includes diagnoses for subtypes of mania and depression. Each of these disorders can be subtyped as occurring with or without psychotic features. If psychotic features are evident, they can be subtyped as either mood congruent or incongruent. Mood-congruent psychotic features are consistent with the patient's mood. Examples include a manic patient who believes he is the most powerful being in the universe and a depressed patient who hears voices telling her she is worthless and should commit suicide. The major mood disorders are subclassified as having a seasonal pattern if the following four criteria are present: (1) the onset of an episode regularly occurs within the same 60-day period of the year, (2) full remission also occurs regularly within a specific 60-day period, (3) three episodes of mood disturbance in three separate years have displayed the seasonal pattern (two of these years must be consecutive), and (4) seasonal mood episodes are at least three time more likely than are nonseasonal episodes. An example of a seasonal pattern is a patient who usually becomes depressed between mid-October and mid-December but recovers during the following March or April.

Major depressive episode is subclassified as occurring with or without melancholia. The melancholic subdiagnosis is very similar to what has been termed endogenous depression in RDC and elsewhere. The melancholic subdiagnosis requires five of the following: loss of pleasure in all or almost all activities, a lack of reactivity to usually pleasurable stimuli, depression worse in the morning, early morning awakening, marked psychomotor retardation or agitation, significant anorexia or weight loss, no significant personality disturbance preceding the first depressive episode, one or more previous major depressions followed by recovery, and a good response to antidepressant therapy.

Patients experiencing a *DSM III-R* manic episode are diagnosed as having bipolar disorder, mixed if their current episode involves the full symptomatic picture of both mania and depression. They are diagnosed as having bipolar disorder, manic if their current or most recent episode was a manic episode. Patients meeting criteria for a *DSM III-R* depressive episode are classified as having bipolar disorder, depressed if they have had one or more manic episodes in the past. Otherwise they are classified as having major depression, single episode, or major depression, recurrent, depending on the number of depressive episodes in their history. If a patient with a major depressive history also has a history including some manic features (hypomanic) but not a full manic episode, he or she is classified as having bipolar disorder not otherwise specified, also known as bipolar II.

Schizoaffective disorder is diagnosed if the patient experiences a full depressive or manic syndrome concurrently with the psychotic symptoms characteristic of schizophrenia. The diagnosis of schizophrenia must first be ruled out and the patient must have had an episode including delusions or hallucinations for at least two weeks without prominent mood symptoms. The *DSM III-R* diagnosis of schizoaffective disorder is explicitly longitudinal. That is, one must observe the relative prominence of psychotic and mood symptoms over time before a diagnosis can be definitively established.

DSM III-R also includes diagnostic categories for mood disorders that are less severe than bipolar disorder or major depression. Individuals who meet neither bipolar nor major depressive diagnoses will be classified as having cyclothymic disorder if they have at least a two-year history of numerous periods during which some of the characteristic symptoms of depression and mania were evident. The symptomatic periods may be separated by periods of normal mood lasting as long as two months. Dysthymic disorder is diagnosed in an individual with at least a two-year history of symptoms characteristic of the depressive syndrome who does not meet the criteria for a major depressive episode. Periods of normal mood may last a few days to a few weeks but no more than two months at a time for this diagnosis. Depressive disorder not otherwise specified will be diagnosed in an individual who exhibits depressive symptoms without meeting the criteria for any specific mood disorder.

In summary, the classification of mood disorders can be represented as a hierarchical structure (see fig. 1.1). As reviewed above, the subdivisions within the structure have been validated to varying degrees through clinical, laboratory, and follow-up studies. The distinctions made at higher levels of the hierarchy are, for the most part, more widely accepted than distinctions made at lower levels. The different clinical manifestations of affective disorder evident in figure 1.1 *may* correspond to different genetic influences. It is the goal of psychiatric genetic studies to determine the importance of genetic factors, their manner of intergenerational transmission, and the degree to which they are shared among disorders having different clinical manifestations.

METHODOLOGIC ISSUES IN PSYCHIATRIC DIAGNOSIS

Although the structured diagnostic criteria described above represent an important advance over previous approaches (e.g., *DSM II*), they represent only the beginnings of a reliable, valid, and clinically meaningful diagnostic system. As Carroll (1984) argued, the

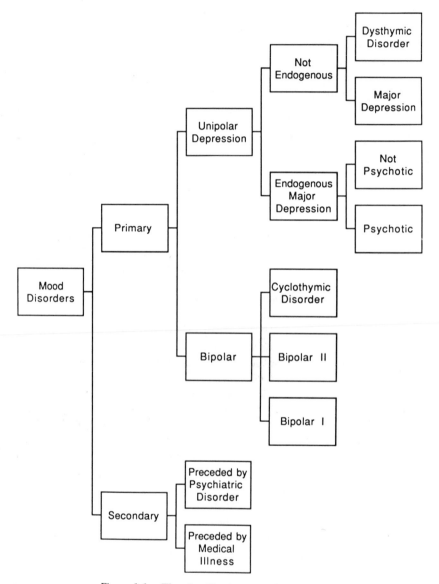

Figure 1.1. The classification of mood disorders

algorithmic and semiquantitative features of these structured diagnostic systems can lead to unrealistic expectations about their usefulness in clinical and research settings. He described six common misconceptions about structured diagnostic criteria that limit their

Table 1.3. Misconceptions about Structured
Diagnostic Criteria

1. They eliminate diagnostic variance
2. They are easy to learn and apply
3. They are based on coherent constructs
4. They ensure homogeneity of patient groups
5. They are reliable
6. They are valid

Source: Based on Carroll, 1984.

usefulness if not controlled for by appropriate research techniques
(see table 1.3). Ideally, a measurement instrument should not add
variability to the natural variability of the objects of measurement
or classification. In other words, the measured value of a variable
should reflect only the "true" value. Irrelevant factors should not
influence the result. This is true for simple measurements such as
height and weight. However, the measurement procedure known as
psychiatric diagnosis involves a complicated interaction between a
patient and an observer. The results will be influenced by characteristics of both participants and the environment in which the interaction takes place. Patient characteristics such as severity of symptoms, quality of memory, presence of substance abuse, and
cooperativeness will add to diagnostic variance, as will observer characteristics such as degree of training and style of the interview.

The second misconception about structured diagnostic criteria
is that they are easy to learn and apply. Interviewers with little clinical
or formal training in psychiatric diagnosis are likely to produce diagnoses of dubious quality even if they are using a structured checklist
approach (Spitzer, Fleiss, and Endicott, 1978). Structured criteria
may reduce the need for seasoned clinical judgment, but this need
cannot be completely eliminated. The application of structured criteria may also be problematic. Although personal interviews with
patients are highly desirable, adjunctive information from medical
records and relatives may be necessary. Clearly, variations in the
training of interviewers and the information available to make diagnoses will add to the problem of increased diagnostic variance.

Structured diagnostic criteria often appear to be based on coherent constructs. However, it must be emphasized that the majority
of psychiatric diagnoses are empirically derived clusters of signs and
symptoms of unknown etiology or pathophysiology. The empirical
approach to psychiatric classification, although appropriate given our
current state of knowledge, does not guarantee intraclass homo-

geneity in descriptive features. For example, according to *DSM III-R* criteria, a patient with dysphoric mood, poor appetite, insomnia, psychomotor agitation, and loss of energy and one who feels worthless, has a pervasive loss of interest, complains of difficulty concentrating, and has suicidal ideation and hypersomnia will both receive the same diagnosis, major depression.

Carroll (1984) also noted that structured criteria are not necessarily reliable. In this context, reliability refers to the ability of two diagnosticians to agree on the diagnoses of the patients. Spitzer and co-workers (Spitzer, Endicott, and Robins, 1975) identified five sources of disagreement that lead to the unreliability in diagnoses. The first source is variability in the patient over time. This occurs when patients have different disorders at different times. They give the example of a patient with acute alcohol intoxication at admission who develops delirium tremens several days later. A second source of diagnostic unreliability occurs when the patient is evaluated during different stages of the same condition. They suggest the example of bipolar disorder; a patient might be in a manic episode during one evaluation and a depressive episode during another. The third source of unreliability leads to differences between diagnosticians because they did not have identical information about a patient. For example, one diagnostician may inquire about suicidal behavior, while another does not. The fourth source of disagreement is due to differences in what two observers notice when presented with the same patient. One observer may judge a patient's affect to be depressed, while another judges it to be blunted. The final source of unreliability they describe is due to differences in the criteria that diagnosticians apply to summarize information into a psychiatric diagnosis.

Spitzer, Endicott, and Robins (1975) pointed out that sources of unreliability due to changes in the patient over time represent true fluctuations and are not due to errors in the diagnostic process. The effect of the other sources of unreliability can be reduced through improvements in diagnostic methodology. The largest source of diagnostic unreliability is variable diagnostic criteria (Ward, 1962). The development of structured diagnostic criteria such as *DSM III*, the Washington University Criteria (Feighner et al., 1972), and the Research Diagnostic Criteria (Spitzer, Endicott, and Robins, 1977) was motivated by a desire to improve the reliability of psychiatric diagnosis by reducing this source of disagreement. The use of specific diagnostic criteria has become standard in research methodology. Although many of the structured diagnostic categories are statistically differentiable from one another regarding response to treat-

Table 1.4. Procedural Characteristics of
Psychiatric Diagnosis

1. Source of information:
   Personal interview
   Relative interview
   Medical records
2. Type of interview:
   Structured
   Unstructured
3. Training of interviewer/diagnostician
4. Interviewer/diagnostician blindness

ment, outcome, course, laboratory findings, and family psychiatric history, this differentiation is far from perfect.

The above discussion does not argue that structured diagnostic criteria are less preferable than previous nonstructured approaches; the structured approach is clearly superior. The goal of this discussion is to emphasize to the reader unfamiliar with psychiatric nosology that, although psychiatric disorders are clearly defined, the psychiatric disorders that are the subject of this book are much less well-defined than other disorders familiar to students of human genetics. Due to the difficulties inherent in psychiatric diagnosis, the results of genetic studies can be interpreted and compared with one another most effectively if the procedures for obtaining psychiatric diagnoses are clearly specified. The four important characteristics of diagnostic procedures as outlined in table 1.4 are these: source of information, type of interview, training of the interviewer, and interviewer blindness.

Ideally, the diagnosis would be based on a personal interview with the individual being examined, an interview with a relative who knows the individual, and an examination of psychiatric medical records. Since most psychiatric genetic studies examine both ill and well relatives, medical records will not be sufficient for a comprehensive study. From a practical standpoint, personally interviewing all index patients (probands) and their relatives can be difficult. Interviewing only one or two members of each family about the entire family is more practical. However, a growing body of research indicates that the use of relative interviews (the family history method) substantially underestimates the amount of psychiatric disorder in the family in comparison to the use of personal interviews (the family study method).

Mendlewicz et al. (1975) interviewed all available spouses and first-degree relatives of 140 unipolar and bipolar probands. These family study diagnoses were compared with family history diagnoses based on interviews with the probands and other family members. The prevalence of mood disorder in the family was underestimated by the probands; the age of onset of relatives with mood disorder was overestimated by the probands. Agreement between the two methods of diagnosis was best when the proband was a child or spouse of a study relative. Agreement between the two methods was also improved when the family history diagnosis was based on the most severe diagnosis provided by any relative. Nevertheless, agreement was still poor, with Kappa coefficients ranging from 0.50 for siblings of relatives to 0.73 for spouses of relatives. Similar results were reported by Andreasen et al. (1977), who collected family history data with a semistructured interview, the Family History–Research Diagnostic Criteria (FH-RDC). FH-RDC criteria are similar to but less stringent than the Research Diagnostic Criteria. FH-RDC interviews with probands estimated the lifetime prevalence rate of mood disorder among relatives to be 11 percent. This estimate increased to 17 percent when probands and other relatives were jointly used as informants, but this was still an underestimation of the 25 percent prevalence rate derived from the family study method. Only 59 percent of the relatives given a diagnosis of mood disorder by the family study method were given that diagnosis by the FH-RDC. The underestimation of psychiatric disorder in the family is less of a problem for the FH-RDC than it had been for previous methods that did not use specialized family history diagnostic criteria (Rimmer and Chambers, 1969; Winokur, Clayton, and Reich, 1969). In contrast to the FH-RDC's low probability of correctly classifying ill individuals (sensitivity), the probability of correctly classifying well individuals (specificity) was high.

The utility of the family history method for the study of depression was examined by Orvaschel et al. (1982). They compared the RDC diagnoses of 696 individuals based on the family study and family history methods. Consistent with the study by Andreasen et al. (1977), the sensitivity of the family history method was low while the specificity was high. The sensitivity was better for reports about female relatives (57 percent) than for reports about male relatives (48 percent). It was substantially higher for reports about probands (73 percent) in comparison to reports about other relatives (33 percent), suggesting that the family history method is more accurate when the relative being discussed is presently experiencing a depressive episode. The specificity of the family history method was uniformly high, ranging from 92 to 98 percent, indicating that the misclassification of a well relative as depressed was infrequent. Another study using the same data set reported that sensitivities for major depression and alcoholism were much higher than for generalized anxiety, drug abuse, phobic disorder, and depressive personality (Thompson et al., 1982). Furthermore, diagnoses based on spouse or offspring reports were more sensitive than those based on parent or sibling reports. The sensitivity of the family history method improved when data were obtained from multiple informants. However, this was not substantial.

Gershon and Guroff (1984) compared family history and family study data collected from 172 mood-disordered probands, 43 normal control probands, and all available first-degree relatives of the probands. Consistent with the results of Andreasen et al. (1977), the family history method was highly sensitive (96 percent) when the individual being diagnosed was a proband. Sensitivity was substantially lower (48 percent) for the diagnosis of major mood disorder when the individual being diagnosed was not a proband. Sensitivity increased linearly from 15 percent when family history was based on one informant to 67 percent with five or more informants. Specificity decreased from 99 percent to 92 percent with increasing numbers of informants. However, increasing the number of informants did not improve agreement on hypomanic or schizophrenic-like symptoms.

The family history and family study methods were compared by Andreasen et al. (1986) using data from a family study of 609 mood disordered probands. FH-RDC family history data were obtained for 4,373 first-degree relatives; direct structured interviews were obtained from 2,216 relatives. Overall, the results of this methodologically sophisticated study were consistent with previous work. The FH-RDC–estimated lifetime prevalence of specific psychiatric disorders was almost always less than the direct interview estimate. For example, the FH-RDC rate of depressive disorder was 22.8 percent, while the direct interview estimate was 32.1 percent. The specificity of the FH-RDC diagnoses was uniformly high, ranging from a low of 84 percent for probable depressive disorder to a high of 100 percent for schizophrenic and schizoaffective disorders. In contrast, the sensitivity of the diagnoses was relatively low, ranging from 31 percent for schizophrenia to 69 percent for psychotic disorder. The sensitivities for depression and mania were 50 percent and 59 percent, respectively. The diagnostic consequences of low sensitivity and high specificity were examined by computing false-positive and false-negative rates. The false-positive rate indicates the percentage of subjects classified as ill by the FH-RDC and well by the direct interview. The false-negative rate is the percentage classified as well by the FH-RDC and ill by direct interview. The rate of false-positive diagnoses ranged from a low of 32 percent for depressive disorder to a high of 82 percent for antisocial personality. All the false-negative rates were close to 0 percent, with the exception of that for depression, which was 21 percent.

Andreasen et al. (1986) found that the sensitivity of the FH-RDC was best when the informant was the parent of the person being diagnosed. For example, the sensitivity for the diagnosis of depression was 62 percent for parent informants, 51 percent for sibling informants, and 37 percent for child informants. The sensitivity of the FH-RDC was also better than those of the modified RDC approach (Orvaschel et al., 1982) or modified WU approach (Winokur, Clayton, and Reich, 1969). These modifications use the RDC and WU methods of diagnosis but require one less symptom for a positive diagnosis. For example, the sensitivity of the family history diagnosis of depression was 56 percent for the FH-RDC probable diagnosis, 33 percent for the modified RDC, and 43 percent for the modified WU. However, although the FH-RDC and modified RDC had similar false-positive rates (38 percent versus 39 percent), the modified WU diagnosis had a substantially lower false-positive rate (10 percent). Increasing the number of informants increased the estimated rate of illness. For example, the rate of FH-RDC depression was 14.9 percent based on one informant and 22.8 percent based on two informants. Since the FH-RDC tends to underestimate rates of illness relative to direct interview, this suggests that multiple informants should be used when possible.

Overall, these methodological studies suggest that the family history method is a poor substitute for the family study method because it seriously underestimates the prevalence of psychiatric disorders, even when multiple informants are used. This conclusion tacitly assumes that diagnoses from personal interviews are more valid than diagnoses made with family history method. As Thompson et al. (1982) and Andreasen et al. (1986) argued, this may not be the case, especially if the presence of a psychiatric disorder impairs a patient's ability to provide relevant diagnostic information or if the disorder has a pejorative connotation (e.g., substance abuse, antisocial personality). Some support for this latter suggestion is seen in Andreasen et al.'s (1986) finding that the FH-RDC estimated rate of antisocial personality was three times that of the direct interviewer estimate. Leckman et al. (1982) examined this question in a methodological study. In a case-controlled family study of major depression they diagnosed 1,878 individuals with a "best-estimate" diagnostic procedure that combined information from personal interviews, relative interviews, and medical records. Diagnostic agreement was greater for individuals for whom personal interview data was available in comparison to noninterviewed individuals. Diagnoses based on personal interviews alone closely approximated the best-estimate diagnoses; using the best-estimate diagnoses as the criterion, the sensitivity of the interview diagnoses of major depression was 86 percent and the specificity was 98 percent. The analyses of Gershon and Guroff (1984) are consistent with the results of Leckman et al. (1982) in agreeing that diagnoses based on personal interviews are close approximations of those based on information from all sources. Gershon and Guroff also concluded that a diagnosis based upon medical record information was a satisfactory alternative to a personal interview or a best-estimate diagnosis. However, diagnoses based on family history data alone were not a satisfactory substitute for best-estimate diagnoses.

The style of the psychiatric interview can vary from being totally unstructured to totally structured. In an unstructured interview, there is no preset format or sequence for questions about psychiatric signs and symptoms. The interviewer is permitted to ask those questions that he or she believes to be appropriate during the interview. In contrast, fully structured interviews, like the Diagnostic Interview Schedule (Robins et al., 1981), provide a complete specification of how questions should be worded and the sequence in which they should be asked. Compromises between complete structure and no structure are seen in semistructured interviews such as the Schedule for Affective Disorders and Schizophrenia (Endicott and Spitzer, 1978). Semistructured interviews give the interviewer more freedom to choose how to word questions and which questions to ask. However, the interviewer must cover a preselected series of topics, usually in a specific order. For research purposes some structure in an interview is desirable to guarantee that all important areas of psychiatric functioning are assessed. The use of a structured interview also makes a diagnostic research procedure easier to replicate.

The choice of how much structure is enough is determined to some extent by the previous experience of the interviewer. Semistructured interviews are appropriate for interviewers who have had clinical experience in the diagnosis of the psychiatric disorders of interest in the study; fully structured interviews are more appropriate when using interviewers with no special training, as is often necessary in large-scale epidemiological or family studies. In either case, some training with the interview schedule to be used is necessary to assure that it is used in a reliable and valid manner. The issue of interviewer training was examined directly in the study of Robins et al. (1981).

Using psychiatric diagnoses as a criterion, they reported the sensitivity and specificity of Diagnostic Interview Schedule (DIS) diagnoses obtained by interviewers who had been trained in the administration of the DIS but had no special clinical psychiatric training. In this context the sensitivity of a DIS diagnosis indicates the percentage of patients given the diagnosis by a psychiatrist who were also given the diagnosis by the lay DIS interviewer. Specificity refers to the percentage of patients who did not have a disorder as determined by the psychiatrist who were also not given the diagnosis by the lay interviewers. Sensitivity was 65 percent for bipolar disorder, 80 percent for major depression, and 63 percent for schizophrenia. Specificity was 97 percent for bipolar disorder, 84 percent for major depression, and 94 percent for schizophrenia. That is, even with a fully structured interview like the DIS, lay interviewers are not in complete agreement with psychiatric diagnoses. However, the degree of disagreement between lay interviewers and psychiatrists cannot be totally attributed to deficiencies with the lay interview method. As Robins (1985) noted, deficiencies in the test-retest design will tend to deflate estimates of agreement and the lack of agreement may be due to the less-than-perfect reliability of psychiatric diagnoses.

In the context of genetic research, psychiatric diagnostic procedures must control for the experimenter bias effect (Rosenthal, 1966). A wide variety of behavioral studies have indicated that in some situations the expectancies of a researcher may intentionally or unintentionally bias the data-collection procedure. Some believe this is not a widespread phenomenon (e.g., Barber and Silver, 1968) and there is some evidence that the experimenter effect does not substantially affect psychiatric diagnosis. For example, McDonald-Scott and Endicott (1984) reported substantial agreement in ratings of psychopathology between blind and nonblind raters. In this study of 50 mood-disordered patients, the blind rater had no previous knowledge of the patients, whereas the nonblind rater had extensive knowledge of the patients' psychiatric history, course, and treatment. As measured by the intraclass correlation, the reliability between blind and nonblind raters was very high for summary scores of depressive features (0.95), endogenous features (0.96), and anxiety (0.91). The reliability of the manic syndrome rating (0.79) was lower but nevertheless reflects a high level of agreement. Despite these findings, the current methodological standard is for interviewers to be unaware of (blind to) psychiatric diagnoses of the interviewees' relatives. Mazure and Gershon (1979) also suggested that diagnoses be made by someone other than the interviewer because interpersonal effects during the interview have been observed to bias some interviewers toward less severe diagnoses.

SUMMARY

In this chapter we have provided an overview of the classification and methodologic issues relevant to genetic studies of mood disorders. As we show in figure 1.1, the mood disorders encompass a heterogeneous class of syndromes ranging from severely debilitating manic and depressive psychoses to milder manifestations such as dysthymia and hypomania. How does one account for the wide range of phenomenologic variability among disorders that share disturbance of mood as a primary component of the clinical picture? At one extreme, it is possible that the various mood syndromes and, perhaps, their subclassifications correspond to etiologically distinct disorders. While not parsimonious, other areas of medicine suggest that similar clinical syndromes are often produced by a variety of etiological pathways. Edema, once believed to be a homogenous disorder, is now known to result from a variety of conditions ranging from pregnancy to heart disease. Anemias and glycogen-storage diseases provide additional examples, but perhaps the most remarkable is mental retardation. This syndrome of low intellectual and behavioral functioning can be caused by one of hundreds of genetic defects or environmental insults. For mood disorders, the presence of etiologic heterogeneity is clearly seen in the distinction between those that are secondary to the biological effects of a medical illness (e.g., hypothyroidism) and those that are not.

At the other extreme, the clinical heterogeneity of mood disorders may reflect what geneticists call pleiotropy, the ability of a single gene to be expressed in a variety of manifestations in different individuals. Matthysse (1985) gave the example of neurofibromatosis, the manifestations of this single-gene disease range from mild cases limited to the presence of cafe-au-lait spots to severely disabled cases with peripheral nerve tumors, bony deformities, and mental retardation. Pleiotropy occurs because genes do not express themselves independently of other influences, both genetic and environmental. The development and functioning of the central nervous system involves a complex sequence of gene-gene and gene-environment interactions. Thus, it is not unreasonable to assume that genetic disorders of the central nervous system, such as mood disorders, are mediated by genes that have pleiotropic effects.

The task of the psychiatric geneticist is hindered by the likelihood that both etiologic heterogeneity and pleiotropy play a role in the clinical heterogeneity of mood disorders. Fortunately, as we can infer from the data in tables 1.1, 1.2, and 1.3, psychiatry has converged upon a *reasonably* reliable means of classifying these disorders. We emphasize the word "reasonably" to indicate that, although diagnostic agreement between raters is well above chance, the degree of disagreement is not negligible and is likely to increase unless great care is taken in the interviewing and diagnostic process. For psychiatric genetic research projects, the following methodologic maxims should be considered: (1) use clearly defined diagnostic criteria, such as those specified by the WU, RDC, and *DSM III-R* diagnostic systems; (2) use structured or semistructured interviewing techniques to collect psychiatric data; (3) assess the reliability of interviewers before and during the project; (4) although diagnostic data collected from an informant are an important adjunct to the diagnostic process, study diagnoses should include data from a direct interview; and (5) whenever possible, keep interviewers and diagnosticians blind to the psychiatric diagnosis of other family members.

Chapter Two

Family Studies

The family study is one of the most widely used tools in psychiatric genetics. We can use the data from such studies to answer the question, does a psychiatric illness run in families? If genes are etiologically important to a disorder, then relatives of ill individuals (probands) should be at greater risk of the illness than are relatives of well individuals (control probands). Furthermore, under a genetic hypothesis the risk to relatives of ill probands should be related to the amount of genes they have in common with the proband. Parents, children, and siblings of probands are called first-degree relatives; they share 50 percent of their genes with the proband. Grandparents, uncles, aunts, nephews, and nieces are second-degree relatives; they share 25 percent of their genes with the proband. If a disorder has a genetic etiology, first-degree relatives should be at greater risk for the disorder than are second-degree relatives. Thus, a genetic hypothesis predicts that relatives of ill probands are at greater risk for the disorder than are relatives of control probands and that the risk to relatives of ill probands decreases as the degree of the relationship increases.

Compared to twin and adoption studies, family studies are relatively easy to implement. Thus, they are commonly used to determine if a disorder is familial. Unfortunately, the interpretation of family studies is limited. Although a genetic hypothesis predicts that a disorder will be familial, a disorder may be familial for other reasons. Family members share a common culture and a common environment. The similarity of these factors tends to increase as the degree of the relationship decreases. Thus, familial environmental factors may confound genetic relationships. For example, if cigarette smoking is a habit that children learn from parents, then one might observe that smoking-related disorders such as emphysema run in families. However, the familial aspect of such a disorder may be due entirely to relatives sharing a common environmental pathogen. Possible sources of cultural and environmental transmission include bacteria, viruses, learned responses to stress, cultural differences in emotional expression, and others. Since a disorder can run in a family for nongenetic reasons, the finding of familial transmission cannot be unambiguously interpreted. However, the failure to find familial transmission can be taken as a strong sign that a disorder does not have a substantial genetic component.

The ideal family study uses double-blind, case-controlled methodology in which diagnoses of relatives are made independent of any knowledge of the proband's diagnostic status. Given the many factors that influence the outcome of a psychiatric diagnosis, controlled studies are preferable. However, in the absence of a control group, the risk to relatives of ill probands can be compared to population risks from epidemiologic studies.

THE EPIDEMIOLOGY OF MOOD DISORDERS

Early epidemiologic studies did not make a distinction between unipolar and bipolar forms of affective disorders. Instead, all cases were grouped under the term "manic-depressive psychosis." Population rates for manic-depressive psychosis from these early studies are given in table 2.1.

All these studies except the American work of Kallmann (1954) were conducted in Europe, primarily England, Germany, and the Scandinavian countries. These early studies did not use structured diagnostic criteria and did not differentiate unipolar and bipolar forms. Thus, it is difficult to know exactly how manic-depressive psychosis was defined. However, many of these authors were clearly aware of the importance of clinical homogeneity in scientific studies. For example, Slater (1936) clearly recognized that the diagnosis of some clinically defined manic-depressive cases was complicated by the presence of schizophrenic or characterologic features. He foreshadowed future methodologic maxims by suggesting that psychiatric genetic studies would be more fruitful if such disputed cases were examined separately from the "indisputable cases." Slater argued that although the disputed cases may have "near or remote genetic connections with what one might call the central group of manic depressives," studies of homogeneous groups would be needed to provide a solid empirical foundation for psychiatric genetics. Slater (1936) was also sensitive to the problem of confusing mild, remitting cases of schizophrenia with mood disorders, given the Kraepelinian approach of using a deteriorating course as a primary sign of schizophrenia and an episodic, remitting course as a primary sign of manic depression. He emphasized that the clinical phenomenology of acute episodes could not be ignored in arriving at a psychiatric diagnosis.

Table 2.1. The Risk of Major Mood Disorder among the
General Population

Study	Risk (%)
Slater, 1938[a]	0.4
Strömgren, 1938[b]	0.6
Luxenburger, 1942[c]	0.4
Fremming, 1947[b]	1.7
Sjögren, 1948[b]	0.8
Schulz and Rudin, 1951[d]	0.4
Stenstedt, 1952	0.6
Kallmann, 1954	0.4
Mean of all studies	0.7

[a]From Slater and Cowie, 1971.
[b]From Stenstedt, 1952.
[c]From Rosenthal, 1970.
[d]From Kallman, 1954.

Stenstedt (1952) endorsed Slater's approach to diagnosis. He clearly excluded cases with schizophrenia-like symptoms, pronounced personality disorders, or evidence of exogenous etiologic factors (e.g., precipitating life events, medical conditions). This last exclusion, also used by Slater, anticipated the contemporary distinction between primary and secondary mood disorders. Kallmann (1954) restricted his diagnosis of manic-depressive psychosis to "cyclic cases which showed periodicity of acute, self-limited mood swings before the fifth decade of life and no progressive or residual personality disintegration before or after psychotic episodes of elation or depression. Clearly reactive or largely situational depressions in a habitually maladjusted setting were excluded in the same way as hallucinatory episodes, or agitated anxiety states associated with hypertension" (p. 9).

Overall, the early studies of manic-depressive psychosis appear to have been sensitive to the necessity of creating homogeneous study groups by appropriate exclusion criteria. Although definitions of manic-depressive psychosis are not clearly stated in most of the studies in table 2.1, the similarity of results across one and one-half decades is remarkable. With the exception of Fremming's (1947) finding of a 1.7 percent risk of manic-depressive psychosis in the general population, these studies all cluster in the range of 0.4-0.8 percent. The mean general population risk in these studies is 0.7 percent if Fremming's results are included and 0.5 percent if they are excluded. In any case, it is reasonable to conclude that, given

Table 2.2.   The Risk of Bipolar Disorder among General Population and Control Samples

Study	Sample	Risk (%)
Fremming, 1951	general population	0.6
Parsons, 1965	general population	0.9
James and Chapman, 1975	general population	0.2
Gershon et al. 1975	relatives of medical patients	0.2
Smeraldi, Negri, and Melica, 1977	general population	0.1
Helgason, 1979	general population	0.8
Tsuang, Winokur, and Crowe, 1980	relatives of surgical patients	0.3
Gershon et al., 1982	relatives of medical patients	0.0
Robins et al., 1984	general population:	
	New Haven	1.1
	Baltimore	0.6
	St. Louis	1.1
Weissman et al., 1984	general population	0.2
Mean from all studies		0.5

early definitions of manic-depressive psychosis, the risk to the general population is less than 1 percent.

The results of epidemiologic studies focusing on bipolar disorder are given in table 2.2. These data come from two types of studies. The general population studies examine the risk of bipolar disorder among individuals randomly selected from a specified catchment area. Case-controlled studies have selected specified medical or surgical patients as probands and have examined the risk of bipolar disorder among their relatives. In general population studies the risk of bipolar disorder ranges from 0.1 percent to 1.1 percent. For case-controlled studies the range is 0.0 percent to 0.3 percent. The mean risk across all studies is 0.5 percent. Similar data for unipolar disorder are presented in table 2.3.

The risk of unipolar disorder in the general population ranges from 3.4 percent to 18.0 percent. For case-controlled samples, the range is 0.7-7.5 percent. The mean risk of unipolar disorder across all studies in table 2.3 is 6.2 percent.

A comparison of tables 2.3 and 2.2 clearly indicates that unipolar disorder is more prevalent than bipolar disorder. All of the studies that examine both unipolar and bipolar disorders find a greater prevalence of unipolar disorder. Based on the means from all studies, a randomly selected individual is 12 times more likely to develop unipolar than bipolar disorder. There is a surprising inconsistency between table 2.1 and tables 2.2 and 2.3. Although the

Table 2.3. The Risk of Unipolar Disorder among General Population and Control Samples

Study	Sample	Risk (%)
Fremming, 1951	general population	16.3
Essen-Moller and Hagnell, 1961	general population	3.4
Helgason, 1961	general population	6.0
James and Chapman, 1975	general population	0.7
Gershon et al., 1975	relatives of medical patients	0.7
Smeraldi, Negri, and Melica, 1977	general population	0.4
Weissman and Myers, 1978	general population	18.0
Helgason, 1979	general population	12.0
Tsuang, Winokur, and Crowe, 1980	relatives of surgical patients	7.5
Gershon et al., 1982	relatives of medical patients	5.8
Egeland and Hostetter, 1983	general population	0.5
Robins et al., 1984	general population:	
	New Haven	6.7
	Baltimore	3.7
	St. Louis	5.5
Weissman et al., 1984	general population	5.9
Mean from all studies		6.2

studies in table 2.1 combine unipolar and bipolar disorders under the term "manic-depressive psychosis," their estimates of population risk are relatively low and similar to those for bipolar disorder in table 2.2. The cause of this discrepancy is not clear. It may be the case that the early studies had a very restricted definition of unipolar disorder. As noted above, cases with exogenous precipitating factors, pronounced personality disorders, or hallucinatory phenomena were often excluded. It is likely that many of these excluded cases would be considered unipolar according to current nomenclature.

Another possibility is that the population risk for mood disorders has increased over time. In fact, a substantial number of independent investigators have observed an increasing lifetime risk for major depression during the twentieth century (Gershon et al., 1987; Hagnell et al., 1982; Klerman, 1976; Klerman et al., 1985; Robins et al., 1984; Srole and Fischer 1980; Weissman and Myers, 1978). A similar trend for bipolar disorder has also been reported (Gershon et al., 1987; Rice, Reich, et al., 1987). For example, the study by Klerman et al. (1985) found increases in the rate of depression in successive birth cohorts through the twentieth century and an earlier age of onset of depression with each birth cohort. This study examined depression in 2,289 relatives of 523 probands with mood disorders. The lifetime risk of major depression was less than 20 percent for relatives born before 1910. The risk rose steadily to more than 60 percent for relatives born after 1949. These results have been called the "birth cohort effect" because the year of birth is predictive of the risk of depression, with successive birth cohorts being at increased risk for the disorder. However, as Lavori et al. (1986) discussed, a putative cohort effect may also be due to a period effect. A pure cohort effect occurs when some factor exerts a different effect on different birth cohorts. The size of the effect for each cohort is stable over the lifetime of the members of the cohort. A pure period effect occurs when some factor affects all individuals for a limited period of time. Lavori et al. used the rate of cancer observed among the survivors of the atomic bombs in Hiroshima and Nagasaki as an example of a pure period effect. People who lived in these areas during the period of high radiation exposure have an increased risk of cancer regardless of their birth cohorts. A period effect will be difficult to disentangle from a cohort effect when there is an age-period interaction. This occurs when the likelihood of developing the disorder is related to the age of the individual. Thus, although the increasing risk of major depression through the twentieth century is consistent with a birth cohort effect, it is equally likely that some recent period of time has been associated with an increase in depressogenic factors that exert stronger effects on younger individuals.

Before comparing these two hypotheses, Lavori et al. ruled out the possibility that the observed effect was due to some confound related to advanced age (e.g., impaired recall, institutionalization, mortality). The effect could also not be explained by the presence of many short or insubstantial depressive episodes recalled by younger subjects or by changes in the severity of the disorder over time. Subsequent analyses indicate that the increasing risk of depression was more consistent with a period effect than with a cohort effect. The results indicated the presence of a marked leap in the risk of depression during the period 1965-75 to a new plateau extending into the 1980s. This effect was particularly prominent for females. Because this period effect interpretation has not been supported by other data (Gershon et al., 1987), it is not possible to attribute definitely the rising risk of depression to a birth-cohort effect or to an age-period interaction.

The presence of a period effect on the risk for unipolar depression has implications for the genetic study of the disorder. The effect may explain the discrepancies between table 2.1 and tables 2.2 and 2.3, since the two sets of studies are separated by several decades.

Firm conclusions are not possible, given that earlier studies differ in many ways (methodology, location) from later ones. Nevertheless, the rising risk of mood disorders must be taken into account when comparing studies. For the presentation of family studies it is convenient to separate those performed before 1960 and those reported after 1960. These two sets of studies differ in several ways. The early studies are primarily of European origin and were completed before the development of structured interviews, structured diagnostic criteria, and standardized research techniques. It is nonetheless humbling to recognize that the pioneers in psychiatric genetics laid a firm scientific foundation for future work.

EARLY FAMILY STUDIES

Like their epidemiologic counterparts, the early family studies do not make the distinction between unipolar and bipolar disorders and do not provide detailed methodologic information regarding the procedural characteristics of psychiatric diagnosis. Table 2.4 gives the risk of major mood disorders among the parents, children, and siblings of mood disorder probands. The risk to parents ranges from 3.2 percent to 23.4 percent, with a mean of 11.3 percent. The risk to children ranges from 6.3 percent to 24.1 percent, with a mean of 14.6 percent. The risk to siblings ranges from 2.7 percent to 23.0 percent, with a mean of 10.9 percent. It is notable that the studies reporting the lowest risks, Pollock, Malzberg, and Fuller (1939) and Humm (1932), did not adjust their risk estimates for the age of the relatives. Age corrections are important, because mood disorders have a variable age of onset. Thus, if a study included many relatives who have not passed through a substantial portion of the age of onset, relatives who eventually will become ill will be defined as well.

None of the studies examined a control group of normal probands and their relatives. The psychiatric diagnoses of relatives in these studies were not blind to the fact of their having a relative with mood disorder. Thus, they may be tainted by the effects of experimenter bias. Although a case-controlled comparison is not possible, the risk to relatives reported in table 2.4 can be compared with that of the general population reported by the same investigators. In table 2.5 this comparison is expressed in terms of the relative risk, the risk to relatives of ill probands divided by the risk to the general population. For authors who do not provide population risk data, the mean from table 2.1 has been used to compute the relative risk. The range of relative risks given in table 2.5 is based on the highest and lowest risks to parents, children, or siblings given in table 2.4.

Table 2.4. The Risk of Major Mood Disorder (MD) among First-Degree
Relatives of MD Probands, Studies before 1960

Study	Relationship (% Risk)		
	Parent	Child	Sibling
Banse, 1929[a,b]	10.8	—	18.1
Humm, 1932[c]	—	—	4.4
Röll and Entres, 1936[a]	13.0	10.7	—
Weinberg and Lobstein, 1936[c,d]	9.9	6.3	7.2
Slater, 1936[c]	15.4	15.8	—
Strömgren, 1938[a,b]	7.5	—	10.7
Pollock et al., 1939[c]	3.2	—	2.7
Luxenburger, 1942[c,d]	—	24.1	12.7
Hoffman and Wagner, 1946[c,e]	—	13.8	10.0
Sjögren, 1948[a,b]	7.0	—	3.6
Schulz and Rudin, 1951[c,e]	15.7	—	13.3
Stenstedt, 1952[f]	7.5	17.1	14.1
Kallmann, 1953, 1954	23.4	—	23.0

[a]From Stenstedt, 1952.
[b]Weinberg correction.
[c]Not age corrected.
[d]From Rosenthal, 1970.
[e]From Kallmann, 1954.
[f]Strömgren correction.

Table 2.5. The Relative Risk of Major Mood Disorder (MD) among First-Degree
Relatives of MD Probands, Studies before 1960

Study	Relative Risk (%)
Banse, 1929	15.4–25.9
Humm, 1932	6.3
Röll and Entres, 1936	15.3–18.6
Weinberg and Lobstein, 1936	9.0–14.1
Slater, 1936	38.0–39.5
Strömgren, 1938	12.5–17.8
Pollock, Malzberg, and Fuller, 1939	5.3–6.0
Luxenberger, 1942	31.8–60.3
Hoffman and Wagner, 1946	14.3–19.7
Sjögren, 1948	4.5–8.8
Schulz and Rudin, 1951	33.3–39.3
Stenstedt, 1952	12.5–28.5
Kallmann, 1953, 1954	57.5–58.5

Note: The relative risk is the risk to relatives of ill probands (see table 2.4) divided
by the risk to the general population (see table 2.1). The mean from table 2.1 is
used for studies not included in table 2.3. The range given is based on the highest
and lowest morbid risks to parents, children, or siblings.

It is notable that all of the relative risks are greater than 1. That is, each of the studies finds relatives of manic-depressive probands to be at greater risk for manic-depressive psychosis than individuals from the general population. The lowest estimate of relative risk comes from Sjogren's (1948) study, which suggested that relatives of ill probands are 4.5-8.8 times more likely to develop manic-depressive psychosis than individuals in the general population. The highest relative risk is reported by Kallmann, whose data suggested that relatives of ill probands are approximately 58 times more likely to become ill than one would expect from general population risk estimates.

Taken together, the early family studies of major mood disorders consistently suggested that manic-depressive psychosis runs in families. Although this consistency is impressive, these results could be due to methodologic artifacts such as lack of interviewer blindness, no control groups, and no systematic application of age corrections to population and family risk figures. The extent of these problems is difficult to assess because most of these early studies do not provide sufficient methodologic detail for their evaluation.

LATER STUDIES OF MAJOR MOOD DISORDERS

Most of the studies reported in this section were performed during the 1970s and 1980s. Due to an increased rigor in scientific writing, these reports allow for a careful evaluation of methodologic aspects. In addition, results are broken down by unipolar and bipolar subtypes and therefore allow the examination of the familial association of these two disorders. Table 2.6 presents the risks for unipolar and bipolar disorders among relatives of bipolar probands, broken down by the relationship of the relative to the proband. Perris's (1966) study was carried out in Sweden. Proband diagnoses were based on personal interviews and medical record data. Although he did not use a structured interview or a structured diagnostic system, his methods are notable in that unipolar disorder was diagnosed only in patients who had suffered as least three depressive episodes. The 138 bipolar probands had 1,077 first-degree relatives. At least one relative from each family was personally interviewed, but the majority of family diagnoses appeared to have been based on the family history method of diagnosis. Assuming a population risk of approximately 0.5 percent (see table 2.2), Perris's data indicate an elevated risk of bipolar disorder among relatives of bipolar probands; relatives of unipolar probands do not have elevated risks.

Reich, Clayton, and Winokur (1969), working in St. Louis,

Table 2.6. The Risk of Major Mood Disorder among Relatives of Bipolar Probands, Studies after 1960

Study	Relative Diagnosis	Relationship (%)		
		Parent	Child	Sibling
Perris, 1966[a]	BP	6.4	4.6	14.1
	UP	0.9	0.0	0.3
Reich, Clayton, and Winokur, 1969[a]	MD	26.9	—	17.0
Winokur et al., 1972[a]	MD	10.3	—	12.0
Mendlewicz and Rainer, 1974[b]	BP	12.1	24.6	21.2
	UP	22.0	41.3	18.6
Goetzl et al., 1974[a]	MD	18.4	52.6	18.9
Helzer and Winokur, 1974[c]	BP	3.3	—	5.5
	UP	13.3	—	8.8
Shopsin et al., 1976[b]	MD	40.0	16.0	25.0
Petterson, 1977[a]	BP	2.4	2.4	5.0
	UP	2.4	4.8	1.3
Smeraldi, Negri, and Melica, 1977[a]	BP	1.2	5.7	7.1
	UP	3.5	5.7	1.4
Trzebiatowska-Trzeciak, 1977[b]	BP	9.8	24.9	10.3
	UP	0.0	0.0	0.0
Angst et al., 1980[b]	BP	2.5	4.0	2.3
	UP	9.4	0.0	6.0

Note: BP = bipolar disorder, UP = unipolar disorder, MD = mood disorder.
[a]Weinberg age correction.
[b]Strömgren age correction.
[c]Not age corrected.

diagnosed 59 bipolar probands through personal interviews and medical record reviews. They used structured interviews and applied the Washington University diagnostic criteria in assessing probands. Relatives were diagnosed through a combination of personal interviews and a collection of family history data. Although relatives' diagnoses were not broken down by polarity, the risk of any mood disorder was 17 percent in siblings and 27 percent among parents of probands, suggesting the importance of familial factors. Winokur et al. (1972) reported a medical record study of mood disorder in more than 300 relatives of 100 bipolar probands. Diagnoses were based on information in the probands' medical records. However, diagnoses of probands and relatives were made independently. The risk of mood disorders among relatives was approximately 11 percent. This is higher than expected from epidemiologic studies, but not markedly so. Given the limitations of medical record–based diagnoses, these results must be interpreted with caution.

Mendlewicz and Rainer (1974) studied the 781 first-degree relatives of 134 bipolar probands. Proband diagnoses were based on personal interviews and reviews of medical records. Although this investigation did not use a structured interview or a contemporary structured diagnostic system, the approach to diagnosis appears to have been similar to current methods. Interviews and diagnoses of relatives were blind to proband diagnosis; 82 percent of the relatives' diagnoses were based on personal interviews. Among relatives, the risk of unipolar disorder was consistently greater than the risk of bipolar disorder for each type of relationship examined. No control group was used, but the risks of both disorders are substantially greater than one would expect from epidemiologic studies. These results contrast sharply with those of Perris (1966), who did not find an increased risk of unipolar disorder among relatives of bipolar probands. A notable diagnostic difference between the two studies is that Perris required three or more depressive episodes before making a unipolar diagnosis. Patients with fewer depressive episodes are considered uncertain cases because there is still a reasonable chance that they are bipolar patients who have not yet experienced their first manic episode. Mendlewicz and Rainer did not make this distinction and classified as depressed anyone who had never experienced mania or hypomania but had experienced one or more depressive episodes. Thus, Mendlewicz and Rainer's unipolar relatives may include bipolar patients who have not yet had a manic episode, possibly inflating the observed risk for unipolar disorder.

Goetzl et al. (1974) examined 245 first-degree relatives of 39 bipolar probands. Probands were diagnosed using unstructured personal interviews and data from medical records. Diagnoses were based on a modification of the Washington University criteria. Assessments of relatives and probands were not blind to one another. Diagnoses of relatives were based upon the proband interview and a self-report questionnaire. The results, not broken down by the polarity distinction, indicate a high rate of mood disorder among relatives of bipolar probands. They are not easily comparable with epidemiologic data, given the unusual means of obtaining relative psychiatric diagnoses. Helzer and Winokur (1974) examined 151 relatives of 30 male bipolar probands. Diagnoses of probands were based on a structured personal interview and a review of medical records using the Washington University diagnostic criteria. The assessment of relatives was blind to proband diagnosis. Approximately half the relatives' diagnoses were based on personal interviews and half on family history data collected from the proband or another relative. The morbidity risks are probably underestimated because they are not age corrected. Nevertheless, the risk of bipolar disorder is clearly greater than what one would expect from epidemiologic studies. The risk of unipolar disorder is greater than the risk of bipolar disorder but is not markedly different from the population expectation. Shopsin et al. (1976) reported results from 76 relatives of 25 bipolar probands. The diagnostic approach was similar to that of Mendlewicz and Rainer but assessments of relatives and probands were not blind to one another. Some diagnoses of relatives were based on personal interviews, some on family history data, and others on medical record data. The proportions in these categories are not stated. Results indicate high rates of mood disorder among the relatives, but information pertaining to the unipolar bipolar distinction is not provided.

Petterson (1977) studied a Swedish sample of 123 bipolar probands and 668 first-degree relatives. Proband diagnoses were based on unstructured personal interviews and medical record reviews. The diagnostic definitions are not well specified but appear to be fairly broad, including patients with "paranoid or confusional elements" in the bipolar group. An unstated proportion of the relatives' diagnoses were based on personal interviews; the rest were based on the family history method. Petterson found a familial risk of bipolar disorder among relatives of bipolar probands greater than four times the population expectation. However, the risk of unipolar disorder is no greater than one would expect from epidemiologic studies, a finding that suggests there is no familial relationship between unipolar and bipolar disorder. Similar results were reported in Smeraldi, Negri, and Melica's (1977) study of an Italian sample of 306 first-degree relatives of 50 bipolar probands. Proband diagnoses were based on personal interviews and the diagnostic system of Perris (1966). Relatives' diagnoses were based on a combination of personal interview and family history assessments that were not blind to the diagnosis of proband. A control group was not used but prevalence rates from Italian epidemiologic studies are provided (tables 2.2 and 2.3). These figures, although age corrected, are based on hospitalized patients only. Thus, they are an underestimate of the lifetime prevalence of mood disorder. Smeraldi's results found increased risk for bipolar disorder among the relatives of bipolar probands. The risk among relatives is 10-70 times the risk from the Italian epidemiologic study and 2-14 times the risk suggested by the mean of the reviewed epidemiologic studies. The risk of unipolar disorder is 3-14 times greater than expected from the Italian epidemiologic study, but less than the mean of all the reviewed epidemiologic studies. Thus, Smeraldi's data support the hypothesis that bipolar disorder runs in families but are not strongly supportive of a familial association between unipolar and bipolar disorders. However, the risk of unipolar disorder in families of bipolar probands is greater than that reported by Perris (1966), even though Perris's criteria for unipolar disorder were used.

These criteria were also used by Trzebiatowska-Trzeciak (1977) in a study of 69 Polish bipolar probands and their 421 first-degree relatives. Probands were diagnosed by personal interviews. Other methodologic aspects of the research are difficult to determine from the report. The risk of bipolar disorder among relatives ranged from 10 to 25 percent, markedly higher than the population expectation. No relatives of bipolar patients were diagnosed as having unipolar disorder. Angst et al. (1980) studied a Swiss sample of 95 bipolar probands and their 641 first-degree relatives. The diagnoses of probands were based on a long prospective follow-up from 1959 to 1975. Information was obtained from personal interviews, medical records, and interviews with relatives. The diagnosis of bipolar disorder appears to have included both bipolar I and bipolar II disorders. The diagnosis of unipolar disorder did not require three depressive episodes. However, the probands had a mean age of 61, suggesting that most of their unipolar parents and siblings would have been old enough to have experienced a manic episode if they had truly been bipolar. Consistent with previous studies, Angst et al. found an increased risk of bipolar disorder among relatives of bipolar probands. The overall risk of unipolar disorder among these first-degree relatives was 7 percent, not markedly higher than the general population expectation.

Table 2.7 reviews family studies of bipolar probands that do not break down risk figures by the relationship to the proband. Results from a New Zealand sample of 46 bipolar probands and 360 first-degree relatives were reported by James and Chapman (1975). Probands were diagnosed through personal interviews and medical record reviews. A structured interview was used and diagnoses were similar to the Washington University criteria. Assessments of relatives were not blind to proband diagnosis. Approximately 40 percent of the relatives were personally interviewed. The risk of bipolar disorder (6.4 percent) was more than 30 times greater than the population expectation. The risk of unipolar disorder among relatives of bipolar probands (13.2 percent) was nearly 20 times greater than the risk to the general population. Gershon et al. (1975) studied an Israeli sample of 54 bipolar probands and their 411 relatives. Four of these probands were bipolar II cases. Probands were diagnosed through personal interviews and medical record reviews using the

Table 2.7. The Risk of Major Mood Disorder among First-Degree Relatives of Bipolar Probands, Studies after 1960

Study	Relative Diagnosis	Risk (%)
James and Chapman, 1975[a]	BP	6.4
	UP	13.2
Gershon et al., 1975[a]	BP	3.5
	UP	8.6
	UP	13.2
Johnson and Leeman, 1977[a]	BP	15.5
	UP	19.8
Abrams and Taylor, 1980[b]	BP	8.5
	UP	6.4
Tsuang, Winokur, and Crowe, 1980[c]	BP	5.3
	UP	12.4
Jakimow-Venulet, 1981[a]	BP	11.8
	UP	6.1
Scharfetter, 1981[a]	BP	2.2
	UP	7.7
Gershon et al., 1982[c]	BP	4.5
	UP	14.0
Endicott et al., 1985[d]	BP	2.3
	UP	8.3
Andreasen et al., 1987[d]	BP	3.9
	UP	22.8

Note: BP = bipolar disorder, UP = unipolar disorder.
[a]Strömgren correction.
[b]Age corrected, method not stated.
[c]Weinberg age correction.
[d]Not age corrected.

Washington University diagnostic system. Eighty-five control probands and their 619 first-degree relatives were also studied. Controls were selected from internal medicine wards of a general hospital. Patients were excluded from the control group if they had a history of any psychotic or neurotic disorder including mild depression in relation to their medical illness. Relatives were assessed with personal interviews and family history information. The final diagnoses of relatives were made blind to the diagnostic status of the proband. This well-controlled family study found an increased prevalence of bipolar and unipolar disorders among the relatives of bipolar probands. These disorders were 10–20 times more likely to be observed among relatives of bipolar probands in comparison to relatives of controls.

Johnson and Leeman (1977) found high rates of bipolar and

unipolar disorders among 213 first-degree relatives of 35 bipolar probands in their Australian sample. Probands were diagnosed with personal interviews and medical record reviews. These authors used a structured but idiosyncratic approach to diagnosis similar to currently used diagnostic systems. Sixty-seven percent of the relatives were diagnosed through personal interviews. Although they provide no control group and no Australian population expectation, the high rate of bipolar disorder among the relatives (15.5 percent) is clearly supportive of familial transmission, as is the 19.8 percent risk of unipolar disorder. Abrams and Taylor (1980) performed a double-blind, uncontrolled study of 14 bipolar probands and their 107 relatives. Patients were diagnosed with a semistructured interview and reviews of medical records. The authors used their own structured diagnostic system for obtaining diagnoses. Relatives' diagnoses were based on a combination of personal interview and family history data. The results indicate a high risk of bipolar disorder (8.5 percent) among relatives of bipolar probands. The risk of unipolar disorder (6.4 percent) is not much greater than one would expect from epidemiologic studies.

A double-blind, controlled study including more than 200 relatives of bipolar probands and more than 500 relatives of control probands was performed by Tsuang, Winokur, and Crowe (1980). Controls were selected from consecutive admissions of appendectomy and herniorrhaphy patients. Patients were diagnosed with a structured psychiatric interview and a review of medical records. Diagnoses were based on the Washington University diagnostic criteria. Assessments and diagnoses of relatives were blind to the diagnostic status of probands. Seventy-three percent of the relatives were personally interviewed. The 5.3 percent risk of bipolar disorder among the relatives was significantly greater than the 0.3 percent risk observed among controls. The 12.4 percent risk of unipolar disorder among the relatives was greater than the 7.5 percent among controls, but the difference was not statistically significant. This provides strong evidence that bipolar disorder is familial, with only weak evidence for a familial relationship between unipolar and bipolar disorders.

Jakimow-Venulet (1981) studied a Polish sample of 150 bipolar probands and their 804 relatives. Proband diagnoses were based on structured personal interviews and medical record reviews. The diagnostic system employed is not clearly stated although Perris's criteria for depression were used. Relatives were diagnosed through a combination of personal interviews and family history interviews. Although we have no population rates from Polish studies to use for comparison, the 11.8 percent risk of bipolar disorder among the relatives strongly suggests familial transmission. In contrast, the 6.1 percent risk of unipolar disorder does not provide strong evidence for a familial association between the two disorders.

A Swiss sample of 30 bipolar probands and their first-degree relatives was examined by Scharfetter (1981). The Present State Examination, a structured psychiatric interview, was the basis for psychiatric interviews and diagnoses. Relatives were evaluated blind to the proband's diagnosis, based on personal interviews and medical reports. The age-corrected risk for bipolar disorder among relatives was 2.2 percent. The risk of unipolar disorder was 7.7 percent.

Gershon et al. (1982) reported a controlled study of more than 500 relatives of bipolar probands. Probands were diagnosed through structured personal interviews based on the research diagnostic criteria. Approximately 75 percent of the evaluations of relatives were blind to the diagnosis of the proband. All but 75 percent of the relatives were personally interviewed, with other diagnoses being based on family history information. The control probands were medical patients who had no history of diagnosable psychiatric disorder according to a structured psychiatric interview and a medical record review. The 4.5 percent risk of bipolar disorder among relatives of bipolar probands is substantially higher than both epidemiologic expectations and the 0 percent risk to the control group. Similarly, the 14 percent risk of depression among relatives of bipolar probands is at the high end of the population expectation and more than twice the risk observed among relatives of controls (5.8 percent). Thus, this well-designed study found an increased risk for both bipolar and unipolar forms among relatives of bipolar probands.

Endicott et al. (1985) studied 122 bipolar probands and their 389 first-degree relatives. Proband diagnoses were based on structured personal interviews and the research diagnostic criteria. Assessments of relatives were primarily made with structured personal interviews in combination with family history information. Diagnoses of the relatives were blind to the diagnosis of the proband. The 2.3 percent risk of bipolar disorder among relatives is higher than the population expectation even though the figure is not corrected for variable age of onset. The risk of unipolar disorder among the relatives of bipolar probands was 8.3 percent. This definition of unipolar disorder required at least two episodes of major depression for a positive diagnosis. When no restriction is made on the number of episodes of depression, the risk increases to 21.9 percent. Thus, consistent with other studies, recurrent unipolar depression does not show a familial association with bipolar disorder. However, such an association emerges when nonrecurrent depressions are included in the category of unipolar disorder.

Andreasen et al. (1987) reported familial rates of mood disorders from the National Institute of Mental Health's (NIMH) Collaborative Study of the Psychobiology of Depression. Probands were sampled from five centers in the United States. The research methods adhered to high standards of quality for family study research. Among the 569 relatives of bipolar probands, 3.9 percent were diagnosed with bipolar depression and 22.8 percent were diagnosed with unipolar depression. These rates clearly exceed population expectations and strongly suggest familial transmission of unipolar and bipolar disorders in bipolar proband families.

Overall, family studies of bipolar probands strongly support the hypothesis that their first-degree relatives are at greater risk of bipolar disorder than is the general population. The risk to relatives ranges from a low of 1.2 percent to a high of 24.9 percent. All of these values are greater than the general population risk of 0.5 percent suggested by epidemiologic studies (table 2.2). More important, each of the three double-blind, controlled studies found high rates of bipolar disorder among relatives of bipolar probands in comparison to control probands. Conclusions regarding the relationship between unipolar and bipolar subforms are more ambiguous. Studies that limit the definition of unipolar depression to recurrent forms tend to find no familial relationship between the two subforms. Studies that do not exclude nonrecurrent unipolar depressives tend to find a familial association but not consistently so. Most of the double-blind, controlled studies find higher rates of unipolar disorder among relatives of bipolar probands in comparison to relatives of controls. However, these studies included nonrecurrent unipolar depressive and may therefore be confounded if many of the unipolar cases are actually bipolar cases who have not yet experienced a first manic episode.

The familial relationship between unipolar and bipolar disorders can also be assessed by studying unipolar probands and their families. Table 2.8 presents studies of unipolar families that provide risk estimates broken down by the type of relationship with the proband. Some of these studies were performed in conjunction with the studies of bipolar probands reported in table 2.6. Methodologic descriptions of those studies are equally applicable to the unipolar proband studies. Perris (1966) reported results from 1,203 first-degree relatives of 139 recurrent unipolar probands. Their risk of bipolar disorder was less than 0.5 percent, much lower than the previously discussed risk for bipolar disorder among relatives of bipolar

Table 2.8.   The Risk of Major Mood Disorder among Relatives of Unipolar
Probands, Studies after 1960

Study	Relative Diagnosis	Relationship (%)		
		Parent	Child	Sibling
Perris, 1966[a]	BP	0.4	0.0	0.3
	UP	5.0	1.8	8.9
Winokur et al., 1971[a]	UP	23.0	26.0	21.0
Winokur et al., 1972[b]				
	AD	12.8	—	15.3
Shopsin et al., 1976[a]	AD	16.0	0.0	17.0
Smeraldi, Negri, and				
Melica, 1977[a]	BP	0.0	4.5	0.0
	UP	4.7	9.1	6.4
Trzebiatowska-	BP	0.3	0.3	0.3
Trzeciak, 1977[a]	UP	8.0	6.3	7.1
Baron et al., 1981[c]	BP	1.6[d]	1.6[d]	2.8
	UP	15.6[d]	15.6[d]	21.1

Note: MD = mood disorder, BP = bipolar disorder, UP = unipolar disorder.
[a]Weinberg age correction.
[b]Not age corrected.
[c]Strömgren age correction.
[d]Parents and children combined.

probands (4.6–14.1 percent, table 2.6) and not much different from
what one would expect from general population studies. The risk of
unipolar disorder among relatives of unipolar probands was 5–30
times greater than the risk to relatives of bipolar probands. These
results led Perris to suggest that unipolar and bipolar subforms were
genetically distinct disorders. However, these results are somewhat
ambiguous because the unipolar risk to relatives of unipolar probands
is not markedly different from the general population expectation.
Thus, without information from a control group, it is difficult to say
whether or not Perris's data showed unipolar disorder to be familial.

Evidence for the familial nature of unipolar disorder was provided by Winokur et al. (1971) in a family history study of 108
unipolar probands and their 529 first-degree relatives. Although the
probands were diagnosed through personal interviews and medical
record reviews using the Washington University criteria, the relatives
were assessed with the family history technique and these assessments
were not blind to the status of the probands. The results indicate
high rates of unipolar disorder among the relatives of unipolar probands (21–26 percent). These rates are clearly higher than the population expectation but, given the lack of blindness, the use of the
family history method, and a lack of a control group, strong conclu-

sions cannot be drawn. Winokur et al. (1972) studied 225 unipolar probands and their 1,187 first-degree relatives. Rates of mood disorder among the relatives were significantly greater than those observed among relatives of a schizophrenic control group. The risk of mood disorder among relatives of unipolar probands was not significantly different from the risk to relatives of bipolar probands. Since polarity distinctions are not made among relatives, it is not possible to draw inferences about unipolar-bipolar relationships from this study.

Shopsin et al. (1976) studied 71 first-degree relatives of 12 unipolar probands. There was no mood disorder among children of unipolar probands, but a moderately high risk among parents and siblings. For all classes of relatives, the risk of mood disorder was greater among relatives of bipolar as compared with unipolar probands. Smeraldi, Negri, and Melica (1977) studied 49 recurrent unipolar probands and their 318 first-degree relatives. They found no bipolar disorder among the parents and siblings of the probands but a 4.5 percent risk to their children. The overall risk to first-degree relatives was 0.5 percent if only definite bipolar cases are included and 1.0 percent if probable bipolar cases are included. This risk is higher than the risk they cited from an Italian epidemiologic study (0.1 percent), but not substantially higher than the mean risk across all the epidemiologic studies (table 2.2). It is, however, lower than the 4.0 percent risk of bipolar disorder among relatives of bipolar probands. In contrast, the unipolar risk to relatives of unipolar probands (4.7–2.9 percent) was greater than the risk to relatives of bipolar probands (1.4–5.7 percent) for all classes of relatives examined. Thus, using Perris's criteria for recurrent depression, Smeraldi found results that parallel those of Perris (1966). As with Perris (1966), the unipolar risk to unipolar relatives is not markedly greater than the mean general population expectation. The pattern of apparent independent segregation of unipolar and bipolar disorders was also observed by Trzebiatowska-Trzeciak (1977). Her study included 53 recurrent unipolar probands and their 379 first-degree relatives. The bipolar risk to relatives of unipolar is not broken down by relationship. Only one case was found, suggesting an overall morbidity risk to first-degree relatives of only 0.3 percent, well within the population expectation and substantially lower than the risk she found to relatives of bipolar probands. The unipolar risk to unipolar probands (6.3-8.0 percent) contrasts sharply with her finding of no unipolar disorder among relatives of bipolar probands.

Baron et al. (1981) extended the bipolar proband series of Mendlewicz and Rainer (1974) by adding 110 unipolar probands and their nearly 500 first-degree relatives. Proband diagnoses were based on structured personal interviews and the Washington University diagnostic criteria. Most of the relatives (79 percent) were personally interviewed. Evaluations of the relatives were blind to the diagnostic status of the proband. Unlike the previously discussed studies, the risk of bipolar disorder (1.6–2.8 percent) among relatives of unipolar probands was high enough to suggest a familial link between the disorders. The risk of unipolar disorder among the relatives of unipolar probands (14.6–21.1 percent) is fairly high, suggesting familial transmission of unipolar disorder. Unlike in other studies, the unipolar risk for relatives of unipolar probands is not greater than the risk to relatives of bipolar probands. A comparison with Mendlewicz and Rainer's (1974) original report indicates the unipolar risk to bipolar probands to be greater than the risk to relatives of unipolar probands. If the comparison is made using Baron et al.'s (1981) extended series, the unipolar risks appear to be equivalent.

Studies that do not provide a risk estimate breakdown by the type of relationship are presented in table 2.9. The double-blind, controlled study of Gershon et al. (1975) included 16 unipolar probands and their 113 first-degree relatives. None of the first-degree relatives had bipolar disorder. The risk of unipolar disorder among relatives of unipolar probands was 1.5 times greater than the risk to relatives of bipolar probands and 20 times greater than the risk to the relatives of controls. The low risk of bipolar disorder argues against a familial relationship between unipolar and bipolar disorders. However, approximately 2 percent of the relatives of unipolar probands had bipolar II disorder. Abrams and Taylor (1980) reported results from 26 unipolar probands and their first-degree relatives. The 4.7 percent risk of bipolar disorder among the relatives is higher than the population expectation but less than the risk to relatives of bipolar probands (8.5 percent). The 7.5 percent risk of unipolar disorder among relatives of unipolar probands is greater than the 6.4 percent risk to bipolar probands but not markedly so. The unipolar risk is also within the range of values employed for the general population. The small sample size renders these data difficult to interpret. However, the high risk of bipolar disorder among unipolar relatives is consistent with a unipolar-bipolar familial association, as is the finding of essentially equal rates of unipolar disorder among relatives of bipolar and unipolar probands.

Tsuang, Winokur, and Crowe (1980) included 225 unipolar probands and their 500 first-degree relatives in their double-blind, controlled family study. The 3.0 percent risk of bipolar disorder among relatives of unipolar probands was significantly different from the

Table 2.9. The Risk of Major Mood Disorder among First-Degree Relatives of Unipolar Probands, Studies after 1960

Study	Relative Diagnosis	Risk (%)
Gershon et al., 1975[a]	BP	0.0
	UP	14.2
Abrams and Taylor, 1980[b]	BP	4.7
	UP	7.5
Tsuang, Winokur, and Crowe, 1980[b]	BP	3.0
	UP	15.2
Angst et al., 1980[a]	BP	0.1
	UP	5.9
Jakimow-Venulet, 1981[a]	BP	0.5
	UP	9.5
Scharfetter et al., 1981[a]	BP	2.2
	UP	9.0
Gershon et al., 1982[b]	BP	1.5
	UP	16.6
Weissman et al., 1984[a]	BP	0.8
	UP	18.4
Endicott et al., 1985[c]	BP	0.7
	UP	11.1
Andreasen et al., 1987[c]	BP	0.6
	UP	28.4

Note: BP = bipolar disorder, UP = unipolar disorder.
[a]Strömgren correction.
[b]Weinberg correction.
[c]Not age corrected.

risk to the control group of 0.3 percent. The 15.2 percent risk for unipolar disorder among relatives of unipolar probands was significantly different from the 7.5 percent risk to relatives of controls. Thus, these results support the contention that unipolar disorder has a familial component and that unipolar and bipolar disorders coaggregate in families.

Angst et al. (1980) studied 161 unipolar probands and more than 1,000 first-degree relatives. The 0.1 percent risk of bipolar disorder among the relatives is well within the population expectation and substantially less than the 2.5 percent risk for relatives of bipolar probands. The 5.9 percent risk of unipolar disorder among relatives of unipolar probands is not markedly different from either the population expectation or the 7.0 percent risk to relatives of bipolar probands. The low bipolar risk in the unipolar families argues against the unipolar-bipolar link, while the equal rates of unipolar disorder support such a hypothesis. Jakimow-Venulet (1981) included 50 unipolar probands and their 306 first-degree relatives in her family study of mood disorder. Perris's (1966) criteria for recurrent unipolar disorder were applied. The risk for bipolar disorder in the relatives was 0.5 percent. This is consistent with general population studies and much less than the 11.8 percent risk found in relatives of bipolar probands. The 9.5 percent risk of unipolar disorder was greater then the unipolar risk to bipolar families (6.1 percent) but not markedly different from general population studies. Thus, these results are consistent with other studies of recurrent unipolar probands in finding a low risk of bipolar disorder and a possibly elevated risk of recurrent unipolar disorder among their first-degree relatives.

Scharfetter's (1981) study reported psychiatric data from relatives of 59 unipolar probands. The unipolar diagnosis did not require recurrent episodes. The risk of bipolar disorder among relatives was 2.2 percent. The risk of unipolar disorder was 9.0 percent. The risk of bipolar disorder is suggestive of a unipolar-bipolar familial link. The risk of unipolar disorder is difficult to interpret in the absence of a control group.

The double-blind, controlled study of Gershon et al. (1982) included 166 first-degree relatives of unipolar probands. The 1.5 percent risk of bipolar disorder was greater than the 0.0 percent risk for controls but less than the 4.5 percent risk for relatives of bipolar probands. The 16.6 percent risk of unipolar disorder to relatives of unipolar probands was not much greater than the 14.0 percent risk of unipolar disorder to relatives of bipolar probands but was nearly three times the risk observed in the control group. These results are similar to those of the controlled studies of Tsuang, Winokur, and Crowe (1980) and Gershon et al. (1975) in finding strong evidence for a familial component to unipolar disorder and weaker evidence for the coaggregation of bipolar disorder in unipolar families.

Weissman et al. (1984) studied psychiatric disorders in 2,003 first-degree relatives of 335 unipolar probands. Probands were diagnosed with structured personal interviews based on the research diagnostic criteria. Relatives were diagnosed primarily through structured personal interviews based on the research diagnostic criteria along with family history evaluations from multiple informants. Approximately 75 percent of the evaluations of relatives were blind to proband diagnostic status. Similar diagnostic methodologies were applied to a community sample of 82 normal controls. The 8.1 percent risk of bipolar disorder among relatives of unipolar probands was four times the risk observed in the community. The 18.4 percent risk of unipolar disorder was three times the risk reported in the community. Thus, consistent with other double-blind, controlled studies, there is evidence for a familial component to unipolar disorder and some suggestion of a familial coaggregation of unipolar and bipolar disorders.

The study of Endicott et al. (1985) included 121 recurrent unipolar probands and their 424 first-degree relatives. The 0.7 percent risk of bipolar disorder among the relatives is not much greater than the population expectation and is less than the 2.3 percent reported for relatives of bipolar probands. The risk of unipolar disorder to relatives of unipolar probands (11.1 percent) was not much greater than the 8.3 percent risk to relatives of bipolar probands. These results are difficult to interpret, since the risks to relatives have not been corrected for variable ages of onset.

The results from the NIMH Collaborative Study of Depression (Andreasen et al., 1987) found a 0.6 percent risk of bipolar disorder and a 28.4 percent risk for unipolar disorder among relatives of unipolar probands. Although the unipolar diagnosis did not require recurrent episodes, the relatives' risk of bipolar disorder does not suggest a familial link between the two disorders. In contrast, the 28.4 percent risk of unipolar disorder provides strong evidence for familial transmission.

We can identify several trends from the data in tables 2.6–2.9. The reported risks of bipolar disorder among relatives of bipolar probands are consistently greater than the risk to the general population, the risk to relatives of normal controls, and the risk to relatives of unipolar probands. Thus, there is strong evidence that bipolar disorder is familial. If unipolar and bipolar disorders are familially related, the lower risk of bipolar disorder among relatives of unipolar probands suggests that the two disorders do not have completely identical familial substrates. The results of studies of unipolar probands demonstrate the importance of control groups in psychiatric genetic studies. Since the epidemiologically reported risks of unipolar disorder in the general population are highly variable, it is difficult to state whether the risk of unipolar disorder to relatives of unipolar probands in uncontrolled studies is greater than one would expect. However, the four double-blind, controlled studies consistently found higher rates of unipolar disorder among relatives of unipolar probands in comparison to controls. These provide strong evidence favoring the hypothesis that major depression is familial.

The reviewed data provide several means for examining the putative familial relationship between unipolar and bipolar disorders. One approach is to focus on the four rigorous, double-blind, controlled family studies. Table 2.10 indicates the relative risk for unipolar and bipolar disorders among first-degree relatives of bipolar

Table 2.10. The Relative Risk of Unipolar and Bipolar Disorders among First-Degree Relatives of Unipolar and Bipolar Probands, Double-Blind Case-Controlled Studies

		Relative Risk of	
Study	Proband Diagnosis	Unipolar Disorder (%)	Bipolar Disorder (%)
Gershon et al., 1975	BP	9.7	17.5
	UP	18.9	0.0
Tsuang, Winokur, and Crowe, 1980	BP	1.7	17.7
	UP	2.0	10.0
Gershon et al., 1982	BP	2.4	4.5/0
	UP	2.9	1.5/0
Weissman et al., 1984	UP	3.1	4.0

Note: The relative risk is the risk to relatives of ill probands (tables 2.7 and 2.9) divided by the risk to the control sample (tables 2.2 and 2.3). BP = bipolar disorder, UP = unipolar disorder.

and unipolar probands. The relative risk is computed by dividing the risk to the relatives of the ill probands by the risk to the relatives of control probands. These results indicate that a unipolar disorder is 1.7–9.7 times more likely to be found among relatives of bipolar probands than among relatives of control probands. Thus, all the controlled studies found an excess of unipolar disorder in bipolar proband families. The results of examining bipolar disorder in unipolar proband families are less conclusive. Three studies found relative risks greater than or equal to 4; one study reported a relative risk of zero. However, the zero relative risk would increase to 10.5 if bipolar II disorder is considered to be a bipolar variant. Overall, there are seven relative risk figures in table 2.10 that evaluate coaggregation. Six of these relative risks are consistent with a familial association between bipolar and unipolar disorders and one is possibly consistent. Unfortunately, all these studies share one major problem of interpretation: none of the double-blind, controlled studies required more than one episode of depression in the definition of unipolar disorder. It is possible that their unipolar samples are contaminated by cases of latent bipolar patients who have not yet experienced a manic episode. There is a remarkable consistency of results from studies limiting the diagnosis of unipolar disorder to recurrent forms (i.e., two or more episodes). As a group, these studies indicate little evidence of unipolar-bipolar concordance in families. Most remarkable in this regard are the studies of Perris (1966) and Trzebiatowska-Trzeciak (1977). They found very little unipolar disorder among relatives of bipolar probands and very little bipolar disorder among relatives of unipolar probands. It is difficult to reconcile these findings with the hypothesis that the two subforms are genetically related. Unfortunately, there are no double-blind, controlled family studies of recurrent unipolar disorder. Resolution of this issue must await further research or, possibly, reanalyses of previous data sets omitting nonrecurrent unipolar cases.

RISK FACTORS FOR FAMILIAL MOOD DISORDERS

In the preceding sections, we have unequivocally demonstrated that mood disorders are familial. In this section we examine three variables proven to be robust familial risk factors. That is, the measurement of the risk factor increases the ability to predict the degree of risk to relatives of ill individuals.

Degree of Relationship

Under a genetic hypothesis, the risk for a disorder among second-degree relatives should be greater than the population prevalence but less than the risk to first-degree relatives. Morbidity risks to second-degree relatives of mood disorder probands are presented in table 2.11.

All of these early family studies reported risks to second-degree relatives that are greater than the general population prevalence but less than the risk to first-degree relatives.

The three more recent data sets pertaining to second-degree relatives in table 2.11 can be compared to general population risks in tables 2.2 and 2.3 and to first-degree relative risks in tables 2.6–2.9. Smeraldi, Negri, and Melica (1977) studied 660 second-degree relatives of unipolar probands and 669 second-degree relatives of bipolar probands. The prevalence of mood disorders among these relatives was clearly less than the prevalence among first-degree relatives but not markedly different from the population expectation. The overall risk for bipolar disorder among second-degree relatives of unipolar probands was only 0.2 percent; the corresponding risk for unipolar disorder was 0.5 percent. The overall risk for bipolar disorder among second-degree relatives of bipolar probands was 0.9 percent; the corresponding risk for unipolar disorder was 0.7 percent. Thus, there is some evidence for an increased risk of bipolar disorder among second-degree relatives of bipolar probands, but no apparent increased risk for other proband-relative comparisons.

Table 2.11.   The Risk of Major Mood Disorder among Second-Degree Relatives

Study	Proband Diagnosis	Relative Diagnosis	Relationship	Risk (%)
Röll and Entres, 1936[a,b]	MD	MD	nephews and nieces	3.6
Schaedler, 1938[a,b]	MD	MD	grandchildren	3.4
Schulz, 1930s[c]	MD	MD	half-siblings	1.4
Luxenburger, 1930s[d]	MD	MD	nephews and nieces	2.6
			uncles and aunts	4.8
Kallmann, 1954	MD	MD	half-siblings	16.7
Smeraldi, Negri, and Melica, 1977[a]	UP	BP	uncles and aunts	0.0
			nephews	0.0
			grandparents	0.7
	UP	UP	uncles and aunts	0.8
			nephews	0.0
			grandparents	0.0
	BP	BP	uncles and aunts	1.2
			nephews	0.0
			grandparents	0.7
	BP	UP	uncles and aunts	1.2
			nephews	0.0
			grandparents	0.0
Trzebiatowska-Trzeciak, 1977[e]	UP	MD	grandchildren	3.4
	BP	MD	grandchildren	5.3
Gershon et al., 1982[e]	UP	BP	grandparents, uncles, and aunts	0.0
	UP	UP	uncles and aunts	3.7
	BP	BP	uncles and aunts	1.1
	BP	UP	uncles and aunts	5.4

Note: MD = mood disorder, BP = bipolar disorder, UP = unipolar disorder.
[a]Weinberg method of age correction.
[b]From Stenstedt, 1952.
[c]From Kallmann, 1954.
[d]From Slater, 1936.
[e]Strömgren method of age correction.

Trzebiatowska-Trzeciak (1977) studied mood disorders in 330 grandchildren of unipolar probands and 252 grandchildren of bipolar probands. These data are difficult to interpret because the diagnoses of relatives were not classified by polarity. However, this author did find unipolar and bipolar disorders to breed true among first-degree relatives (tables 2.6 and 2.8). If it is assumed that these disorders also breed true among the second-degree relatives, then the data in table 2.11 would indicate an increased risk of bipolar disorder among second-degree relatives of bipolar probands but no increased risk of unipolar disorder among second-degree relatives of unipolar probands.

The study of Gershon et al. (1982) is the only double-blind, controlled study to include second-degree relatives. These results are similar to those of Smeraldi, Negri, and Melica in that the risks to second-degree relatives are clearly less than the risks to first-degree relatives but not consistently greater than the population prevalence. In fact, the only risk of morbidity to second-degree relatives that is substantially greater than the risk to the control group is the risk for bipolar disorder among second-degree relatives of bipolar probands. Thus, all of the three recent family studies of second-degree family relatives find evidence for an increased risk of bipolar disorder among relatives of bipolar probands. There is no strong evidence for an increased risk of unipolar disorder among second-degree relatives of either unipolar or bipolar probands. There is no evidence for an increased risk of bipolar disorder among the second-degree relatives of unipolar probands. Thus, studies of second-degree relatives are consistently supportive of a genetic component to bipolar disorder. They provide little evidence of a genetic component to unipolar disorder or of a genetic association between unipolar and bipolar disorders. In interpreting these data it is, of course, important to remember that family studies of second-degree relatives are more difficult and probably less methodologically sound than family studies of first-degree relatives. This is because the more distant relatives are more difficult to contact and less likely to be recruited for personal interviews. Thus, data on second-degree relatives are often based on the family history method. To compound the problem, the family history method is less reliable when informants are reporting about distant relatives. Since none of these studies provided data on second-degree relatives of control probands, the extent of such potential biases is difficult to determine. However, the direction of the bias would be to lower the observed risk to second-degree relatives. Since the bias should not differentially affect diagnoses of unipolar and bipolar disorder, the differences observed between these two disorders are probably not artifactual.

Gender

Epidemiologic studies have consistently found women to be at greater risk than men for unipolar disorder. The comprehensive review by Weissman and Boyd (1984) indicated that this gender effect is more pronounced for unipolar than for bipolar disorder. The unipolar/bipolar difference in the robustness of the gender effect is clearly seen in the data of Robins et al. (1984), indicating women to be twice as likely as men to experience a major depressive episode but equally likely to have experienced a manic episode. This difference was observed in three large community samples and is consistent with Winokur and Crowe's (1983) review of 14 family studies of bipolar probands indicating that, among affected female relatives, the ratio of unipolar to bipolar disorder is approximately two, whereas, among affected male relatives, the ratio is approximately one. As Winokur and Crowe (1983) noted, the gender effect may hold a clue to clarifying the observed familial transmission and suspected genetic heterogeneity of the mood disorders.

The possibility that the gender effect is due to the transmission of a gene on the X-chromosome has received much attention. A dominant X-linked gene is consistent with greater prevalence among females. The mathematics of population genetics has shown that, assuming a dominant X-linked gene, the ratio of ill males to ill females should be $1/(2 - p)$, where p is equal to the probability of the pathogenic gene in the population. Low values of p would be consistent with the population male/female sex ratio of 0.5 reported in epidemiologic studies (Weissman and Boyd, 1984). A hallmark of X-linkage is the absence of father-to-son transmission, because fathers cannot transmit an X-chromosome to their sons. There have been reports of no father-son transmission of bipolar disorder in some samples (see, e.g., Winokur, 1970). However, one comprehensive review found 73 cases of father-son transmission in 11 family studies of bipolar disorder (Zerbin-Rudin, 1980). Thus X-linkage cannot account for all cases of mood disorder.

Autosomal inheritance can lead to sex differences in the presence of a nonfamilial, environmental effect that differentially affects males and females. For example, if certain maternal child-rearing experiences increase vulnerability to mood disorders, then a sex difference will be observed. The autosomal model with nonfamilial effects predicts that the male/female sex ratio among relatives of female probands is expected to equal the sex ratio among relatives of male probands, and both are expected to equal the population sex ratio.

Faraone, Lyons, and Tsuang (1987) examined the gender effect by presenting data from 16 informative family studies that provided the morbidity risk by the sex of the proband and the sex of the relative. Their results are presented in figures 2.1 and 2.2 as ratios of the form IJ/KL; here the ratio expresses the morbidity risk of a relative of sex J given a proband of sex I, divided by the risk to relative of sex L given a proband of sex K. The second sex ratio in

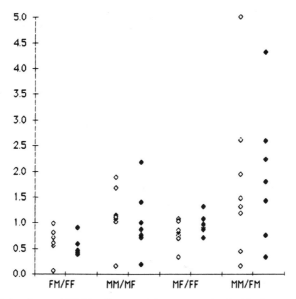

Figure 2.1.   Parent/child family resemblance sex ratios (◇ bipolar, ◆ unipolar)

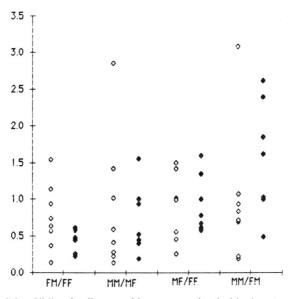

Figure 2.2.   Sibling family resemblance sex ratios (◇ bipolar, ◆ unipolar)

figure 2.1 (MM/MF) has the most straightforward interpretation. It should be equal to the gene frequency, p, under the X-linked model and to the population male/female sex ratio under the nonfamilial effects model. Since the general population risk for mood disorder is less than 10 percent in most studies, the gene frequency must be relatively low. This is especially obvious for dominant X-linked disorders, where the male population risk of the disorder equals the gene frequency times the penetrance (the probability of expressing the disorder if one has the ill genotype).

For the X-linked model, the risk to females should be $p(2 - p)$ times the penetrance. Since monozygotic twin concordance rates for mood disorder are greater than 50 percent, it is unlikely that mood disorders are a low-penetrant phenotype. The MM/MF sex ratios in figure 2.1 are highly variable for both the unipolar and the bipolar studies. They are not consistent with the suggestion that either X-linkage or a nonfamilial effects model accounts for a large majority of the mood disorders in the 16 studies reviewed.

Consistent with mathematical modeling studies (see chap. 5 below), the data in figures 2.1 and 2.2 are not consistent with the hypothesis that males (the less frequently affected sex) require more multifactorial familial liability to develop the disorder than do females. Such a model predicts relatives of male probands to be at a greater risk than relatives of female probands. As the MF/FF and MM/FM sex ratios in each figure indicate, this is not true for many of the data sets examined.

The first two sibling sex ratios (FM/FF and MM/MF) in figure 2.2 indicate that the ratio of ill brothers to ill sisters is larger when the proband is male. If the population sex ratio is due to a nonfamilial effect, the brother/sister ratio should not depend on the sex of the proband. Thus it is likely that some familial sex-specific effect is operating. X-linkage is a reasonable candidate; it predicts that the brother/sister sex ratio among female probands will be less than the comparable ratio among male probands.

The sibling effect was examined from another perspective by comparing same-sex sibling risks with opposite-sex sibling risks (Faraone, Lyons, and Tsuang, 1987). Opposite-sex morbidity risks were less than both same-sex morbidity risks for 10 of the 12 proband groups in studies that did not report the polarity of the disorder. That is, the opposite-sex risks were significantly less than the brother/brother risks and the sister/sister risks. The studies examining diagnoses of relatives by polarity produced more ambiguous results. Although 9 of 15 comparisons indicated lower opposite-sex than same-sex risks, the differences are not statistically significant.

The sibling data reviewed by Faraone et al. are consistent with the involvement of cultural transmission. For example, Rice, Cloninger, and Reich (1980) described a multifactorial polygenic model with cultural transmission from same-sex identification. If, through social learning, children are more likely to develop the behavior patterns of the same-sex parent, then same-sex sibling concordance should be greater than opposite-sex sibling concordance. This model is also consistent with data in figure 2.1 that can be interpreted to mean that mother-daughter transmission is greater than mother-son transmission for most studies. However, the model makes the incorrect prediction that father-son transmission will be greater than father-daughter transmission.

Age of Onset

That mood disorders have a variable age of onset has been known for many years. The cause of this variability is unknown, but its significance as a predictor of familial risk has not gone unobserved. Stenstedt (1952) reported that relatives of early-onset unipolar probands had more than twice the risk of mood disorders than relatives of late-onset unipolar probands. The onset was considered early if the first episode of illness was before age 40. First episodes after age 40 defined late-onset probands. This finding has been frequently replicated and extended to include relatives of bipolar probands. Table 2.12 compares morbidity risks among relatives of early- and late-onset probands. Of the 19 studies in table 2.12, 17 found relatives of early-onset probands to be at greater risk for mood disorder than relatives of late-onset probands. All of the 10 comparisons from unipolar proband studies found the effect, as did 2 studies combining unipolar and bipolar probands. Only 2 of the 7 bipolar proband studies did not. Thus, the age-of-onset effect has overwhelming support. Recent reports from the NIMH Collaborative Study of Depression have confirmed the effect for bipolar (Rice, Reich, et al., 1987) but not for unipolar (Reich et al., 1987) probands.

The age-of-onset effect appears to be independent of both the gender of the proband and the gender of the relative. The effect is consistently observed among relatives of male and female probands (table 2.13) regardless of the relative's gender (table 2.14).

Furthermore, when methods analogous to multiple regression are used to predict illness among relatives, the age-of-onset and gender effects are found to be independent for both unipolar (Weissman et al., 1986) and bipolar (Rice, Reich, et al., 1987) disorders in relatives. These analyses also indicate that the age-of-onset effect

Table 2.12. The Risk of Illness by the Age of Onset of the Proband

| Study | Proband/Relative Diagnosis | Age Cutpoint[a] | Risk (%) by Age of Onset of Proband | |
			Early[a]	Late[a]
Stenstedt, 1952[b,c]	UP/MD	40	16.6	7.9
Hopkinson, 1964[d]	AD/MD	50	21.1	9.1
	BP/MD	40	9.6	12.0
Winokur and Clayton, 1967[b,c]	UP/MD	40	23.0	8.7
	BP/MD	40	34.8	20.6
Hopkinson and Ley, 1969[c]	AD/MD	40	28.8	12.5
Winokur et al., 1971[d]	UP/UP	40	19.6	13.6
Marten et al., 1972[c]	UP/MD	40	12.2	6.3
Taylor and Abrams, 1973[d]	BP/MD	30	30.6	7.9
Winokur et al., 1973[c]	UP/MD	40	16.5	7.6
(parents then sibs)	UP/MD	40	17.3	13.8
Goetzl et al., 1974[c]	BP/MD	40	17.4	19.8
James, 1977[d]	BP/MD	30	26.0	12.3
Johnson and Leeman, 1977[d]	BP/MD	30	31.4	28.8
Winokur, 1979[c]	UP/UP	40	23.0	8.1
Angst et al., 1980[d]	BP/MD	50	13.2	10.3
Mendlewicz and Baron, 1981[d]	UP/UP	40	21.4	14.3
Weissman et al., 1984[c]	UP/UP	40	16.6	7.6
McGuffin, Katz, and Bebbington, 1987[d]	UP/UP	32	43.1	35.2

Note: MD = mood disorder, BP = bipolar disorder, UP = unipolar disorder.
[a]Early (Late) onset is less (greater) than cutpoint.
[b]As tabulated by Cadoret et al., 1970.
[c]Weinberg method of age correction.
[d]Strömgren age correction.
[e]No age correction.

Table 2.13. The Risk of Illness by the Sex and Age of Onset of the Proband

| Study | Proband/Relative Diagnosis | Risk (%) to Relatives | | | |
| | | Male Proband | | Female Proband | |
		Early Onset	Late Onset	Early Onset	Late Onset
Hopkinson and Ley, 1969	MD/MD	30.7	14.8	27.9	10.9
Winokur et al., 1973	UP/MD	15.4	9.1	17.4	6.4
James, 1977	BP/MD	27.6	12.1	25.8	15.5

Note: MD = mood disorder, BP = bipolar disorder, UP = unipolar disorder.

Table 2.14 The Risk of Illness by the Sex and Age of Onset of the Proband and the Sex of the Relative

			Risk (%) to Relative			
			Male Proband		Female Proband	
Study	Proband/Relative Diagnosis	Sex of Relative	Early Onset	Late Onset	Early Onset	Late Onset
Stenstedt, 1952	BP/MD	M	7.7	0.0	11.8	0.0
		F	6.5	0.0	11.8	33.8
	UP/MD	M	20.0	0.0	12.0	9.0
		F	22.2	7.1	18.2	13.9
Winokur and Clayton, 1967	BP/MD	M	14.3	0.0	12.5	45.5
		F	85.7	26.7	43.8	0.0
	UP/MD	M	24.0	14.9	20.9	5.8
		F	16.8	6.5	29.0	9.3
Cadoret et al., 1971	UP/MD	M	—	—	7.2	6.9
		F	—	—	11.1	17.8
Winokur et al., 1971	UP/UP	M	16.0	19.0	9.0	6.0
		F	37.0	12.0	29.0	9.0
Marten et al., 1972	UP/MD	M	6.9	11.8	7.9	2.8
		F	17.5	5.1	17.0	8.1
Mendelwicz and Baron, 1981	UP/UP	M	10.0	8.0	8.0	6.0
		F	17.0	8.0	17.0	10.0

Note: MD = mood disorder, BP = bipolar disorder, UP = unipolar disorder.

cannot be attributed to either the birth cohort effect or the presence of anxiety or alcohol use disorders in the probands.

There are several competing explanations for the age-of-onset effect. Perhaps the simplest is that the older-onset probands are contaminated by cases of mood disorder that are secondary to another disorder. The older-onset group would be more susceptible to contamination because the aging process is associated with an increased likelihood of having an illness that may present as a mood disorder. Since the mood disturbance may be apparent before the diagnosis of the primary illness, one would expect that even the most rigorous diagnostic criteria would be prone to such misdiagnosis. Another possibility is etiologic heterogeneity. That is, early- and late-onset cases may correspond to different forms of primary mood disorders. The age-of-onset distinction has been useful in clarifying the etiologic heterogeneity of other illnesses, such as diabetes. It may also provide a useful marker of discrete subtypes for mood disorders.

If mood disorders are homogeneous, then early-onset probands may have a more severe form of the same disorder that affects late-onset probands. This explanation is consistent with a multifactorial polygenic model of familial transmission (see chap. 5 below for details). Briefly, the multifactorial model asserts that the onset of a disorder is caused by the additive action of numerous genetic and environmental factors. In this formulation a more severe disorder is one that is accompanied by a greater number of these factors.

It is reasonable to expect that severe cases have an earlier age of onset than milder cases, because the latter's onset may be forestalled until an environmental stress occurs. Since severe cases, by definition, also have a higher genetic loading (i.e., more polygenes), one would expect their relatives to be at greater risk for the disorder. Although none of these alternative explanations for the age-of-onset effect can be definitively chosen, it is unequivocally clear that the age of onset is a familial risk factor that deserves further exploration.

Summary

The family study is the workhorse of psychiatric genetics. The systematic evaluation of families where illness is known to affect one member provides a relatively straightforward means of testing the hypothesis of genetic transmission. In this chapter we have provided a context for interpreting family studies by reviewing the epidemiology of mood disorders. An accurate estimate of the population rate of illness is essential to a meaningful interpretation of the rate of illness among families of ill individuals. As we can discern from table 2.1, the pioneering European studies suggested that the lifetime risk for what was then called manic-depressive psychosis was less than 1 percent. Although these studies did not use explicitly defined, structured diagnostic criteria, they were sensitive to the necessity of creating homogeneous study groups using appropriate exclusion criteria.

More recent epidemiologic studies focusing on bipolar disorder report rates of illness ranging from 0 percent to 1.1 percent, with a mean of 0.5 percent (table 2.2). It is notable that there is relatively little variability among the 12 studies examined. In contrast, estimated population rates of unipolar disorder are highly variable, ranging from a low of 0.5 percent to a high of 18.0 percent (table 2.3). These results could indicate that population rates of unipolar disorder are truly more variable across time and location than are rates of bipolar disorder. However, a more parsimonious methodologic explanation should be considered. There may be more agreement among investigators regarding the definition of bipolar disorder, leading to more agreement in estimates of prevalence.

It is also notable that the early European studies report population rates of manic-depressive psychosis that are in the same range as the more recently reported rates of bipolar disorder but well below the range of rates reported for major depression. This may indicate that the early definition of manic-depressive psychosis was essentially limited to bipolar cases and, perhaps, the more severe cases of recurrent unipolar disorder. Alternatively, these differences may reflect true increases in rates of mood disorders during the twentieth century. Systematic evaluations of trends in the rates of mood disorders support this latter interpretation. A growing number of investigators have observed an increasing lifetime risk of mood disorders during the twentieth century. Although further work is needed before this phenomenon is completely understood, the effect does not appear to be due to simple confounds such as impaired recall of early episodes by older individuals. It is more likely that the presence of a true cohort effect or age-period interaction has been established. Choosing between these alternatives is difficult for a variety of reasons. Nevertheless, the work of Lavori et al. (1986) from the NIMH Collaborative Study of Depression provided compelling evidence that there was a marked leap in the risk of depression during the decade from 1965 to 1975, suggesting the presence of a period effect that increased the risk of illness to individuals who had not passed through the age-of-onset range for the disorder. Follow-up data from the collaborative study should provide more definitive evidence for the proposed period effect.

The early European family studies of mood disorders used methods and diagnostic practices similar to those employed in the early European epidemiologic studies. In fact, many of the same investigators produced both epidemiologic and family study data. These investigators consistently found that manic-depressive psychoses were much more prevalent among the parents, children, and siblings of manic-depressive patients than among the general population (table 2.5). For most studies, the risk to relatives was more than 10 times the risk to the general population. In four studies there was a fortyfold increase in the risk to relatives (table 2.5).

The more methodologically sophisticated family studies completed in recent decades have confirmed observations made by the pioneers of psychiatric genetics. Family studies of bipolar probands (tables 2.6 and 2.7) strongly support the hypothesis that their parents, siblings, and children are at greater risk for bipolar disorder than the general population. Each of the three double-blind, controlled studies found increased rates of bipolar disorder among relatives of bipolar probands compared to relatives of normal control probands (table 2.10). Findings regarding the relationship of unipolar and bipolar disorders were ambiguous. Studies limiting the definition of unipolar to recurrent cases tend to find no familial relationship between the two disorders. Studies including nonrecurrent cases tend to find a familial association, but not consistently. All of the double-blind, controlled studies find a familial association but none of these excludes cases of nonrecurrent depression. It is difficult to determine whether increased rates of depression among families of bipolar probands are due to bipolar cases that have not yet experienced a manic episode.

Family studies of unipolar probands provide less consistent evidence than do bipolar proband studies (tables 2.8 and 2.9). Given the high variability of estimates in population prevalence, uncontrolled studies are difficult to interpret, because in many cases the risk to parents, siblings, and children is within the range observed in epidemiologic studies. Fortunately, all of the double-blind, controlled studies consistently found elevated rates of depression among relatives of unipolar probands when compared to relatives of normal control probands or population samples. Thus, the familial nature of unipolar depression has been definitively established. The unipolar proband studies do not conclusively establish a familial link to bipolar disorder. Some studies find increased rates of bipolar disorder in the relatives; others do not. The increased rates are usually found in studies that include nonrecurrent cases of unipolar depression and are usually not found when such cases are excluded. Case-controlled, double-blind family studies separating recurrent and nonrecurrent depressions are needed to clarify this issue.

In this chapter we have examined three factors known to affect strongly the familial risk of mood disorders. Under any genetic transmission hypothesis, the risk to relatives should decrease as the number of shared genes decreases. With the data in table 2.11 we can demonstrate that, for the early European studies of manic-depressive psychosis, the risk to second-degree relatives (who share 25 percent of their genes with probands) is greater than the population risk but less than the risk to first-degree relatives (who share 50 percent of their genes with probands). The three recent studies of second-degree relatives all suggest an increased risk for bipolar but not unipolar disorder among second-degree relatives of bipolar probands. The risk to second-degree relatives tends to be less than the risk to first-degree relatives. There is little evidence for an increased risk of unipolar or bipolar disorders among second-degree relatives of unipolar probands. Thus, although the degree of genetic relatedness appears to be a risk factor for familial mood disorders, further double-blind, case-controlled studies of second-degree relatives are needed to provide more definitive evidence.

The role of gender as a risk factor for depression was first suggested from epidemiologic data finding consistently higher rates of depression among females. Within bipolar families, father-son transmission is less frequently observed than is mother-son transmission, suggesting that gender is related to familial risk in a manner consistent with X-chromosome transmission. However, X-chromosome transmission cannot explain the observed sibling effect—that is, that the risk to siblings of the same sex is greater than the risk to opposite-sex siblings. Such a pattern raises the question of cultural transmission due to same-sex identification or related processes. We discuss issues of genetic transmission more fully in subsequent chapters and we suggest that there may be a role for both X-linked and culturally transmitted factors in the transmission of mood disorders.

An early age of onset in probands has been frequently observed to be associated with increased risk to relatives. Although there are some inconsistent results, this age-of-onset effect is surprisingly robust. It has been reported for both unipolar and bipolar disorders and is independent of the sex of both proband and relative. The age of onset of mood disorder may be a marker of etiologic heterogeneity. That is, as is the case with diabetes, an early age of onset may characterize a more familial form of the disorder. An alternative hypothesis is that the age of onset is associated with a multifactorial polygenic liability that underlies mood disorders. Under this hypothesis, earlier-onset patients have more polygenes than do late-onset patients and are therefore more likely to transmit the illness to relatives.

Chapter Three

Twin Studies

The occurrence of twinning provides a natural experiment in human genetics. Monozygotic (MZ) twins have 100 percent of their genes in common. Thus, differences between MZ twins must be due to environmental influences. Dizygotic (DZ) twins have only 50 percent of their genes in common; their genetic similarity is the same as that between siblings. Since DZ twins are not genetic copies of each other, differences within a twin pair can be due to environmental or genetic factors. Thus, a comparison of the co-occurrence of a psychiatric disorder in MZ and DZ twins provides information about the relative importance of genetic and environmental factors in the etiology of the disorder.

METHODOLOGIC CONSIDERATIONS

Twin data for all-or-none traits like psychiatric disorders are usually expressed as concordance rates. These rates are based on a sample created by first identifying ill individuals (the probands) from twin births and then evaluating the co-twin. The pairwise concordance rate is defined as the proportion of twin pairs in which both twins are ill. If X is equal to the number of concordant twin pairs (i.e., both twins are ill) and Y is equal to the number of discordant twin pairs (i.e., only one twin is ill), then the pairwise concordance rate is given by:

$$\frac{X}{X + Y}$$

Although intuitively appealing, the pairwise concordance rate is appropriately used only when the mode of sampling is single selection—that is, the probability of sampling an ill individual is so low that two ill co-twins are never independently ascertained as probands. The proband method of computing concordance rates is appropriate when the mode of sampling is multiple selection—that is, for some concordant pairs both twins were probands (Cavalli-Sforza and Bodmer, 1971). The proband concordance rate is defined as the proportion of proband twins that have an ill co-twin. If X and Y are defined as before and if Z is the number of concordant pairs in which both the twins are probands, then the proband concordance rate is defined as:

$$\frac{X + Z}{X + Y + Z}$$

Slater and Cowie (1971) demonstrated that the results of the proband method are independent of the ascertainment probability if it can be assumed that the probability of ascertaining a proband is independent of the condition of the co-twin.

We can use the information collected from MZ and DZ twins to estimate the heritability of a disorder. Heritability is a measure of the degree to which the phenotypic variability of a disorder is influenced by genetic factors. A value of zero indicates that the phenotypic variability is due entirely to environmental influences. A value of one indicates that the phenotypic variability of a disorder can be explained entirely by genetic factors. Heritability (h^2) is defined mathematically as a ratio of variances. The phenotypic variability (V_p) can be partitioned into two sources of variance—genetic variance (V_g) and environmental variance (V_e)— if it can be assumed that genetic and environmental factors are statistically independent and do not interact (i.e., $V_p = V_g + V_e$). Heritability, in the broad sense, is defined as the ratio of genetic and phenotypic variances (i.e., $h^2 = V_g/V_p$). From this definition it is clear that a heritability of zero indicates that there is no genetic variability in the sample under consideration. It does not mean that the etiology of the phenotype can be explained solely by environmental influence. Several methods of estimating heritability from twin data have been suggested. Holzinger (1929) suggested that heritability be computed as follows:

$$H = \frac{CMZ - CDZ}{100 - CDZ}$$

where CMZ and CDZ are the proband concordance rates for MZ and DZ twins, respectively. Smith (1974) suggested a definition of heritability appropriate to the case when a disorder is due to an unobservable, continuous liability. Individuals with a liability greater than a certain value develop the disorder; individuals below this threshold value are not afflicted. The formula is

$$G = 2(rmz - rdz),$$

where rmz and rdz are the correlations of liability between MZ and DZ twins, respectively. These correlations can be computed from the proband concordance rates in conjunction with the population prevalence of the disorder (Reich, James, and Morris, 1972; Smith 1974).

In addition to heritability, two environmental variance components can be calculated from the correlations of liability. Common environmental variance (Vc) is calculated by the formula

$$Vc = 2\,rdz - rmz.$$

Unique environmental variance is calculated by the formula

$$Vu = 1 - rmz.$$

Under the assumptions of this model, these three variance components (G, Vc, Vu) account for the total amount of variance contributing to the variability of a trait. The calculation of G, Vc, and Vu assumes that the effects of the relevant genes are additive and that the effects of epistasis (interaction among genes) and assortative mating are negligible.

THE LIMITATIONS OF THE TWIN METHOD

The ability of the twin method to provide meaningful results is inextricably linked with the ability to diagnose zygosity correctly. If a substantial misclassification of MZ and DZ twins occurs, an examination of concordance rates and heritability estimates is meaningless. Fortunately, precise methods of determining zygosity exist. These take advantage of the fact that a twin pair can be classified as dizygotic if the twins differ on any known genetic marker. Thus, a determination of blood groups, serum proteins, isoenzymes, and HLA antigens can increase the certainty of the zygosity classification. Given the large number of genetic markers available, it is possible to make the probability of misclassification arbitrarily low (Vogel and Motulsky, 1979). In the absence of comprehensive genetic marker data, similarity of physical characteristics such as eye color and dermatoglyphics can provide accurate estimates of zygosity. In fact, a determination of zygosity by a response to questions about the degree of physical similarity and the degree to which the twins were mistaken for one another as children has been shown to be reasonably accurate in comparison to genetic marker classifications (Cederlof et al., 1961; Kasriel and Eaves, 1976; Nichols and Bilbro, 1966). Although zygosity can theoretically be determined with high accuracy, even sophisticated methods using genetic markers are subject to experimental and laboratory error. Thus, some confusion between MZ and DZ twins is to be expected, although it appears unlikely that errors will greatly influence the results if appropriate procedures are followed.

Inferences from twin studies to nontwin populations may be inappropriate if biological or psychosocial factors associated with twinning are etiologically important in the development of psychiatric disorders. Kringlen's (1967) data suggested that this is not the case. His tabulation of the age-specific rates of first admissions for functional psychosis for twins and the general population indicated that twins are not more or less likely to develop schizophrenia, manic-depressive disorder, or reactive psychosis then are members of the general population. These results apply to both males and females and are based on data collected between 1921 and 1960. In a study of 22 MZ and 13 DZ pairs, the degree of depression reported by twins on the Zung Depression Scale was similar to levels reported by nontwins (Paluszny et al., 1977). Despite these empirical results, there are theoretical reasons to believe that there are important differences between twins and nontwins. For example, twins have lower birth weights than nontwins, twins' births suffer from higher rates of pregnancy and delivery complications, and congenital malformations are more common in twin than singleton births (Vogel and Motulsky, 1979). Since pregnancy and delivery complications can have neurologic sequelae relevant to the etiology of psychiatric disorders, these environmental influences may play a greater role in twin than in nontwin populations. For example, Paluszny and Abelson (1975) found that although twins were less likely to be referred to a child psychiatric clinic, they were more likely to show evidence of minimal brain dysfunction in comparison to a matched nontwin group. Thus, estimates of heritability from MZ and DZ concordance rates may not be generalizable to the general population.

The cornerstone of the twin method is the assumption that differences between MZ and DZ twin similarity are due to genetic factors. That is, the environmental determinants of similarity are assumed identical for the two types of twin pairs, whereas the genetic determinants of similarity are greater for MZ pairs. However, if the similarity of MZ twin environments is greater than that of DZ twin environments with regard to etiologically relevant factors, then the twin method will overestimate the importance of genetic influences. Several studies indicate that the social environments of MZ twins are more similar than those of DZ twins. For example, habits, activities, personal preferences, parental treatment, and self-image have been found to be more similar between MZ twins (Scarr, 1968;

Smith, 1965). MZ twins are more likely to be dressed alike (Koch, 1966; Loehlin, 1973) and are more likely to be mistaken for one another in childhood (Cederlof et al., 1961; Kasriel and Eaves, 1976; Nichols and Bilbro, 1966).

These results suggest that twin studies may overestimate heritability because the similarity of MZ environments appears to be greater than that of DZ environments. However, as Matheny, Wilson, and Dolan (1976) noted, this criticism of twin studies assumes the following causal pathway: (1) similarity of appearance causes greater similarity of treatment by others, and (2) similarity of treatment by others causes greater similarity of behavior. If this is true, then the physical and behavioral similarity of twins should be correlated. Matheny, Wilson, and Dolan found no substantial evidence for such an association for 18 cognitive and personality measures of behavior. Scarr and Carter-Saltzman (1979) tested the environmental bias hypothesis from a different perspective by taking advantage of the fact that twins and their parents often make wrong judgments about their zygosity. If behavioral similarity is caused by genetic factors, then it should not be influenced by incorrect perceptions of zygosity. In contrast, if behavioral similarity is due to environmental similarity that was induced by physical similarity, then perceived zygosity, not true zygosity, should determine the degree of behavioral similarity. In Scarr's (1979) study, 40 percent of 400 twin pairs either disagreed or were wrong about their zygosity. The similarity of cognitive measures was related to true, not perceived zygosity. For measures of personality, both true and perceived zygosity were related to co-twin similarity. MZ personalities were more similar than DZ personalities, but DZ twins who thought they were MZ were more similar than DZs who disagreed and DZs who perceived their correct zygosity. However, Scarr also found that, compared to other DZs, DZs who thought they were MZs were more similar genetically based on blood-group similarities. This suggests that the observed "perceived zygosity" effect may actually be genetic. Overall, methodologically oriented twin research does not strongly indicate that environmental biases vitiate the twin study method. Furthermore, the etiologic importance of purported environmental bias factors for psychiatric disorders has not been clearly demonstrated. Therefore it is reasonable to conclude that the twin method can provide interpretable information about the genetics of mood disorders.

Greater physical and environmental similarity between MZ twins may actually lead to a decrease in behavioral similarity. MZ twins may work harder to develop a persona that clearly differentiates each from the other. Such effects may lead to what Vogel and Motulsky (1979) referred to as role differentiation, where each twin performs different behavioral functions for the twin pair (e.g., one twin may be dominant, the other submissive). These effects may explain the result of Farber (1981), that similarity of personality is greater among MZ twins reared apart than among those reared together.

Biological factors may also act to decrease the estimate of genetic influence derived from the twin method. Unlike DZ twins, a substantial proportion of MZ twins share a common chorion in utero. Monochorionic twins may develop transfusion syndrome, in which blood from one twin enters the circulatory system of the other through their common placenta (Benirschke and Kim, 1973). This condition may lead to differences in the size and health of MZ co-twins. Transfusion syndrome and other prenatal factors may explain why MZ twins tend to have lower and more variable birth weights than DZ twins (Vogel and Motulsky, 1979).

As we indicated in chapter 2, assortative mating may be substantial for the mood disorders. As Kendler (1983) noted, assortative mating will tend to make DZ twins more similar to one another than would be expected under random mating. Since MZ twins are always genetically identical, assortative mating has no effect on their genetic similarity. Thus, the presence of assortative mating will increase DZ concordance rates, leading to an underestimate of heritability.

Although twin studies are not without interpretive limitations, there is no conclusive evidence that these limitations substantially bias the results of twin studies of mood disorders. Thus, the twin method provides an informative source of converging evidence in determining the importance of genetic factors in mood disorders.

Twin Studies of Major Mood Disorders

Most twin studies of mood disorders were performed before 1960. Although they provided a firm foundation for subsequent work in psychiatric genetics, they could not benefit from the recent advances in psychiatric diagnosis and research methodology that we discussed in chapter 1. Luxenburger (1928, 1930) selected 38 twin probands from more than 2,000 patients hospitalized with manic depression. As in most of the earlier studies, no distinction between bipolar and unipolar forms of the disorder was made. The determination of zygosity was made by consulting a birth register and by judgments of physical similarity. His results (table 3.1) excluded cases of uncertain zygosity. In table 3.1 a single probandwise concordance

Table 3.1. Concordance Rates and Heritability Estimates from Twin Studies

Study	Diagnosis	Monozygotic			Same-Sex Dizygotic			Opposite-Sex Dizygotic			H	G[a]
		N	N_c	CR	N	N_c	CR	N	N_c	CR		
Luxenburger 1928, 1930	MD	4	3	0.80	5	0	0	8	0	0	0.80	—
Rosanoff, Handy, and Rosanoff Plesset, 1935	MD	23	16	0.69–0.82	35	8	0.23–0.37	32	3	0.17[b]	0.77	0.45
Slater, 1953	MD	7	4	0.57–0.73	16	3	0.19–0.32	16	3	0.32[b]	0.60	0.47
Kallmann, 1953, 1954[c,d]	MD	27	25[e]	1.00	55	13[e]	0.26	—	—	—	1.00	0.64
	IP	—	—	0.61	—	—	0.06	—	—	—	0.59	—
Da Fonseca, 1959[f]	MD	21	—	0.60	39	—	0.31	11	0	0	0.42	0.33
Kringlen, 1967	MD	6	2	0.33–0.50	9	0	0	—	0	0	0.50	—
	BP	3	2	0.67–0.80	—	—	—	—	—	—	0.80	—
Juel-Nielsen and Videbeck, 1970	S	19	4	0.21–0.35	58	0	0	—	—	—	0.35	—
Pollin et al., 1969	MD	24	1	0.04–0.08	58	0	0	—	—	—	0.08	—
Allen et al., 1974	MD	15	5	0.33–0.50	34	0	0	—	—	—	0.50	—
	UP	10	4	0.40–0.57	19	0	0	—	—	—	0.57	—
	BP	5	1	0.20–0.33	15	0	0	—	—	—	0.33	—
Bertelsen, Harvald, and Hauge, 1977	MD	55	32	0.67	52	9	0.20	—	—	—	0.59	0.61
	UP	28	11	0.43	16	2	0.18	—	—	—	0.30	—
	BP	27	14	0.62	36	2	0.08	—	—	—	0.59	—
Torgersen, 1986	MD	37	14	0.38–0.56	65	8	0.12–0.22	—	—	—		0.56
	UP	33	10	0.30–0.47	59	8	0.14–0.24	—	—	—		—
	BP	4	4	1.00	6	0	0	—	—	—		—
All combined[g]	MD	195	114	0.58–0.74	255	40	0.17–0.29	67	6	0.09–0.16	0.69	—

Note: N = number of twin pairs, N_c = number of concordant twin pairs, CR = concordance rate, H = Holzinger's heritability, G = Smith's heritability, MD = mood disorder, BP = bipolar disorder, UP = unipolar disorder.

[a] As calculated by Faraone et al. (1988).

[b] A single figure indicates an exact probandwise estimate, otherwise the range from pairwise to highest possible probandwise is given.

[c] Concordance rates are age corrected.

[d] Same- and opposite-sex dizygotic twins are not reported separately.

[e] N_c derived from Kallmann's (1954) incidence figures.

[f] Based on Tienari (1963) and Kringlen (1967).

[g] Excluded Pollin et al. (1969).

rate is given when it has been provided by the author or is computable from available data. Otherwise a range is given; the lower end is the pairwise rate and the higher end is the probandwise rate if all affected twins were probands. Heritability estimates use the high end of the range and do not include information from opposite-sex DZ twins when same-sex data are available. Smith's estimate of heritability (*G*) and variance components *Vc* and *Vu* were calculated by Faraone et al. (1988).

Kringlen (1967) noted that Luxenburger's definition of manic-depressive psychosis was fairly wide, including atypical mixed conditions, minor mood disturbances, and some paranoid and obsessive-compulsive reactions. Three of four monozygotic pairs were concordant for manic-depressive illness and none of the thirteen dizygotic pairs was concordant, suggesting a heritability of 0.80.

The probands in the study by Rosanoff, Handy, and Rosanoff Plesset (1935) were also collected from a hospitalized population, but the definition of manic-depressive illness was not clearly specified. This report also does not specify how zygosity was determined, but uncertain cases were apparently excluded. The MZ concordance rate of 0.82 is similar to that reported by Luxenburger; however, the higher DZ concordance rate found by Rosanoff results in a lower estimate of heritability (0.45–0.77). Only 3 of 32 opposite-sex DZ pairs were concordant, resulting in the pairwise concordance rate of 0.17. This is consistent with the data from nontwin siblings that we discussed in chapter 1. Although concordance rates for MZ and same-sex DZ twins did not vary with gender, it is notable that in 83 percent of the discordant opposite-sex DZ pairs, the afflicted twin was female.

The twin probands collected by Slater and Shields (1953) were hospitalized cases. Our presentation of his data differs from the original based upon our review of the twins' case studies. We excluded one discordant MZ pair because the case study indicates the proband had a brain tumor. In current diagnostic practice, this proband would clearly be considered as a case of mood disorder secondary to physical illness. We reclassified three of the concordant DZ twins as discordant because, although the probands satisfied criteria for major mood disorder, the co-twins did not. In one case the most appropriate diagnosis would appear to be panic disorder complicated by dysthymic disorder. In another case the co-twin had cyclothymic personality disorder. In the third case dysthymic disorder appears to be the most appropriate diagnosis. The degree of genetic determination in Slater's series appears to be less than that in previous reports, with heritability ranging from 0.47 to 0.60. There are no concordance differences between same- and opposite-sex dizygotic twins, and females are not more likely to be affected among discordant opposite-sex DZ pairs. Thus, the gender effect reported by Rosanoff, Handy, and Rosanoff Plesset was not replicated in Slater's data. Although his data set is too small to be conclusive, Slater noted that concordant MZ pairs are more likely to be similar with regard to the presence or absence of environmental stresses in comparison to concordant DZ pairs. Thus, Slater suggested that genetic factors may help to determine the susceptibility to environmental stresses. His results may also reflect a deficiency of the twin method—that is, the environmental similarity between twins may be greater for MZ pairs.

The twin probands collected by Kallmann (1953, 1954) were all hospitalized cases. His definition of manic-depressive psychosis was fairly strict, excluding cases that had any schizophrenic component and cases that were "clearly reactive or largely situational depressions in a habitually maladjusted setting" (1954, p. 9). Thus, Kallmann's twins are probably more diagnostically homogeneous and are not likely to include what would currently be called schizoaffective disorder, mood disorder with mood incongruent psychosis, adjustment reactions with depressed mood, and depressions in the context of a chronic dysthymic or personality disorder. Unfortunately, Kallmann did not provide a clear presentation of his data. No discrimination between same- and opposite-sex dizygotic twins was made. Although age-corrected pairwise concordance rates are given, the raw numbers of concordant twins are not given; those presented in table 3.1 are approximations reconstructed from his data. His results indicate perfect age-corrected concordance in MZ twins and a relatively low (0.26) age-corrected concordance rate in DZ twins, resulting in a heritability estimate between 0.64 and 1.0.

Kallmann also presented twin data on "involutional psychosis," which includes menopausal, presenile, and other depressions with the first onset after age 50. The breakdown of his 96 involutional probands between MZ and DZ twins is not given, but the respective age-corrected probandwise concordance rates are 0.61 and 0.06, suggesting heritability to be 0.59. His involutional group was probably fairly heterogeneous, given that 3 percent of the MZ co-twins were schizophrenic.

The twin series of Da Fonseca (1959, 1963) consisted of "endogenous" manic-depressive cases. We do not present a detailed description of his study because most of the work is reported in Portuguese. The difference in MZ and DZ concordance rates is not as substantial as reported in previous studies leading to heritability estimates ranging from 0.33 to 0.42.

Kringlen (1967) ascertained his twin series through the twin and psychiatric registries available in Norway. For 71 percent of his twin sample, zygosity was established on the basis of genetic markers. For other cases, zygosity was determined by comparisons of physical characteristics and responses to questions. The majority of diagnoses were based on a personal interview by the author. Specific diagnostic criteria were not used. However, Kringlen indicated that "atypical" cases were included. These were cases that were difficult to differentiate from "reactive psychosis" and "schizophreniform psychosis of a catatonic type." The resulting category of manic-depressive psychosis was a broad definition similar to that used to make hospital diagnoses at the time. Of six monozygotic pairs, only two were concordant. The zero concordance rate for dizygotic pairs suggests a heritability of 0.50. Although Kringlen did not use an age-of-onset correction, he did note that the age range of the discordant MZ pairs (55-59 years) suggests that the MZ concordance rate would not substantially increase with further observation of the sample. Although Kringlen did not subdivide his sample in terms of bipolar and unipolar forms, he indicated that both twins in the concordant MZ pairs had experienced both depression and elation during the course of their illness. One twin from each pair appears to have had a course characterized primarily by severe depressive episodes and hypomanic episodes. These cases would probably be classified as bipolar II using current nomenclature. Given that only one of the four discordant pairs exhibited the bipolar form and assuming that some of the dizygotic probands had the bipolar form, these results suggest a heritability for bipolar disorder of approximately 0.80. Data for the unipolar form are more difficult to interpret. Kringlen stated that three MZ pairs were concordant for a "clean" depressive syndrome. Only one pair was discordant for this syndrome. However, these numbers are not consistent with the numbers given for bipolar disorder and the manic-depressive group as a whole. This is probably due to the inclusion of depressive twin pairs from the nonmanic-depressive samples reported in his monograph (e.g., reactive psychosis, neurotic depression). Since only one of the clean depressive pairs was discordant for depression, the other depressive patients in his manic-depressive MZ sample must have been atypical.

Juel-Nielsen and Videbech (1970) used the Danish Psychiatric Twin Register to perform a systematic twin study of suicide. Although the psychiatric status of the sample is not specified, their study is of interest, given the known relationship between mood disorders and suicide. Zygosity was established through interview data and questionnaires concerning the degree of similarity between twins. Of the 19 MZ pairs, 4 were concordant; none of the 58 DZ pairs were concordant, suggesting a heritability of 0.35 for suicide.

Pollin et al. (1969) obtained their twin series from a sample of 15,909 pairs of same-sex veteran twins collected by the National Academy of Sciences National Research Council. Zygosity was determined by anthropometric measures, questionnaires, and dermatoglyphic data. Diagnoses were based upon questionnaire responses and clinical diagnoses resulting from the twins' contact with military or VA medical services. Only 1 of 24 monozygotic pairs was concordant for mood disorder. None of the 58 dizygotic pairs were concordant. The rate of MZ concordance is much lower than expected from previous studies. This is probably due to the relative dearth of information used by Pollin et al. (1969) to make diagnoses. Using the same sample and using a better method of diagnosis, Allen et al. (1974) found higher MZ concordance rates. To determine the diagnosis, they reviewed the VA medical records for all twin pairs in which one or both had a clinical diagnosis of affective reaction, involutional psychotic reaction, other psychoses, or paranoid reaction. They classified the twins into unipolar and bipolar subforms according to criteria that were similar to current conceptions of this dichotomy. The MZ concordance rate for unipolar disorder (0.40–0.57) was higher than that for bipolar disorder (0.20–0.33). The DZ concordance was 0 for both, indicating heritabilities of 0.57 for unipolar disorder and 0.33 for bipolar disorder. Corrections were not made for the age of onset; the age range of the sample was 45–55 years. A comparison of results between Pollin et al. (1969) and Allen et al. (1974) underscores the importance of the methodology for obtaining psychiatric data. The former study used questionnaire responses and clinical diagnoses to estimate an MZ concordance rate in the range 0.04–0.08. Collecting additional information by screening medical records increased this estimate to 0.33–0.50 in Allen et al.'s study.

The largest and most methodologically sophisticated twin study to date was performed in Denmark by Bertelsen, Harvald, and Hauge (1977). They identified twins through the Danish Psychiatric Twin Register. Of the 220 twin partners identified from the register as suitable for the study of manic-depressive psychosis, 138 were alive and 133 were personally interviewed. Final diagnoses were based on interview information and case histories available through the twin register. The authors stated that their diagnostic criteria "were made quite wide in accordance with the concept of Kraeplin." Probands and their partners had to have been admitted to a hospital because of a disorder with "predominating mood disturbances of universal character, not restricted to the sphere of recent psychic traumas, supported by the presence of disturbances of psychomotor and mental activity, characteristic sleep disturbances and diurnal variations, and furthermore, by a periodic course of illness and a tendency to recovery without defect" (Bertelsen, 1985). For 53 pairs, zygosity was based on 16–25 systems of blood types, tissue types, serum protein variants, and isoenzymes. For the remaining pairs, zygosity was determined anthropometrically based upon questions regarding similarity and cases of mistaken identity. Unlike many earlier studies, the Danish twin study provided exact probandwise concordance rates. Although age correction was not used, the majority of the twins were elderly at the time of diagnosis, suggesting that age correction would not greatly modify the results. The MZ proband concordance rate of 0.67 is more than three times greater than the DZ rate of 0.20, suggesting a heritability range of 0.59 for the diagnosis of mood disorder. After stratification by polarity, results differ from those of Allen et al. (1974) in finding higher MZ concordance rates for bipolar (0.62) than for unipolar (0.43) disorder and suggesting a higher heritability of the bipolar form. These overall results did not change substantially when diagnoses were made more stringent by excluding cases that, in addition to a manic-depressive syndrome, exhibited pronounced neurotic or schizophrenic-like symptoms. Concordance rates for males and females were not significantly different. However, there was a marked difference between the male MZ proband concordance rate for unipolar disorder (0.29) and the corresponding female rate (0.61). Sex comparisons for DZ pairs and for bipolar cases indicated no differences. The results indicated the heritability of unipolar disorder for females (0.59) to be approximately twice that observed in males (0.31). However, the relatively small sample of males (5 MZ and 5 DZ pairs) makes it difficult to draw firm conclusions.

Table 3.2 presents proband concordance rates for unipolar and bipolar disorder subdivided by "degree of polarity." The heritability of bipolar disorder is greater for probands who have had manic episodes than for those who have only hypomanic episodes. Both MZ and DZ concordance rates are greater for probands having had three or more episodes of depression. Heritability is also greater for these probands. Overall, these results partially suggest that the severity of illness in the proband is associated with increased risk to the co-twin. These results have implications for the multifactorial

Table 3.2.   Probandwise Twin Concordance Rate and Degree of Polarity

Diagnosis of Proband	Monozygotic	Dizygotic	H
Bipolar I	0.80	0.13	0.77
Bipolar II	0.78	0.31	0.68
Unipolar			
≥ 3 episodes	0.59	0.30	0.41
< 3 episodes	0.33	0.14	0.22

Source: Adapted from Bertelsen, Harvald, and Hauge, 1977.

polygenic (MFP) transmission hypothesis. The MFP model assumes that the severity of the illness increases with the number of polygenes inherited. Thus, individuals with a severe illness should have many of the pathogenic polygenes, so their relatives should be at greater risk for the illness than relatives of individuals with a milder form of the disorder. It is also possible that the severe cases have a single-gene disorder with greater probability than the mild cases.

Bertelsen, Harvald, and Hauge presented the distribution of their twin pairs with respect to polarity and zygosity. The results were similar to those reported by Zerbin-Rudin (1969) in finding a relative scarcity of pairs in which one twin was unipolar and the other bipolar (table 3.3).

The observed number of unipolar/bipolar pairs (7) was significantly less than expected under the hypothesis that unipolar and bipolar disorder are genotypically identical (15.9). However, the existence of some unipolar/bipolar pairs suggests some relationship between the two subforms. The existence of this cross-concordance cannot be due simply to the misdiagnosis of unipolar patients, because 5 of the 7 unipolar twins with bipolar co-twins had had three or more episodes of depression, suggesting that they are truly unipolar.

Torgersen (1986) examined 151 same-sex twin pairs with the Present State Examination and a review of medical records. Zygosity was determined by genetic marker analysis for 75 percent of the sample. All twins responded to questions regarding their similarity of appearance and confusion of identity in childhood. The agreement between genetic marker and questionnaire determinations of zygosity was 95 percent. Therefore, the questionnaire was used to diagnose zygosity when genetic marker analysis was not possible.

Ten of the twin probands received a diagnosis of bipolar disorder. Three of 4 MZ co-twins of these probands had a bipolar disorder; the fourth had a diagnosis of major depression. Thus, 100 percent of the MZ co-twins of bipolar probands had a major mood

Table 3.3.   The Distribution of Twin Pairs by Zygosity and Subtype

Diagnosis	Bertelsen, Harvald, and Hauge, 1977		Zerbin-Rüdin, 1967[a]	
	Monozygotic	Dizygotic	Monozygotic	Dizygotic
Both unipolar	11	2	22	8
Both bipolar	14	2	21	1
One unipolar and one bipolar	7	5	7	4
Partially concordant	14	9	9	7
Discordant	9	34	24	36

[a]As reported by Slater and Cowie, 1971.

disorder. In contrast, no mood disorder was found among the 6 DZ co-twins of bipolar probands. Major depression was diagnosed in 102 of the probands. Among the 33 MZ co-twins of these probands, there was 1 case of bipolar disorder and 9 cases of major depression, indicating a 30 percent concordance rate for major mood disorders. For the 59 co-twins among the DZ pairs, there was 1 bipolar case and 7 diagnoses of major depression, leading to a 9 percent concordance rate. When bipolar and unipolar probands are combined, the heritability is estimated to be 0.56.

The phenomenon of monozygotic twins reared apart provides a rare but important naturalistic experiment in human genetics. Price (1968) catalogued 12 MZ pairs where one or both twins had some form of mood disorder. These twin pairs had originally been ascertained by one of four investigators (Juel-Nielsen 1965; Rosanoff, Handy, and Rosanoff Plesset 1935; Shields 1962; Stenstedt 1952). Eight of the 12 pairs were concordant for mood disorder, indicating a pairwise concordance rate of 0.67. From Price's case studies, it appears that all of the ill individuals in this sample were cases of major depression. The only possible exception is one concordant pair in which both twins had psychoses characterized by irritability, assaultiveness, and distractibility. Price noted that the follow-up period of examination for this pair was short and that a final diagnosis might have been schizophrenia rather than mood disorder. Another problem with this collection of MZ twins "reared apart" is that 4 of the pairs had a substantial amount of contact during their lives. One pair was not separated until age 8, another was separated only from birth to the age of 12, a third was separated only from age 1 to 7, and a fourth was separated at age 3 but brought up in the same town. If one excludes these four pairs, then 5 of the 8 remaining pairs are concordant, resulting in a pairwise concordance rate of 0.63. Thus, even when questionable cases are removed, MZ concordance rates for twins reared apart are similar to those found for MZ twins reared together. This finding suggests that MZ concordance for major depression is not substantially increased by common environmental factors.

As we can determine from table 3.1, when one combines data from all available twin studies, 100 of 158 pairs are concordant for mood disorder, suggesting a pairwise concordance rate of 0.63 and a probandwise rate of up to 0.78. The combined results for same-sex DZ twins indicate that 32 of 190 pairs are concordant, resulting in a pairwise rate of 0.17 and a probandwise rate as high as 0.29. Based on the probandwise concordance rates, the combined data suggest a heritability of approximately 0.63. The combined results also suggest that opposite-sex DZ concordance rates are somewhat lower than same-sex DZ concordance rates. This difference is statistically significant if the pairwise rates are compared using the normal approximation to the binomial distribution ($z = 2.66, p < 0.01$). This is consistent with the gender effect observed among nontwin siblings reported by family studies (chap. 2). The effect is most likely due to the environments of same-sex DZ twins being more similar to one another than are those of opposite-sex DZ twins. As we discussed in chapters 1 and 2, epidemiologic and family study data suggest that the gender effect in mood disorders is limited to unipolar disorder. This is consistent with Bertelsen, Harvald, and Hauge's (1977) twin study, in which gender effects were limited to unipolar cases. Their results suggested the sex difference in unipolar disorder to be familial, because females had a higher heritability for unipolar disorder than males. Such a difference is clearly inconsistent with the hypothesis that nonfamilial environmental factors are responsible for the increased prevalence of unipolar disorder among females.

Faraone et al. (1988) computed variance components from the nine available twin studies of major mood disorders. To quantify the relative contribution of genetic and environmental factors in these disorders, they calculated values of G (heritability), Vc/V (common environmental influences), and Vu/V (unique environmental influences) from six of these studies along with the weighted mean value from all nine studies. The three studies reporting DZ concordance rates of 0 were not presented individually because the variance components cannot be calculated if either the MZ or DZ concordance rate is 0. These three studies were included in the calculation of the weighted means. The weighted means were calculated by weighting the concordance rates in each study by the number of pairs included

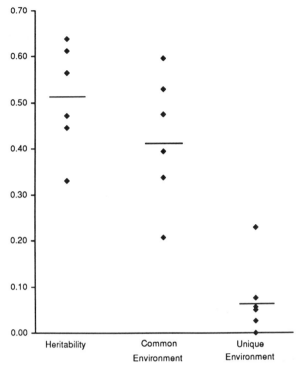

Figure 3.1. The relative contribution of genetic (G), common environmental (Vc/V), and unique environmental (Vu/V) variance for each study (—— denotes mean)

in the study. The weighted means were based on 195 MZ pairs and 310 DZ pairs.

Figure 3.1 presents the relative contribution of the three variance components for each of the six studies having nonzero DZ concordance rates. Generalizing from these studies, it appears that a substantial proportion of the variance in mood disorders is due to G, a smaller but still sizable proportion is due to common environment, and a small or negligible contribution is due to unique environment. These relative contributions are reflected in the six-study mean values of 0.51 for heritability, 0.42 for common environment, and 0.07 for unique environment.

Figure 3.2 depicts variability in the three variance components across the six studies. The values of G ranged from 0.33 for the Da Fonseca (1959) study to 0.64 for the Kallman (1953, 1954) study.

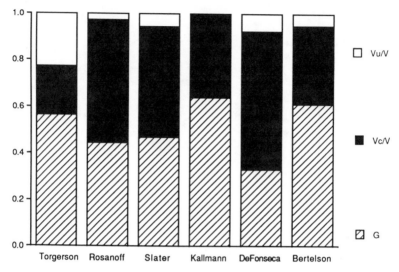

Figure 3.2. The variability of variance components across studies

However, analyses of standard errors for each of the six individual studies indicated that this variation was not statistically significant; the *G* values for five of the six individual studies fall within one standard error unit of the other studies. The weighted mean of *G* for all nine studies (0.62) also falls within one standard error unit of five of the six studies. Thus, while there was some variability in *G* across studies, the analyses of Faraone et al. (1988) suggested that quite a substantial proportion of variance could be attributed to genetic factors.

The pattern of results shown in figure 3.2 for the common environment (*Vc/V*) component indicated a smaller contribution to mood disorder than does heritability. The values of *Vc/V* in five of the six individual studies fell within one standard error unit of the other studies and also fell within one standard error of the nine-study weighted mean (0.32). Given this reasonable degree of stability in findings, the mean values of *Vc/V* suggest that between 30 and 40 percent of the variance in mood disorders is due to common environmental factors.

Unique environmental effects accounted for only a small amount of variance in mood disorders in five of the six studies. Using either the six-study mean or the weighted mean, the results indicated that only 67 percent of variance could be attributed to unique environmental effects.

Twin Studies of Minor Mood Disorders

As we noted in chapter 1, mood disorders range in severity from severe disturbances of mood associated with gross impairments in daily functioning to minor conditions such as dysthymic disorder and cyclothymic personality disorder associated with moderate to mild impairments in functioning. Although no twin study as yet has systematically addressed the relationship between major and minor mood disorders, some data shed light on this issue. Kallmann (1953, 1954) presented the incidence of "cycloid personality types" in the co-twins of his manic-depressive probands. Cycloid personality was described as "a periodic but relatively mild tendency to emotional instability" (1954, p. 6). Among MZ pairs, two of the 57 were discordant for manic depression. In one of these discordant cases, the proband was manic depressive and the co-twin had a cycloid personality. Among the 55 DZ pairs, 42 were discordant, but in 17 of these 42, the proband's co-twin had a cycloid personality. If one considers manic depression and cycloid personality as a common phenotype, the concordance rates for this phenotype would be 100 percent for MZ twins and approximately 63 percent for DZ twin pairs. This leads to a decreased estimate of heritability in comparison to that based on the manic-depressive phenotype only, because the DZ concordance rate has increased substantially whereas the MZ rate cannot go above 100 percent.

The results of Da Fonseca's (1959) twin study have been subject to a similar analysis (Kringlen, 1967). When Da Fonseca's concordance rates are adjusted to include partially concordant cases (i.e., when the co-twin had a depressive or hypomanic personality), MZ pairwise concordance increases from 60 percent to 75 percent and DZ rates increase from 31 percent to 39 percent. These changes do not markedly change the estimate of heritability. In Kringlen's (1967) twin study, pairwise MZ concordance would increase from 0.33 to 0.67 if the manic-depressive phenotype were extended to include "depressive reactions of a neurotic type." Unfortunately, Kringlen did not present similar data for his DZ twin pairs. Thus, the effect on heritability of including milder cases cannot be determined.

Shapiro (1970), using material from the Danish Psychiatric Twin Register, selected probands having a clinical diagnosis of "nonendogenous depression." Probands were not included in the study if they had been given a diagnosis of manic depression and were eligible for the study by Bertelsen, Harvald, and Hauge (1977). Shapiro's probands constituted a heterogeneous group consisting of neurotic depression, reactive depression, and other milder depressions. However, although the depression was relatively mild, it was severe enough for the proband to have been hospitalized. In addition to having access to hospital records, the investigators visited and interviewed all twins individually. Zygosity was established based on a genetic analysis of blood groupings or by physical appearance when data on blood grouping were not available.

There were 18 probands from 16 MZ pairs and 14 probands from 14 DZ pairs. When pairs were considered concordant only if the co-twin had been hospitalized for a nonendogenous depression, the proband concordance rates were 0.22 for MZ pairs and 0 for DZ pairs. If the definition of concordance is expanded to include co-twins who "possibly had a mild nonendogenous depression which did not result in hospitalization," then the MZ proband concordance rate increased to 0.56 and the DZ rate increased to 0.14. If the definition of concordance is further expanded to include two co-twins with other neurotic conditions and one co-twin with an undiagnosed condition requiring psychiatric hospitalization, the MZ concordance rates increased to 0.67 and the DZ rates to 0.21.

Shapiro also provided an assessment of the personality structure of the twins. When the definition of concordance is extended to include co-twins with an "underlying neurotic or personality disorder," the MZ concordance rate increases to 0.72 and the DZ rate remains unchanged. If uncertain cases are also included (i.e., there was not enough information definitively to characterize the co-twins's personality as normal), the MZ concordance rate remains the same while the DZ rate rises to 0.57. We have summarized these results in table 3.4.

Although concordance rates increase when the definition of the phenotype is expanded to include increasingly milder cases, there is no clear trend for the estimate of heritability. Shapiro concluded that genetic factors are less important for mild depressions in comparison to typical manic-depressive illness. A comparison of tables 3.1 and 3.4 suggests that Shapiro's conclusion is valid.

Slater and Shields (1969) presented data on twins with anxiety neuroses and "other" neuroses. In a subsequent report of these data, Slater and Cowie (1971) indicated that the "other" neuroses group consisted primarily of reactive depressions. These twins were ascertained through the Maudsley Hospital twin register. It is not clear whether any of these twins were hospitalized for their disorders. However, it is likely that the sample consisted of milder depressions than the hospitalized, nonendogenous depressions studied by Shap-

Table 3.4. Shapiro's (1970) Twin Study of Nonendogenous Depression

	Proband Concordance Rate		
Condition of Co-twin	Monozygotic	Dizygotic	H
1. Hospitalized nonendogenous depression	0.22	0	0.28
2. #1 plus other nonendogenous depression	0.56	0.14	0.49
3. #2 plus other nonendogenous disorders	0.67	0.21	0.58
4. #3 plus abnormal personality	0.72	0.21	0.65
5. #4 plus ? abnormal personality	0.72	0.57	0.35

iro. All diagnoses were blind to the diagnosis of the partner and the zygosity of the pair.

Among the 12 MZ and 21 DZ probands, no co-twins received the diagnosis of neurotic depression. Among the co-twins of MZ neurotic depressive probands, 25 percent had some other psychiatric diagnosis. The corresponding rate among DZ co-twins was 24 percent. These results suggest that the genetic contribution to neurotic depressions is negligible. The authors demonstrated the ability of their methods to detect differences between MZ and DZ pairs in their results for anxiety neuroses. Based on 17 MZ pairs, the MZ concordance rate for anxiety neurosis was 0.41. This was substantially higher than the DZ rate of 0.04 that was based on 28 pairs. Thus, Slater and Shields (1969) found substantial evidence for a genetic component to anxiety neurosis, but not for depressive neuroses.

Torgersen (1985) used Norwegian twin and psychiatric registers to identify neurotic twin probands. All twins were personally interviewed by a psychologist using a lifetime version of the Present State Examination. For 75 percent of the sample, zygosity was established by blood analysis of 10 genetic markers. For the remainder of the sample, zygosity was determined based on questionnaire responses. Final diagnoses were made by psychiatrists based on interview and medical record information using criteria from the World Health Organization's *International Classification of Diseases,* ninth edition (*ICD 9*). The diagnosis of neurotic depression was appropriate for 30 probands from 30 MZ pairs and 44 probands from 42 DZ pairs. Anxiety neurosis was considered the best diagnosis for 28 probands from 27 MZ pairs and 48 probands from 48 DZ pairs. *ICD 9* neurotic depression is similar to *DSM III-R* dysthymic disorder; *ICD 9* anxiety neurosis is similar to *DSM III-R* panic and generalized anxiety disorders.

The proband concordance rates for neurotic depression were

20 percent and 27 percent for MZ and DZ twins, respectively. These results suggest that heredity has little influence on neurotic depression. Expanding the definition of concordance to include anxiety and other neuroses increases concordance rates to 40 percent for MZ and 41 percent for DZ twins but provides no evidence for a substantial genetic component. Reducing the definition of concordance by excluding cases of mixed anxiety depression in probands and co-twins lowered concordance rates to 18 percent for MZ and 27 percent for DZ. Thus, "purification" of the neurotic depression sample does not markedly affect conclusions.

It is unlikely that Torgersen's results were due to methodologic problems, because evidence for a genetic component in anxiety neurosis was found with the same procedure. Proband concordance rates were 36 percent for MZ and 13 percent for DZ twins, suggesting a heritability of approximately 0.64. The "purification" of the definition of anxiety neurosis by excluding mixed cases of anxiety with depression resulted in a somewhat higher estimate of heritability (0.71). Thus, consistent with the results of Slater and Shields (1969), nonpsychotic disorders with anxiety as the primary problem appear to have an appreciable genetic component in comparison to minor depressive disorders.

Torgersen's (1986) twin study of major mood disorders also examined 35 probands with dysthymic disorder and 14 with depressive adjustment disorder. Among MZ co-twins of dysthymic probands, there was a 25 percent concordance rate for any major or mild mood disorder, compared to a 16 percent concordance for the DZ co-twins. If depressive adjustment disorder is counted as a mood disorder, these rates are 31 percent and 26 percent, respectively. Among MZ co-twins of depressive adjustment disorder probands, there was a 0 percent concordance for any major or mild mood disorder, compared to an 11 percent concordance for the DZ co-twins. If depressive adjustment is counted as a mood disorder, these rates are 21 percent and 22 percent, respectively. Among co-twins of Torgersen's bipolar probands there were no cases of either dysthymic or depressive adjustment disorder. In contrast, 15 percent of the MZ co-twins of major depressive probands had a dysthymic diagnosis and 6 percent had had a depressive adjustment disorder. The rates for the DZ co-twins were 8 percent and 7 percent, respectively. Although the results pertaining to mild mood disorders are difficult to interpret without comparable population rates, there is no compelling evidence in Torgersen's data to suggest that the mild mood disorders are highly heritable. There is a trend for higher rates of dysthymia among MZ as compared to DZ co-twins of dysthymic probands, but this is not marked. The size of the depressive adjustment disorder group is too small to arrive at firm conclusions.

The hypothesis of lower heritability for mild depressive conditions can be examined through twin studies of personality traits using nonhospitalized samples. Young, Fenton, and Lader (1971) examined 17 MZ pairs and 15 DZ pairs with the Middlesex Hospital Questionnaire and the psychoticism, extraversion, and neuroticism questionnaire. The intraclass correlation for the depression score was 0.07 for MZ twins and −0.01 for DZ twins, suggesting a fairly low heritability (0.16). The results for depression were markedly different from results for anxiety, neuroticism, and extraversion, which resulted in statistically significant MZ correlations ranging from 0.47 to 0.61 and nonsignificant DZ correlations ranging from −0.28 to 0.12. These correlations suggest heritabilities greater than 0.65 for these traits.

Vandenberg (1967) presented correlations for depression scores on the Minnesota Multiphasic Personality Inventory (MMPI) derived from the combined adolescent and adult twin samples of Gottesman (1963, 1965) and Reznikoff and Honeyman (1967). His analysis included a total of 120 MZ and 132 DZ twin pairs. The MZ correlation for depression (0.44) was significantly greater than the DZ correlation of 0.14, suggesting a heritability of 0.60. Gottesman's (1963) data suggest that heritability for MMPI depression scores may be greater for males than for females. Both had similar MZ depression correlations (0.48 and 0.44, respectively), but the male DZ correlation (−0.19) was substantially less than the female DZ correlation (0.25).

Clifford et al. (1984) studied 609 MZ twins and 532 DZ twins using the Middlesex Hospital Questionnaire to measure depression. All twins were volunteers from the general population. Zygosity was determined by responses to questions and by blood typing. The twin correlations for depression were 0.31 and 0.07 for MZ and DZ twins, respectively, suggesting a heritability of 0.48. However, there was a notable sex difference, such that the MZ and DZ correlations for males were very low and essentially identical (0.08 and 0.07, respectively). The MZ correlation for females was 0.48 and the DZ correlation was 0.14. These data suggest a heritability of 0.68 for females and 0.02 for males. To understand further the gender effect, mathematical models were applied to the data. These analyses indicated that 79 percent of the correlation between female MZ pairs could be attributed to shared environment and the remainder to genetic factors. When shared environment was taken into account, the heritability for depression scores was reduced to 0.13. The analysis is particularly compelling in that it included data for sibling pairs and parent-offspring pairs. In addition, the cohabitation history of the twins was taken into account when computing the effect of shared environment.

Jardine, Martin, and Henderson (1984) analyzed depression scores from the Delusions-Symptoms-State Inventory from 3,810 twin pairs. Zygosity was determined based upon answers to questions about similarity and by examining photographs. Mathematical models were used to examine the importance of environmental factors unique to individuals, environmental factors shared by co-twins, additive genetic variance, and genetic variance due to dominant gene action. Results indicated the effects of shared environment and dominant genes to be negligible for both males and females. Thus, variability in depression scores among twins could be accounted for by environmental factors unique to individuals and additive genetic variance. The heritability of 0.37 for females was significantly but not markedly greater than that of 0.33 for males. The results also suggested that the genes affecting depression in males were similar to those affecting depression in females, because the correlation of 0.73 between male and female genetic effects was not significantly different from 1. An analysis of the genetic covariation of depression, anxiety, and neuroticism indicated substantial overlap between the genetic factors that affect these traits. The genetic correlation between depression and neuroticism was 0.73 for males and 0.76 for females; the correlation between anxiety and depression was 0.73 for males and 0.80 for females. In contrast, there was much less overlap between traits involving environmental factors. The environmental correlation between depression and neuroticism was 0.45 for both males and females; the environmental correlation between anxiety and depression was 0.48 for males and 0.54 for females. These results suggest that neuroticism, anxiety, and depression share a common polygenic etiology and that differentiation between these traits is due primarily to environmental factors.

Wierzbicki (1986) examined depressive and hypomanic personality traits in 92 adult twin pairs. A self-report measure of similarity was used to diagnose zygosity. The estimated heritability of depressive characteristics was 0.23 for the depression scale of the MMPI. Subscales DR and D30 of the MMPI depression scale had higher heritabilities: 0.41 for DR and 0.43 for D30. Negative and positive mood as measured by the Depression Adjective checklist (DACL) had heritabilities of 0.47 and 0.04. Elation as measured by the W-R Mood Scale had a heritability of 0.67. These highly variable results emphasize that estimates of the heritability of subclinical mood-related traits are highly dependent on the method used to measure the trait.

Kendler, Heath, Martin and Eaver (1986) analyzed the data of Jardine, Martin, and Henderson by applying mathematical genetic models to individual symptom items. The results were consistent with the previous study in finding that additive genetic factors and environmental factors unique to the individual can account for the variability in twin responses to these items. There was only equivocal evidence suggesting an etiologic role of familial environmental factors. Genetic factors accounted for 33–46 percent of the variance in response to the individual items.

SUMMARY

Overall, twin studies of major mood disorders find higher concordance rates for MZ than DZ twins. The only exception to this is the study of Pollin et al. (1969), which is compromised by a questionable means of obtaining psychiatric diagnoses. Twin studies are consistent with family studies in suggesting that genetic factors play a substantial role in the mood disorders. However, the finding of MZ concordance rates lower than 100 percent substantiates the importance of environmental factors. These factors include sources of experimental error (e.g., psychiatric, diagnostic, and zygosity misclassification). Thus, the importance of etiologically relevant environmental factors cannot be fully assessed.

The apparent disparities in concordance rates among the various studies are attenuated when measures that minimize the effects of methodologic differences among studies are applied. In addition to supporting the hypothesis that genetic factors play a major role in the etiology of mood disorders, twin studies also suggest that common environmental factors account for a sizable component of etiology. The effects of common environment will be overestimated and those of heritability underestimated in the presence of assortative mating. Thus, the true magnitude of the genetic effect is likely to be larger than variance components suggest, because assortative mating is common among patients with mood disorders. The sum of the heritability and common environmental components provides an upper limit to the true heritability, free from the effects of assortative mating. This upper limit is 0.93, as calculated by Faraone et al.'s (1988) meta-analysis indicating the prominence of etiologic factors that are shared by twins.

Overall, twin studies of minor mood disorders and depressive personality characteristics suggest that such traits have less of a genetic component than do major mood disorders. The studies of Slater and Shields (1969) and of Torgersen (1985) are strikingly consistent in finding a substantial genetic component for anxiety neurosis but not for depressive neurosis. Twin studies of depressive personality traits have not produced consistent results. Some show heritabilities in the range seen for major mood disorders, while others find low heritabilities. The study by Wierzbicki (1986) demonstrated that estimates of the heritability of a subclinical trait are highly dependent on the method of measurement. The mathematical modeling results of Clifford et al. (1984) suggest that heritability estimates are inflated due to the effects of shared environment. Two of the three depressive personality studies examining gender as a variable agree with the findings from Bertelsen, Harvald, and Hauge's unipolar twin sample that heritability is greater for females than for males. However, Clifford et al.'s results suggest this difference to be due to differences in shared environment between male and female pairs. From their results, one would conclude that the high rate of female-female in comparison to male-male concordance is due to familial environmental effects, not genetic effects. Yet this conclusion is at variance with the results of Jardine, Martin, and Henderson (1984), who found that familial environmental factors were not important even though the heritability for females was significantly, albeit not markedly, greater than that for males. From these mixed series of results, we cannot draw firm conclusions about the etiology of gender effects in mood disorders.

Chapter Four

Adoption Studies

Adoption studies provide one of the few means of disentangling genetic and environmental contributions to the familial aggregation of a disorder. This is because children adopted at an early age have a primarily genetic relationship with their biological parents and an environmental relationship with their adopted parents. The ability to draw inferences from an adoption study is strongest when the adopted children were separated from their biological parents at birth. Any parent-child interaction from the time of birth to the separation will confound genetic and environmental aspects of that relationship to some degree. Furthermore, the environmental circumstances of parents may be associated with pre- and perinatal events relevant to the etiology of mood disorders. For example, low social and economic status may be associated with poor pre- and perinatal care, resulting in environmental insults to the developing fetus and newborn. Although the etiologic relevance of such factors to mood disorders is not clearly established, they must be considered as environmental factors that are difficult to disentangle from the genetic parent-child relationship.

Despite these potential confounds, adoption studies are valuable tools for psychiatric genetics. There are three major designs of adoption studies. The parent-as-proband design compares the rate of illness in the adopted offspring of ill and well individuals. Support for a genetic component is indicated if the risk of illness among adopted children of ill individuals is greater than the risk of adopted children of well individuals. The adoptee-as-proband design uses ill and well adoptees as probands. A genetic component is indicated if the biological relatives of ill adoptees are at greater risk for illness than the adoptive relatives of ill adoptees. In addition, the risk of illness of the biological parents of ill adoptees should be greater than that of the biological parents of well adoptees. The third possible design is the cross-fostering design. This compares rates of illness in two group of adoptees. One group has ill biological parents and is raised by well adoptive parents. The other group has well biological parents and is adopted by ill adoptive parents. This design allows for a direct comparison of environmental and biological transmission in an adoptee sample. Ideally, all three types of adoption study design should be used to find converging evidence for the importance of genetic factors.

A much simpler approach to adoption studies would be to compare rates of illness among adoptees having ill biological parents with general population prevalence rates. A similar approach would be to compare rates of illness among biological parents of ill adoptees with the population prevalence. However, these designs are inappropriate because adoptees and their families are not representative of the general population as regards psychiatric morbidity. For example, children having a *DSM III* diagnosis of attention deficit disorder are eight times more likely to have been adopted than children with no psychiatric disorder (Deutsch et al., 1982). Similarly, adoption studies of schizophrenia have found higher rates of psychopathology in control groups than would be expected from general population prevalence figures (Kety et al., 1975, 1978; Rosenthal et al., 1968, 1975). The causes of increased psychiatric morbidity among adoptees and their relatives is not well understood. Both genetic and environmental factors may be involved. It is likely that parents having a mental disorder are more likely to have their children adopted than are parents who have no mental disorder. It is also possible that the stressors that cause a parent to give up a child are important to the etiology of psychiatric disorders. Furthermore, the stress of being an adoptee may also contribute to the etiology of mental disorders. Whatever the true causal pathway may be, the methodologic maxim is that an adoptee control group is always needed to draw inferences from an adoption study design.

ADOPTION STUDIES OF MOOD DISORDERS

The first reported adoption study of mood disorders was carried out by Mendlewicz and Rainer (1977) in Belgium. They used the adoptee-as-proband design supplemented with two additional control groups. The additional groups were the parents of nonadoptees with mood disorder and the parents of individuals who had contracted poliomyelitis during childhood or adolescence. The purpose of the latter group was to control for the effect on parents of raising a disabled child. A sample of adoptees with mood disorder was obtained by examining the medical records of five outpatient clinics and five inpatient services from admissions that occurred during a five-year period. The authors interviewed potential probands with a semistructured psychiatric interview and made diagnoses using Washington University criteria. To be accepted as an ill proband adoptee, the subject must have met criteria for primary mood disorder and must have been transferred to the adoptive home before one year of age. In addition he or she must have been raised by the adoptive parents until adulthood. The adoptee control group was selected by interviewing individuals obtained through adoption agencies and accepting only those without evidence of psychopathology. The nonadoptee bipolar group was obtained by using the same screening and interview methods applied to the bipolar adoptee group. The poliomyelitis patients were obtained through three pediatricians. The adoptive and biological parents of probands were given a psychiatric interview by individuals blind to the adoptive and clinical status of their children.

The results of the study are represented in table 4.1. Psychiatric morbidity was greater among the biological than among the adoptive parents of bipolar adoptees. The only exceptions are the risks for cyclothymic disorder and schizophrenia, both of which were 0 for each type of parent. The observed differences between the adoptive and biological parents of bipolar adoptees were statistically significant for comparisons of total psychopathology and mood spectrum disorders (unipolar, bipolar, and schizoaffective). Rates of alcoholism and sociopathy were fairly high among biological parents of normal adoptees, suggesting that the risks for these disorders among the biological parents of bipolar adoptees were due to the fact that the adoptee samples were not representative. The results for the biological parents of bipolar nonadoptees are consistent with the results of other family studies of bipolar disorder. It is notable that these parents have less bipolar, unipolar, and schizoaffective disorder but more cyclothymic disorder than do the biological parents of bipolar adoptees. Thus, the bipolar adoptees may have a larger genetic component to their disorders than do the bipolar nonadoptees.

The results for adoptive parents of bipolar adoptees indicate that raising a child who eventually develops bipolar disorder does not increase the parents' risk of developing bipolar or other disorders. Similarly, there is no indication that the stress of raising a child with poliomyelitis substantially increases psychiatric morbidity. Overall, the results of Mendlewicz and Rainer's (1977) adoption study indicate that genetic, not environmental, factors are implicated in the familial transmission of mood disorders.

Using a parent-as-proband design, Cadoret (1978) compared eight adoptees whose biological mothers had mood disorders with 118 adoptees whose biological mothers did not have mood disorders.

Table 4.1. The Number of Affected Parents in Mendlewicz and Rainer's (1977) Adoption Study of Bipolar Disorder

Parental Diagnosis	Parents of Bipolar Adoptees		Parents of Normal Adoptees		Bipolar Nonadoptee Biological Parents (N = 61)	Poliomyelitis Biological Parents (N = 39)
	Adoptive (N = 57)	Biological (N = 57)	Adoptive (N = 42)	Biological (N = 43)		
Bipolar	1 (1.8%)	4 (7.0%)	0 (0%)	0 (0%)	2 (3.3%)	0 (0%)
Unipolar	6 (10.5)	12 (21.1)	3 (7.1)	1 (2.3)	11 (18.0)	4 (10.3)
Schizoaffective	0 (0)	2 (3.5)	0 (0)	0 (0)	1 (1.6)	0 (0)
Cyclothymic	0 (0)	0 (0)	1 (2.3)	0 (0)	2 (3.3)	0 (0)
Schizophrenia	0 (0)	0 (0)	1 (2.3)	0 (0)	1 (1.6)	0 (0)
Alcoholism	2 (3.5)	3 (5.3)	0 (0)	3 (7.0)	2 (3.3)	1 (2.6)
Sociopathy	0 (0)	2 (3.5)	0 (0)	3 (7.0)	1 (1.6)	0 (0)
Total psychopathology	9 (15.8)	24 (40.3)	5 (11.9)	8 (18.6)	20 (32.8)	5 (12.8)

Adoptees were selected from three private adoption agencies. Only those who were eighteen years of age or older at the time of the study were included. All of the other adoption records were searched for evidence of psychopathology in the biological parents. The diagnosis of the adoptees was based on telephone interviews with the adoptive parents and with the adoptee whenever possible. These interviews were blind to the diagnoses of the biological parents. Washington University diagnostic criteria were used with minor modifications.

There were no cases of bipolar disorder among the adoptees. However, 37.5 percent of the eight adoptees whose biological mothers had mood disorder were themselves afflicted with unipolar disorder. In contrast, only 9.3 percent of the adoptees with normal biological mothers had unipolar disorder. Although this difference fell short of statistical significance ($p = 0.067$), it is consistent with a genetic hypothesis for mood disorders. It is difficult to draw strong inferences from this study due to its small sample size and the lack of personal interview data on the biological parents. Furthermore, the adoptees were relatively young. More than 50 percent of them had not attained the age of 24 at the time of the follow-up. Therefore, many of the adoptees had been exposed to only a small portion of the period of risk for mood disorders.

Von Knorring et al. (1983) obtained a sample of 56 adoptees with mood disorder and 115 adoptees with no psychiatric disorder. On the basis of the extensive psychiatric and social welfare records available in Stockholm, Sweden, the adoptees and their parents were diagnosed using the criteria of Perris (1966) for psychotic mood disorders and D'Elia, von Knorring, and Perris (1974) for nonpsychotic depression. The prevalence of mood disorders among the biological parents of ill adoptees (5.1 percent) was nonsignificantly greater then the prevalence among their adoptive parents (2.7 percent). Furthermore, the prevalence among biological parents of ill adoptees (5.1 percent) did not differ from the prevalence among biological parents of normal adoptees (5.4 percent). Thus, this study found little evidence for a familial aggregation of mood disorders. However, it did find that the risk for substance abuse among the biological mothers of ill adoptees (7.1 percent) was greater than the corresponding risk for biological mothers of normal adoptees (0.9 percent). These results are difficult to interpret due to several methodologic limitations. Diagnoses were based on information from medical and other records, not personal interviews. More important, 57 percent of the ill adoptee sample carried a diagnosis of neurotic depressive reaction. As the family and twin data reviewed in previous chapters indicate, such mild depressions may not involve a substantial genetic component.

Cadoret, O'Gorman, Heywood, and Troughton (1985) interviewed 443 adoptees and their adoptive parents with a structured psychiatric interview. Biological relatives of the adoptees were diagnosed based on information contained in adoption agency records and, in some cases, the hospital or court records. A biological relative was considered depressed if there was any evidence of a history of treatment for depression or a history of two or three symptoms of the major depressive syndrome with no other evident diagnosis. Only 48 of the adoptees had had a major depressive episode at some time during their life. Among male adoptees, 15 percent of those with a biological family history positive for mood disorder had major depression. Only 7 percent of those with a negative family history had major depression, but the difference was not statistically significant. Among female adoptees, 29 percent of those with a positive biological family history had major depression, as compared to 14 percent with a negative family history. However, the difference was not statistically significant.

In striking contrast to these negative results, Cadoret et al. found that several environmental factors in the adoptive family were predictive of adoptee depression. Six potential precipitants of adoptee depression were examined: parental alcohol problems, parental antisocial behavior, other parental psychiatric problems, parent death before adoptee age 19, and parental divorce. Alcohol problems, other psychiatric problems, and parental death were all associated with elevated rates of major depression in the adoptee. Parental alcohol problems predicted male adoptee depression, whereas the other two problems predicted female adoptee depression. Overall, these results suggest that stressors in the home environment are more predictive of depression than genetic predisposition. However, the inability to find a genetic component to major depression in this study must be considered tentative due to methodologic problems. The means for diagnosing the mood disorders among biological relatives was limited by a reliance on medical records and the inability to obtain direct interviews with biological parents. Furthermore, most of the biological parents were in their teens and twenties when their psychiatric data were originally collected. Given the variable age of onset of mood disorders, it is likely that many of the biological parents considered to be well would have eventually developed a mood disorder.

In contrast to the results of Cadoret et al., strong support for genetic components to mood disorders has been found by a meth-

odologically sophisticated Danish study using the adoptee-as-proband design (Wender et al., 1986). These investigators identified 71
adult adoptees with mood disorders and 75 control adoptees with no
record of psychiatric illness, alcohol or substance abuse, or attempted
or completed suicide. The ill and control adoptees were matched on
sex, age, time spent with biological mother, age at transfer to adoptive home, and socio-economic class of adopting parents. Since Danish law requires communities to maintain extensive population registers of births, adoptions, and changes of address for adoptive and
biological parents, it was possible to identify 387 biological relatives
of ill adoptees, 344 biological relatives of control adoptees, 180 adoptive relatives of ill adoptees, and 169 adoptive relatives of control
adoptees. The psychiatric status of probands and their relatives was
determined by cross-indexing the information contained in the population registers with information contained in the Danish psychiatric
register. Based on these records, the ill probands were diagnosed as
follows: 27 were unipolar, 10 were bipolar, 21 had neurotic depression (including dysthymic disorder and cyclothymic personality), and
15 had "affect reactions." This latter diagnosis is a Danish diagnostic
term for individuals who manifest histrionic or panicky behavior or
who make an impulsive suicidal attempt in response to an identifiable
event.

The results of the study are presented in table 4.2. Since there
were significant demographic differences between the biological and
adoptive relatives, no statistical comparisons were made in the prevalence of psychopathology between biological and adoptive relatives.
However, it is evident from table 4.2 that among relatives of ill
adoptees, the risk to biological relatives is somewhat greater than

Table 4.2.   The Number of Affected Relatives in Wender et al.'s (1986) Adoption
Study of Mood Disorders

Relatives' Diagnosis	Relatives of Mood-Disordered Adoptees		Relatives of Control Adoptees	
	Adoptive ($N = 180$)	Biological ($N = 387$)	Adoptive ($N = 169$)	Biological ($N = 344$)
Mood disorder spectrum	11 (6.1%)	29 (7.5%)	6 (3.6%)	16 (4.7%)
Unipolar	1 (0.6)	8 (2.1)	1 (0.6)	1 (0.3)
Bipolar	0 (0)	2 (0.01)	1 (0.01)	3 (0.01)
Neurotic depression or affect reaction	6 (3.3)	9 (3.3)	3 (1.8)	8 (2.3)
Alcoholism	3 (1.7)	21 (5.4)	3 (1.8)	7 (2.0)
Attempted suicide	7 (3.9)	13 (3.4)	5 (3.0)	4 (1.2)
Completed suicide	1 (0.6)	15 (3.9)	2 (1.2)	1 (0.3)

the risk to adoptive relatives. Most notable is the fact that biological relatives of ill adoptees were more than six times more likely than the adoptive relatives to have completed suicide. The biological relatives had rates of unipolar disorder and alcoholism that were more than three times the rates for adoptive relatives of ill adoptees. In contrast, suicide, unipolar disorder, and alcoholism were not more prevalent among the biological than the adoptive relatives of control adoptees.

Meaningful statistical comparisons could be made between the relatives of ill and control adoptees, as these groups did not differ on demographic variables. The diagnosis of a mood spectrum disorder (unipolar, bipolar, uncertain major mood disorder, neurotic depression, or affect reaction) was nearly twice as common among the biological relatives of ill adoptees as among the biological relatives of control adoptees, but the difference was not statistically significant. Bipolar disorder was equally prevalent among the biological relatives of the two proband groups, as were neurotic depression and affect reaction. However, unipolar disorder was seven times more prevalent among the biological relatives of ill adoptees and the difference was statistically significant. The biological relatives of ill adoptees also had elevated rates of alcoholism, attempted suicide, and completed suicide in statistical comparisons with biological relatives of control adoptees. The strongest findings were for completed suicide: the rate among biological relatives of ill adoptees was fifteen times the rate among biological relatives of control adoptees.

The differences in psychopathology between the biological relatives of the two proband groups provide compelling evidence for a genetic component to mood disorders, because no differences in psychopathology could be demonstrated between the adoptive relatives of ill adoptees and the adoptive relatives of control adoptees. Thus, the crucial difference between the two groups of adoptees resides in the biological, not the adoptive relationship.

SUMMARY

Of the five available adoption studies of mood disorder, two provide strong support for genetic factors, another is moderately supportive, and two are not supportive. Although the two most methodologically sound studies support the genetic hypothesis (Mendlewicz and Rainer, 1977; Wender et al., 1986), more adoption study is needed to solidify the foundation of converging evidence needed to assert more conclusively that genetic factors play a substantial role in the etiology of mood disorders. It would be of particular interest to conduct a cross-fostering study, because the design has not been used to examine the genetics of mood disorders. Unfortunately, adoption studies are very difficult to implement. Thus, it is unlikely that much more relevant data from adoption designs will soon be forthcoming.

The adoption study results form a pattern that is consistent with what has been learned from family and twin studies. These latter methods have unequivocally demonstrated that the bipolar disorder is more strongly familial than the unipolar disorder. Thus it is comforting for the genetic hypothesis to note that the only adoption study using exclusively bipolar probands found markedly increased rates of both bipolar and unipolar disorders among the biological relatives of bipolar probands. Such high rates are not seen among their adoptive relatives or among either adoptive or biological relatives of control probands. Family and twin studies also lead to the expectation that mild mood disorders are not highly familial. Thus, adoption studies using mildly disordered probands cannot discredit the genetic hypothesis for major mood disorders.

Chapter Five

Quantitative Models of Genetic Transmission

The mode of inheritance of mood disorders has substantial implications for etiologic research and clinical practice. A conclusive demonstration that a single major locus (SML) is involved would hold the promise that a relatively direct biochemical pathway from genotype to phenotype accounts for the pathophysiology of these disorders. If a multifactorial polygenic (MFP) model describes the mode of transmission, the search for a simple biochemical pathway is likely to be less fruitful. This is so because, as Kidd (1981) noted, the MFP model relegates genetic factors to an amorphous pool of small, indistinguishable components that contribute additively to the pathophysiology of the disorder.

Understanding the genetic mechanism in mood disorders will also help researchers develop selection rules to maximize the yield of etiologic research. For example, if this mechanism involves an SML, homozygotes may be more likely to manifest the underlying pathophysiology to a degree that is detectable with current methods; this may not be true for heterozygotes who become ill. Therefore, as Matthysse and Kidd (1976) suggested, sampling for homozygotes may increase the power to detect pathophysiologic abnormalities. However, they also demonstrated that the probability of a patient's being homozygous varies greatly from one SML model to another. Thus, optimal sampling rules will require a precise explication of the mode of inheritance.

In clinical practice, knowledge of the mode of inheritance will facilitate genetic counseling. Currently, such counseling is based on the empirical risk figures observed in family studies. There are several problems with this approach (Morton et al., 1979). These figures do not consider the total family history of the person being counseled. For example, even if we knew the risk for mood disorder among children and nephews of bipolar patients, we would not know the risk to a person with one bipolar parent and one bipolar uncle.

Ideally, genetic counseling should be based on risk figures from a known model of genetic transmission. The model could then be applied to an individual's pedigree to determine the risk of a mood disorder. The importance to genetic counseling of identifying the correct model has been demonstrated by Morton et al. (1979). They constructed hypothetical pedigrees and used SML and MFP models to compute illness risks for possible progeny of the pedigrees. Risk figures were computed under three sets of assumptions corresponding to one MFP and two SML models. These models were equally acceptable in terms of their ability to predict the empirical data of Matthysse and Kidd (1976). Nevertheless, the computed risks varied substantially between models for both simple and complex pedigrees. The authors concluded that risk prediction was model dependent, and that clinically important errors in predictions could be made by incorrect models. Their results emphasized the need to understand the mode of genetic transmission for inherited disorders. Identifying the correct model has important implications for helping afflicted individuals in genetic counseling settings.

STATISTICAL PROCEDURES

The statistical procedures used to model genetic transmission fall into two categories: prevalence analysis and pedigree segregation analysis. The major difference between the two approaches involves the form in which the family data enter the analysis. In prevalence analysis, the data are reduced to a matrix that specifies the prevalence of the disorder in relatives of ill and control probands (Reich et al., 1972; Reich, James, and Morris, 1979). This form of analysis loses important information about the familial pattern of illness in a given sample because it does not treat probands with multiple ill relatives differently from those with only one such relative. The method of pedigree segregation analysis (Elston, 1981) uses all such information available in the pedigree to test genetic hypotheses. Pedigree segregation analysis also has greater statistical power than prevalence analysis (Kidd, 1981). Simulation studies have shown that the former method provides smaller standard errors of parameter estimates and greater power to discriminate between competing models (Reich, James, and Morris, 1979).

The more detailed data used by pedigree segregation analysis enable investigators to use the method to estimate parameters that can adjust the analysis for biases that may have occurred in the sampling procedure. For example, because mood disorders have a variable age of onset, it is necessary to make an adjustment for the fact that many of the relatives involved in the analysis have not yet lived through the period of risk. Another example is ascertainment bias or nonrandom sampling. Corrections have been developed to account for the fact that the families used as data for genetic studies of mood disorders are not randomly sampled from the population but are selected (ascertained) via affected probands. The details of these corrections are discussed by Elston (1981).

Prevalence analysis has one advantage over pedigree segregation analysis. After the parameters of the genetic model have been established, a goodness-of-fit chi-square can be computed to determine how well the model predicts the observed data. Pedigree segregation analysis provides no equivalent test. Instead, a genetic model is defined by a set of parameters, some of which are fixed at a value specified by the genetic hypothesis. Using a likelihood ratio test, this model is compared with a model that allows that parameters fixed by the genetic hypothesis be unrestricted (i.e., instead of being prespecified, they are estimated from the data). Thus, as Elston and Yelverton (1975) noted, the test of the genetic model assumes that the unrestricted model adequately fits the data. If the unrestricted model is wrong, "the test may be either invalid or meaningless" (p. 97).

SINGLE MAJOR LOCUS MODELS

Single major locus models propose that the pair of genes present at a single locus is primarily responsible for the transmission of mood disorders. The major problem facing SML proponents is how to explain the non-Mendelian distribution of the disorders and the variable expression of the affected genotype. To this end, more complex SML models have been developed that include one or all of the following modifications to the classic Mendelian model: (a) reduced penetrance of the pathogenic gene (i.e., some individuals having the pathogenic genotype do not become ill), (b) the existence of phenocopies (i.e., the environmental induction of illness in individuals without the pathogenic genotype), and (c) the addition of an environmentally related liability-threshold construct. In the following discussion, a refers to the pathogenic gene responsible for the disorder, and A refers to the nonpathogenic gene that may be present at the same locus.

A detailed exegesis of mathematical genetic models is beyond the scope of this chapter; such details are presented in many of the cited articles (e.g., Elston, 1981). A genetic model has two major components. The first is a description of the mode of transmission. The second is a procedure for determining whether the predictions made by the model adequately describe the observed familial pattern of illness. For example, the classic recessive Mendelian model would describe the transmission of illness as follows: there are three possible genotypes at the single major locus, *AA, Aa,* and *aa.* All *aa* individuals are affected; none of the other genotypes is affected. This model incorrectly predicts that all children of two ill parents will become ill. In this case the predictions are obviously wrong. When the accuracy of prediction is not clear, statistical techniques are used to determine whether the model adequately describes the observed data.

Prevalence Analyses

An early application of the SML model to mood disorders was provided by Mendlewicz and Rainer (1974). Their data set consisted of 134 bipolar probands, 268 parents of probands, and 327 siblings of probands. Structured diagnostic criteria modeled after Perris (1966) and Winokur, Clayton, and Reich (1969) were used. Although a statistical goodness of fit test could not be applied, it was demonstrated that the observed morbidity risks to parents and siblings could be approximated by a model of single-gene dominant inheritance. It is possible to obtain a statistical test of goodness of fit for SML models by incorporating the liability-threshold concept of Falconer (1965). As Kidd and Cavalli-Sforza (1973) proposed, it can be assumed that all individuals have a liability or predisposition to develop mood disorders. This liability is influenced by genetic and environmental factors. Although not directly measurable, liability is assumed to be a continuous measure that varies from small to large amounts. If a given individual's liability exceeds a threshold, illness occurs. The relationship between the single-gene and the liability-threshold concept is diagrammed in figure 5.1 for a single threshold. In this diagram, *a* is the pathogenic gene; increasing the number of pathogenic genes increases the amount of liability associated with the genotype at the disease locus. It is further assumed that each genotype is associated with a normal distribution of liability. Thus, due to environmental influences, individuals with the same genotypes can have different liabilities. The liability-threshold concept provides a convenient means of modeling variable penetrance. A genotype's penetrance under this model is equal to the proportion of the genotype's liability distribution that is to the right of the threshold.

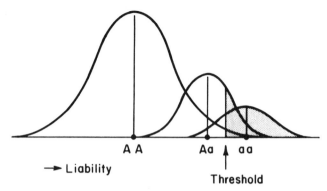

Figure 5.1.   Single major locus liability threshold model

Furthermore, the presence of phenocopies can be accounted for by allowing some portion of the *AA* distribution to be above the threshold.

A statistical goodness-of-fit test becomes possible when a second threshold is added to the model. Furthermore, the addition of a second threshold makes it possible to delineate three different phenotypes. Individuals below a lower threshold are considered to be unaffected, individuals above the highest threshold are considered to be severe cases, and individuals between the two thresholds are considered to be mild cases. The number of related phenotypes can be increased by adding thresholds to the model.

Gershon et al. (1965) tested several SML multiple-threshold models. These models were applied to the family study data of Gershon et al. (1965). A two-threshold analysis assumed that bipolar and unipolar disorders were different phenotypic manifestations of the same single gene. Bipolar disorder was considered to be the severe form and unipolar disorder the mild form. This two-threshold model could not be rejected. That is, the prevalences predicted from the model were not significantly different from the observed prevalences. The best-fitting model was essentially a recessive model with reduced penetrance. In another analysis, a third threshold was incorporated to account for a group of related disorders (cyclothymic personality, undiagnosed major psychiatric disturbance, and neurotic depression). The threshold for the related disorders was assumed to be the lowest threshold. This model could not be statistically rejected. Unlike the two-threshold results, the three-threshold results indicated the disorders to be due to a partially dominant gene. Thus, the Gershon et al. results indicated that SML models can provide good fits to prevalence data. However, the parameter estimates of these models appear to be very sensitive to the number of thresholds assumed and the types of disorder chosen as variant phenotypes of the same genotype.

Similar results are seen in the analyses of Gershon et al. (1976). They applied the two-threshold model of unipolar and bipolar disorders to the data of Angst (1966), Perris (1966), and Gershon et al. (1965). The two-threshold model of unipolar and bipolar disorders could not be rejected for the data of Angst and Gershon but could be rejected for the data of Perris. The results from the Angst and Gershon data sets differed in that the former was suggestive of recessive inheritance whereas the latter indicated codominant inheritance. However, both studies predict a gene frequency of about 5 percent for the pathogenic allele.

Leckman and Gershon (1977) applied the two-threshold SML model to examine the gender effect in bipolar-related major mood disorders. The gender effect refers to the consistent finding from epidemiologic studies that the risk for mood disorders is consistently greater among women than among men (Weissman and Boyd, 1984). In most studies this effect is limited to unipolar disorder. The two-threshold model is applied to the gender effect by assuming that males and females have different thresholds for manifesting illness. The relative scarcity of male cases is explained by assuming that the male threshold is higher than the female threshold. That is, it predicts that fewer males than females will be affected. The model also predicts more illness among relatives of male than female probands, an effect that is not frequently observed (Faraone, Lyons, and Tsuang, 1987). Leckman and Gershon applied the two-threshold model of the gender effect to five data sets: James and Chapman, 1975; Goetzl et al., 1974; Winokur and Clayton, 1967; Mendlewicz and Rainer, 1974; and Gershon et al., 1965. The two-threshold model could adequately predict the prevalence data of Goetzl, Gershon, and James. The model was rejected for the data of Winokur and Mendlewicz. The results from the three data sets that provided acceptable fits did not consistently describe the mechanism of inheritance. The Goetzl data set suggested that the pathogenic gene was codominant, with a gene frequency of 0.22. The James (1975) data set suggested that the pathogenic gene was dominant, with a much lower gene frequency of 0.09. The Gershon et al. (1965) data set agreed with the gene frequency of 0.09 but suggested that the pathogenic gene was partially recessive.

Van Eerdewegh, Gershon, and Van Eerdewegh (1980) examined X-chromosome threshold models of the gender effect in unipolar and bipolar disorders. Three models were examined. Model I assumed one threshold on the liability scale that determined the manifestation of bipolar disorder. Unipolar relatives of bipolar probands were considered to be normal in this model. Model II also included only one threshold, but in this case unipolar and bipolar forms were considered to be genetically and environmentally identical. That is, either disorder could occur if an individual exceeded the threshold. Model III included two thresholds. Individuals above the highest threshold developed bipolar disorder; those between the lower and upper thresholds developed unipolar disorder; those below the lowest threshold remained normal. These three models were tested with and without the gender effect. The gender effect was modeled by including separate thresholds for males and females. Thus, models I and II become two-threshold models, whereas III becomes a four-threshold model. These models were applied to three data sets: Winokur and Pitts, 1965, Gershon et al. 1965, and Mendlewicz and Rainer, 1974.

For the data of Winokur and Pitts, none of these models could be rejected. There was consistency between models in indicating the pathogenic gene to be dominant, with incomplete penetrance and a low gene frequency (0.02). The models incorporating sex-specific thresholds gave a slightly better fit to the data, but this was not statistically significant. For the data of Gershon et al. (1965), models II and III could be rejected. The addition of sex-specific thresholds did not significantly improve or worsen the fit of model I. The results suggested a dominant pathogenic gene with low penetrance and a relatively high gene frequency (0.19). The Mendlewicz and Rainer (1974) data were only adequate for a test of model II. This model was statistically rejected both with and without sex-specific thresholds. Overall, the results of Van Eerdewegh, Gershon, and Van Eerdewegh (1980) indicated substantial heterogeneity between data sets. Sex-specific thresholds do not appear to improve substantially the fit of genetic models to the data sets examined. Similarly, the hypothesis of unique thresholds for unipolar and bipolar disorders was not strongly supported.

Baron (1981) applied the two-threshold model of the gender effect to the combined data from four family studies (Gershon et al., 1965; Marten et al., 1972; Winokur and Cadoret, 1967, 1971). These analyses were able to reject the autosomal, SML model with sex-specific thresholds. Baron (1983) applied a four-threshold model to the family data of Baron (1981). This model allowed unique thresholds for unipolar and bipolar disorders, along with unique thresholds for males and females. The statistical analysis indicated that the four-threshold model could not account for the observed data.

The two-threshold model of the gender effect was used by Smeraldi et al. (1984a) on a data set consisting of 94 bipolar probands, 51 unipolar probands, and their 864 first-degree relatives. The single major autosomal locus model with sex-specific thresholds could not be rejected. The gene frequency of the pathogenic gene was estimated to be very low (0.005) and the mode of inheritance was close to codominance.

Price et al. (1985) analyzed the data of Weissman et al. (1984) using the four-threshold model with sex- and polarity-specific thresholds. Although the statistical fit of this autosomal model to the data was acceptable, the result was biologically uninteresting. As the authors noted, the best-fitting model predicted most cases of unipolar and bipolar disorders to be phenocopies—that is, under this model, most ill individuals do not carry the pathogenic gene.

Overall, the SML prevalence analyses outlined in table 5.1 provide inconsistent evidence regarding the genetic transmission of mood disorders. Four of five relevant studies suggested that models with sex-specific thresholds are not superior to models that assume the location of thresholds to be independent of sex. Multiple threshold modeling of the effects of polarity has resulted in less straightforward results. Some data sets support the hypothesis that bipolar

Table 5.1. Single Major Locus Prevalence Analyses

Study	Conclusion
Mendlewicz and Rainer, 1974	Best-fitting single-threshold model for UP and BP suggests involvement of dominant gene
Gershon et al., 1975	Multiple-threshold models of UP, BP, and related disorders not rejected
Gershon et al., 1976	Two-threshold model of UP and BP not rejected for data of Angst (1966) and Gershon (1975), but rejected for data of Perris (1966)
Leckman and Gershon, 1977	Two-threshold model of gender effect fits 3 of 5 data sets
Van Eerdewegh, Gershon, and Van Eerdewegh, 1980	X-chromosome threshold models do not consistently describe the families of BP probands from 3 data sets
Baron, 1981	Two-threshold model of gender effect rejected
Baron, 1983	Four-threshold model of UP, BP with gender effect rejected
Smeraldi, et al., 1981	Two-threshold model of gender effect not rejected
Price et al., 1985	Four-threshold model of UP, BP with gender effect rejected

Note: UP = unipolar disorder, BP = bipolar disorder.

and unipolar disorders are severe and mild forms, respectively, of the same SML disorder. Other studies have failed to support this hypothesis.

Pedigree Segregation Analyses

A summary of SML pedigree segregation analyses is given in table 5.2. Crowe and Smouse (1977) analyzed the data of Winokur, Clayton, and Reich (1969), which consisted of a series of families ascertained through 61 bipolar probands. Diagnoses were based on a blind structured interview with patients and their relatives. Relatives were considered to be ill if they exhibited either bipolar or unipolar illness. The autosomal recessive model provided a poor fit to the Winokur, Clayton, and Reich data. Both the X-linked dominant and the autosomal dominant model could adequately predict the observed morbidity risks of first-degree relatives. However, the X-linked dominant model provided more accurate predictions and was estimated to be approximately 89 times more likely than the autosomal dominant hypothesis. An examination of the likelihoods for individual families indicated that, of the 55 informative families, 19 favored the X-linked dominant hypothesis, 10 favored the autosomal dominant hypothesis, and 26 were equivocal. Thus, although in the aggregate these results are more suggestive of X-linked inheritance than of autosomal inheritance, they are also consistent with the hypothesis of genetic heterogeneity.

Tanna et al. (1979) examined 111 individuals from families exhibiting depression spectrum disease, defined as a unipolar disorder in which at least one member of the family is ill with unipolar depres-

Table 5.2.   Single Major Locus Pedigree Segregation Analyses

Study	Conclusion
Crowe and Smouse, 1977	X-linked dominant more likely than autosomal models
Tanna et al., 1979	Autosomal models rejected; environmental transmission not rejected
Bucher et al., 1981	X-linked and autosomal models rejected; environmental transmission rejected
Crowe et al., 1981	Neither autosomal nor environmental transmission rejected
Goldin et al., 1983	X-linked, autosomal, and environmental transmission rejected under several phenotypic models
Tsuang, Bucher, Fleming, and Faraone 1985	Autosomal model rejected; environmental transmission not rejected

sion and at least one other first-degree relative has alcoholism and/
or antisocial personality. Families with bipolar disorder were excluded from these analyses. The initial series of analyses rejected
autosomal dominant and recessive models allowing for incomplete
penetrance and corrections for ascertainment bias. In contrast, the
hypothesis of "environmental" transmission could not be rejected.
The environmental model assumes that familial transmission is independent of genotype. Thus, these results suggest that the familial
transmission of depressive spectrum disorder is primarily due to environmental influences.

Bucher et al. (1981) applied pedigree segregation analysis to
three sets of family data (Goetzl et al., 1974; Helzer and Winokur,
1974; Winokur, Clayton, and Reich, 1969). The Helzer and Winokur
families were selected through 30 bipolar probands. Diagnoses were
based on personal interviews with probands and all available first-
degree relatives. The Washington University diagnostic criteria were
used. The Winokur, Clayton, and Reich data consisted of families
selected through 62 bipolar probands. Personal interviews were used
to diagnose probands and all available first-degree relatives with the
Washington University criteria. The Goetzl et al. data consisted of
the families of 39 bipolar probands. Diagnostic information for probands was obtained from personal interviews. Diagnostic information
for relatives was obtained from a mailed questionnaire.

The conclusions drawn from separate analyses of these three
data sets were consistent with one another. It was possible statistically
to reject X-linkage along with dominant, recessive, and codominant
autosomal models. Furthermore, the hypothesis of environmental
transmission was also rejected. Thus, although several SML models
could be rejected, the results suggest that the transmission of bipolar
related mood disorders cannot be primarily attributed to environmental factors.

Crowe et al. (1981) analyzed a single large pedigree ascertained
through a unipolar depressive male. The pedigree included 98 family
members who were interviewed with a structured psychiatric interview. Diagnoses were based on the Washington University diagnostic
criteria. In addition to the proband, the pedigree contained cases of
unipolar depression, bipolar disorder, alcoholism, drug dependency,
schizophrenia, and "undiagnosed illness." The single schizophrenia
case was considered to be unaffected in all analyses. The definition
of the ill phenotype always included unipolar depression; the inclusion of other disorders varied across eight different analyses. None
of these analyses could reject the hypothesis of autosomal SML inheritance, nor could they reject the hypothesis of environmental

transmission. Although the different phenotypic models produced essentially similar results, the best-fitting model included unipolar depression, alcoholism, and drug dependency.

Goldin et al. (1983) examined the distribution of affective illness in the 4,179 relatives of 11 schizoaffective, 96 bipolar I, 34 bipolar II, 31 unipolar, and 43 normal controls. Probands were diagnosed using the Research Diagnostic Criteria based on a structured personal interview. Approximately 25 percent of the relatives were personally interviewed; additional information on relatives was obtained through medical records and interviews with informants. The family data were analyzed according to four phenotypic models, which varied the definitions of normal, mildly affected, and severely affected phenotypes. The four phenotypic models were applied to seven subsamples of the data according to the diagnosis and/or biological characteristics of the proband. These subsamples were schizoaffective proband families, bipolar I proband families, bipolar II proband families, unipolar probands families, "low" MAO bipolar probands and their families, "low" 5-HIAA bipolar probands and their families, and lithium-responsive bipolar probands and their families. These analyses could not produce evidence supportive of either a single autosomal or a single X-chromosome locus. For the smaller subsamples, both the genetic and the environmental hypotheses could not be rejected; for the larger samples both the genetic and the environmental hypotheses were rejected. Thus, this study's attempts to reduce genetic heterogeneity by studying subsamples and to model within family heterogeneity with different phenotypic models could not differentiate genetic and environmental hypotheses.

Tsuang, Faraone, and Fleming (1985) examined autosomal SML hypotheses based on the family data of Tsuang, Winokur, and Crowe (1980). The probands from this study consisted of 100 bipolar and 225 unipolar patients diagnosed according to Washington University diagnostic criteria based on semistructured interviews. Surgical patients matched on sex, pay status (private and public), and age were used as controls. More than 70 percent of the ill and control patients' relatives were personally interviewed with structured psychiatric interviews that were blind to the diagnostic status of the proband. The SML model applied to these data assumed that, within the same family, unipolar and bipolar illnesses are caused by the same autosomal gene having a different penetrance for each disorder. To reduce between-family heterogeneity, unipolar and bipolar probands were analyzed separately. For both sets of families, dominant and recessive models could be statistically rejected; the environmental hypothesis could not be rejected.

Overall, SML pedigree segregation analyses are not consistent with the hypothesis that a majority of mood disorders are caused by the same single gene. The conclusions to be drawn from these studies do not differ greatly from those drawn from SML prevalence analyses. Both methods fail to find substantial evidence for autosomal or X-chromosomal inheritance. Since the pedigree segregation analysis studies tend to reject the hypothesis of environmental transmission, an alternative genetic explanation is required. The presence of substantial genetic heterogeneity always remains a possibility, but becomes less tenable as one considers the various studies that have attempted to reduce such heterogeneity by proband stratification or phenotypic modeling.

Multifactorial Polygenic Models

The failure to find an SML model that accounts for the familial transmission of mood disorders suggests the examination of multifactorial polygenic models. The MFP model, as originally formulated by Falconer (1965), makes the assumption that all individuals have some unmeasurable liability or predisposition to become ill. Greater amounts of liability increase the likelihood that an individual will develop the disorder. If an individual's liability value is greater than a certain threshold value, the individual will become ill. Liability values lower than the threshold correspond to well individuals. As parameterized in the studies to be described, the MFP model is, strictly speaking, a familial model, not a genetic model. That is, it assumes that liability is composed of both genetic and environmental components. Many genetic and environmental factors are presumed to exist and each is assumed to have a small additive effect on liability. The resulting liability is assumed to have a normal distribution (fig. 5.2). The MFP model in figure 5.2 can be generalized to include multiple thresholds placed along the liability scale (Reich et al., 1972, Reich, James, and Morris, 1979). As previously described for the SML liability-threshold models, the use of multiple thresholds allows for the incorporation of related phenotypes into the genetic model.

The earliest application of the MFP model to mood disorders is found in the work of Slater and Tsuang (1968) using a computational model developed by Slater (1966). This model examines the distribution of illness in the maternal and paternal ancestors of ill probands. If a proband's illness is due to a rare, dominant gene, then

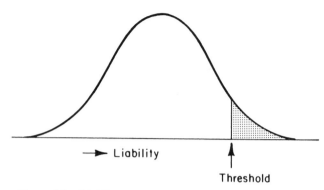

→ Liability

Threshold

Figure 5.2. Multifactorial polygenic liability threshold model

one would expect a unilateral distribution of ill relatives. That is, since the pathogenic gene is transmitted from either the mother or the father, only the maternal or paternal ancestors should be affected. In contrast, the polygenic hypothesis suggests that both parents can contribute pathogenic genes to the proband. Thus, one would expect a bilateral distribution of ill relatives. That is, both maternal and paternal relatives of the proband should be affected. Slater and Tsuang examined the 75 maternal and paternal relatives of 24 mood-disordered probands. The distribution of ill relatives on maternal and paternal sides did not differ significantly from the polygenic expectation.

Perris (1971) applied Slater's model to 138 bipolar and 139 unipolar probands. For both groups, results were compatible with the polygenic hypothesis. Slater, Maxwell, and Price (1971) studied 68 ancestors of 26 bipolar probands. Mood disorders were found on both maternal and paternal sides supporting the polygenic hypothesis.

Baker et al. (1972) sampled unipolar probands from 100 consecutive admissions to an inpatient psychiatric service. Diagnoses of depression, alcoholism, and sociopathy were based on the Washington University criteria. Slater's computational model was applied to several diagnostic subsets of the sample. There were 17 "pure depressive disease" families. These families exhibited at least three cases of unipolar depression and no alcoholism or sociopathy. The results clearly favored polygenic inheritance, even when the 17 families were subdivided according to early versus late onset and male versus female proband. Another subsample consisting of families exhibiting both unipolar depression and alcoholism was analyzed. Again, results favored polygenic inheritance. Additional analyses, stratifying the sample by the age of onset and sex, were also consistent with polygenic inheritance. Thirty families exhibited unipolar disorder, alcoholism, and sociopathy. The observed distribution of maternal and paternal cases did not differ from the polygenic expectation and was not affected by either sex or age of onset.

Mendlewicz et al. (1973) applied the Slater model to subgroups of bipolar proband families. The positive family history probands had at least one relative with bipolar disorder; the negative family history group had no relatives with bipolar disorder. For the Slater analyses, bipolar disorder, unipolar disorder, and alcoholism were considered to be phenotypically equivalent. The involvement of a single dominant gene was suggested by the analysis of the patients with a positive family history. For the subgroup with a negative family history, the results were consistent with polygenic inheritance. James and Chapman (1975) examined 26 bipolar probands and their first-degree relatives. Probands and all first-degree relatives were interviewed and diagnosed based on a method similar to the Washington University criteria. Unipolar and bipolar disorders were considered phenotypic equivalents. Nine probands and 26 of their first-degree relatives were informative for the Slater analysis, which indicated that the polygenic hypothesis could not be rejected.

In contrast to previous studies, Trzebiatowska-Trzeciak (1977) rejected the polygenic hypothesis in her applications of the Slater model to unipolar and bipolar proband families. The 53 unipolar and 69 bipolar probands were diagnosed according to the criteria of Perris (1966); similar criteria were used with the relatives, except three consecutive episodes of depression were not needed for a diagnosis of unipolar disorder among relatives. Suicide in a relative was considered evidence of the ill phenotype.

The polygenic model was not rejected in an application of Slater's model to the family study of James (1977). All of the 46 probands had bipolar disorder as diagnosed by structured interviews. A majority of their first-degree relatives were personally interviewed and diagnosed with criteria similar to the Washington University criteria. Another failure to reject the polygenic hypothesis was reported by Smeraldi, Negri, and Melica (1977). They diagnosed 49 unipolar and 55 bipolar probands according to the criteria of Perris (1966). These same criteria were applied to personal interview data collected on the 624 available first-degree relatives.

Overall, applications of the Slater computational model to mood disorders have failed to reject the polygenic hypothesis. However, these results must be considered suggestive, not conclusive. As Slater, Maxwell, and Price (1971) indicated, the model is subject to several biases that could favor the polygenic hypothesis. Most important, if assortative mating is present, one would expect to observe ill individuals in both the maternal and the paternal ancestries under any genetic hypothesis. Also, since the polygenic hypothesis is the null hypothesis, conditions of low statistical power would favor the polygenic hypothesis. These potential biases are also, to varying degrees, applicable to the more sophisticated prevalence and pedigree segregation analysis approaches.

Prevalence Analyses

Gershon, Baron, and Leckman (1975) applied multiple-threshold MFP models to unipolar, bipolar, and related disorders. This last group included cyclothymic personality, undiagnosed major psychiatric disturbance, and neurotic depression. In the two-threshold model, the related disorders were considered phenotypically normal. In the three-threshold model, they were considered to be the mildly affected phenotype. None of the two- or three-threshold models could be rejected. Gershon et al. (1976) applied the two-threshold MFP model of unipolar and bipolar disorder to three independent data sets (Angst, 1966; Gershon et al., 1965; Perris, 1966). The model was statistically rejected for the data of Perris but not for the other data sets. If the MFP model is correct, these results suggest the heritability to be approximately 0.70–0.94. Leckman and Gershon (1977) applied the two-threshold MFP model of the gender effect to five different data sets (Gershon et al., 1965; Goetzl et al., 1974; James and Chapman, 1975; Mendlewicz and Rainer, 1974; Winokur and Clayton, 1967). The model was rejected for two of the five data sets. For two of the three data sets that provided a satisfactory fit, sex-specific thresholds were not necessary to predict adequately the observed prevalences. Thus, although all of these analyses provide some support of the MFP hypothesis, they do not strongly indicate the need for sex-specific thresholds. These results suggest that the heritability of mood disorders ranges from 0.80 to 1.0.

Smeraldi, Negri, and Melica (1977) could not reject a two-threshold model of unipolar and bipolar disorder. The estimated heritability for these disorders ranged from 0.77 to 0.96. Baron (1981) used the two-threshold MFP model to examine the gender effect in affective disorders. The model was statistically rejected.

Gershon et al. (1982) applied a three-threshold model of unipolar, bipolar, and schizoaffective disorders to their family data set. Their model assumed that schizoaffective disorder resulted when individuals exceed the highest threshold on the liability scale. Those between the second and third thresholds were assumed to develop bipolar disorder, those between the first and second, unipolar disorder, and those below the first threshold were assumed to remain normal. This model could not be statistically rejected. The estimated heritability was approximately 0.78. Smeraldi et al. (1984a) studied the 164 first-degree relatives of 94 bipolar and 51 unipolar probands. The MFP model with sex-specific thresholds could not be rejected. The results suggested that the heritability of mood disorders ranged from 0.52 to 0.88.

Tsuang, Faraone, and Fleming (1985) applied the two-threshold model of unipolar and bipolar disorders to Tsuang, Winokur, and Crowe's (1980) case-controlled, double-blind family study. The results could not statistically reject this version of the MFP model, suggesting that the two disorders share a common genetic liability. Price et al. (1985) combined the unipolar/bipolar distinction and the gender effect in a four-threshold MFP model. They examined the family data set of the Yale-NIMH collaborative study (Gershon et al., 1982; Weissman, Kidd, and Prusoff, 1982). The model was statistically rejected, indicating that multiple-threshold MFP models cannot account for both the unipolar/bipolar distinction and the gender effect. Similar results for the gender effect were reported by Merikangas, Weissman, and Pauls (1985) using the family data of Weissman, Kidd, and Prusoff (1982), a subset of the data used by Price et al. Merikangas, Weissman, and Pauls rejected the two-threshold model of the gender effect because the risk of depression among relatives was independent of the sex of the proband, contrary to the prediction of the two-threshold MFP model.

Reich et al. (1987) examined the transmission of unipolar disorder among families ascertained through the NIMH Collaborative Depression Program. Their model allowed for sex-specific secular trends in lifetime population prevalence, correlations between nontransmissible etiologic factors in siblings, and the transmissibility of the liability to depression. Although there was a trend for the familial transmission of unipolar disorder to be greater in more recently born birth cohorts, this was not statistically significant. Thus, the birth cohort effect observed in these data cannot be attributed to an increased prevalence of nonfamilial, sporadic cases in younger cohorts. However, the degree of transmissability was greater for females (0.62) than for males (0.28). These transmissability estimates are the equivalent of heritability when there are no familial, environmental factors. There was no evidence for nontransmissable environmental factors common to siblings. That is, the degree of concordance be-

Table 5.3.   Multifactorial Polygenic Prevalence Analyses

Study	Conclusion
Gershon et al., 1975	Multiple threshold models of UP, BP, and related disorders not rejected
Gershon et al., 1976	Two-threshold models of UP and BP not rejected for data of Angst (1966) and Gershon et al. (1975) but rejected for data of Perris (1966)
Leckman and Gershon, 1977	Two-threshold model of sex effect fits 3 of 5 data sets
Smeraldi, Negri, and Melica, 1977	Two-threshold model of UP and BP not rejected
Baron, 1981	Two-threshold model of gender effect rejected
Gershon et al., 1982	Three-threshold model of UP, BP, and SA not rejected
Smeraldi et al., 1981	Two-threshold model of gender effect not rejected
Tsuang, Faraone, and Fleming, 1985	Two-threshold model of UP and BP not rejected
Price et al., 1985	Four-threshold model of UP, BP with gender effect rejected
Merikangas et al., 1985	Two-threshold model of gender effect rejected
Reich et al., 1987	MFP model of UP not rejected. Birth cohort not related to transmissibility. Transmissibility greater for females than for males.

Note: UP = unipolar disorder, BP = bipolar disorder, SA = schizoaffective disorder.

tween siblings for depression could be accounted for by transmissable factors. The degree of transmission from mothers to offspring did not differ from that observed between fathers and offspring. Thus, neither maternal nor paternal effects can account for gender difference in this data.

The MFP prevalence analyses listed in table 5.3 can be summarized as follows. Six of seven studies cannot reject the hypothesis that unipolar and bipolar disorders share a common multifactorial liability. Results for the gender effect are more equivocal; four of nine studies reject the two-threshold model of sex differences. Six of the papers that presented MFP prevalence analyses also presented results for SML prevalence analyses (table 5.1). These six studies analyzed a total of 12 data sets. For six of these data sets, both the MFP and SML models could be rejected. For seven of these data sets, neither model could be rejected. Thus, prevalence analyses have not provided strong evidence favoring a specific mode of inheritance.

MIXED MODELS

The mixed model provides a more complicated but perhaps more reasonable alternative to the hypotheses of SML and MFP inheritance (Morton and MacLean, 1974). As the name suggests, the mixed model allows the genetic etiology of a disorder to include both an SML and an MFP component. A major advantage of this approach is that a single model can test both the null hypothesis of no MFP effect and the null hypothesis of no SML effect. These hypotheses cannot be directly compared, but each can be compared with a model including both components. That is, a mixed-model analysis can determine if one of the two components can provide an adequate fit to the data without including the presence of the other component.

The lack of clear-cut results favoring either SML or MFP inheritance in mood disorders suggests that the mixed model may be an appropriate method of analysis. Shaughnessy et al. (1985) examined a 28-member three-generation pedigree selected through a bipolar proband. Family members who had a history of a major or minor mood disorder were considered to be affected. The mixed-model analysis could reject the hypothesis of no familial transmission. However, it could not distinguish between SML and MFP models of transmission. Similar results were obtained when the definition of affected was changed to include only individuals who had been hospitalized for a mood disorder. These mixed model results are very preliminary for two reasons. First, the sample size was relatively small, suggesting that tests of hypotheses were not very powerful. In addition, the analytic model used by these authors did not allow them to correct the data for the variable age of onset of mood disorders.

Rice et al. (1987b) applied the mixed model to 187 families of bipolar patients from the NIMH Collaborative Study of the Psychobiology of Depression. Diagnoses were made according to Research Diagnostic Criteria (RDC) derived from structured psychiatric interviews. All available first-degree relatives were interviewed. Those who were unavailable were diagnosed according to the Family History RDC based on information from an informant. Only bipolar relatives were considered to be ill in these analyses. Bipolar disorder was defined as meeting criteria for bipolar I disorder (149 probands) or schizoaffective disorder-manic subtype (38 probands). The schizoaffective subgroup was included because it was found that schizoaffective-manic and bipolar I probands had the highest rates of bipolar I disorder among their first-degree relatives as compared to probands with schizoaffective disorder-depressed type, bipolar II disorder, or unipolar disorder. Moreover, relatives of probands with schizoaffective disorder-depressed type had higher rates of schizophrenia than relatives of unipolar probands. The rates of schizophrenia did not differ for relatives of schizoaffective-manic and unipolar probands.

The mixed model was examined both with and without different liability classes that would allow the age of onset to reflect severity. The hypothesis of no familial transmission could be rejected. Support for the MFP model did not differ whether or not liability was differentiated on the basis of the age of onset. This was not the case for the SML model. In the analysis without liability classes determined by the age of onset, the SML model was not supported; however, with the inclusion of these liability classes in the mixed model, there was evidence for an SML. There was little support for multifactorial inheritance in this latter mixed model because the polygenic background was quite low.

Consistent with other reports (see chap. 2) indicating that the age of onset reflects the degree of liability, these results suggest that the model using age-of-onset–based liability classes is more meaningful. However, the investigators noted that the results were not conclusive because the estimated transmission probabilities were significantly different from Mendelian expectations. That is, the transmission probabilities differed from their expected values under the Mendelian hypothesis. The expected probabilities of transmitting the normal allele A, for genotypes AA, Aa, and aa are 1.0, 0.5, and 0.0, respectively.

In an effort to reduce heterogeneity and to allow for more complex models of transmission, Price, Kidd, and Weissman (1987) applied mixed-model analysis to subgroups of individuals from the Yale Family Study (Gershon et al., 1982; Weissman, Kidd, and Prusoff, 1982). This data set was discussed above in regard to multiple-threshold SML and MFP analyses of bipolar and unipolar disorders. In those analyses (Price et al., 1985), it was found that the SML model with the gender effect could be fit to the data but most of the unipolar and bipolar cases were phenocopies. The MFP model was rejected. This more recent analysis (Price, Kidd, and Weissman, 1987) included only families of unipolar probands and considered only relatives with unipolar disorder to be affected. The gender effect was modeled in terms of sex-specific penetrances for unipolar disorder. In addition, the authors incorporated into the analyses the presence or absence of early onset (under age 30) and panic disorder in probands as potential etiologic markers.

Three overlapping subsets of families were examined: (1) 105 families selected through 64 early-onset probands; (2) 50 families of 28 unipolar probands with secondary panic disorder (24 families of early-onset probands and 7 families of late-onset probands); and (3) 38 families of 21 probands with both early onset of unipolar disorder and secondary panic disorder. Diagnoses were made according to modified RDC based on direct interview. Different thresholds for unipolar disorder were assumed for men and women and for different age cohorts. Age cohorts were modeled on differences in thresholds because recent evidence indicates that lifetime rates have significantly increased in more recent cohorts (see chap. 2).

Pedigree segregation analyses rejected a model of no familial transmission for all three subgroups. For the early-onset group the best-fitting mixed model indicated a dominant major gene with incomplete penetrance. The frequency of the pathogenic gene was about 4 percent. A large proportion of cases (40 percent) were phenocopies according to the model. Polygenic heritability in the best-fitting mixed model approached 0, making it equivalent to an SML model. These data strongly suggest the presence of a major gene and clearly reject the pure MFP model. On the other hand, the estimated probabilities of transmission were significantly different from expected Mendelian values under the SML model.

In the panic subgroup the best-fitting mixed model was that of a dominant gene with a low gene frequency (0.03) and polygenic heritability (0.25). For the early onset with panic disorder subgroup, the mixed model suggested a partially dominant gene with a gene frequency of 0.03 and no polygenic background. In these subgroups the transmission probabilities were again non-Mendelian.

The authors noted that the age cohort–effect makes the interpretation of the results difficult. The inconsistency of estimated transmission probabilities with Mendelian expectations could have resulted if the cohort effect were due to nongenetic factors, as the work of Lavori et al. (1986) suggests. If so, modeling cohort differences as differences in thresholds would be inaccurate. Conclusions regarding the panic disorder and early onset with panic disorder subgroups are limited by the small sample sizes involved. Overall, there is stronger evidence for an SML as opposed to an MFP process. Because of the inconsistencies noted, findings should be considered suggestive, but not conclusive, of a predominantly SML mode of inheritance for individuals with early-onset unipolar disorder.

SUMMARY

The results of analyses incorporating the unipolar-bipolar distinction are summarized as follows. Of five data sets in which the SML model was examined, two failed to reject the model, two rejected it, and one had equivocal results. The ambiguous results were for the data of Gershon et al. (1965), in which an X-chromosomal model was rejected but an autosomal model was not. There are not enough such comparisons, however, to draw any firm conclusions about the adequacy of the autosomal model versus the X-chromosomal model. The MFP model received stronger support from the six data sets in which it was examined. Five of those six failed to reject the MFP model.

The only study incorporating the unipolar-bipolar distinction that rejects the MFP model is an analysis of the data of Perris (1966) by Gershon et al. (1976). Perris limited the definition of unipolar disorder to recurrent forms. Thus, the rejection of the model is consistent with family studies using the recurrent criteria; such studies have tended to find no familial relationship between bipolar and unipolar disorder (see chap. 2). On the other hand, if one looks at the five instances in which both autosomal SML and MFP models are tested on the same data set, the results suggest that there is a lack of strong evidence favoring a specific model. For only one of these data sets (Tsuang, Winokur, and Crowe, 1980) did the results differ between the SML and MFP models; the former was rejected, whereas the latter was not. For three of the data sets both models could not be rejected and for one of them both models were rejected.

Whereas the results of analyses using polarity-specific thresholds are equivocal, the majority of studies without such thresholds reject the SML model. The autosomal model was rejected for five of seven data sets. The X-chromosomal model was also rejected for five of seven data sets; one failed to reject it and one provided mixed results. There are five data sets in which both the autosomal and X-chromosomal models were tested. In four of these, both models were rejected; in one of them the autosomal model was not rejected but the X-chromosomal model was rejected. Either of these SML models is thus only very weakly supported.

Analyses of the gender effect using polarity-specific thresholds were conducted on only three data sets. Because there are so few of these studies and the results are variable, no firm conclusions can be drawn. Many more studies have been performed in which the gender effect was applied without the use of polarity-specific thresholds. The results of these studies are inconsistent for both SML and

MFP models. Out of 13 data sets in which the SML model with the gender effect was tested, 7 failed to reject the model, 5 rejected it, and 1 had ambiguous results. The MFP model with the gender effect was rejected for 4 out of 8 data sets. Moreover, studies that examined the same data set both with and without the gender effect found little or no differences. Testing these models with the gender effect also failed to produce evidence that would favor a specific model. For 7 out of 8 data sets, either the SML and MFP models were both rejected or were both supported. Regardless of whether or not polarity-specific thresholds are used, neither SML nor MFP models with the gender effect have been superior to the models without it.

For the two studies that applied mixed-model analysis and examined the gender effect, the pure MFP model was not supported (Price, Kidd, and Weissman, 1987; Rice et al., 1987b). Unfortunately, support for the SML model was ambiguous in both studies. Price, Kidd, and Weissman studied only unipolar disorders and included the gender effect in their analyses. On the other hand, Rice et al. studied only bipolar disorders but did not include the gender effect in their tests of the models because there was little support for sex differences in their data. Almost all of the analyses before these two recent studies have applied the gender effect to data sets including both bipolar and unipolar subjects. The use of different thresholds for men and women across both diagnostic categories may have been problematic. Based on the findings of epidemiologic studies, this approach is clearly justifiable for unipolar disorders. But, epidemiologic studies do not tend to find a gender effect for bipolar disorders. At least with regard to gender effects, the results of these two mixed-model analyses are consistent with the epidemiologic findings.

In two of three mixed-model pedigree segregation analyses (Price, Kidd, and Weissman, 1987; Rice et al., 1987b), the pure MFP model was not supported but results for the SML model were ambiguous. The lack of conformation to Mendelian expectations in the two mixed-model pedigree segregation analyses is consistent with the conclusion that alternative genetic explanations are needed because these analyses reject the hypothesis of environmental transmission.

The lack of consistent or definitive results suggests that mathematical genetic modeling studies have reached a limit in their utility for understanding the transmission of major mood disorders. While methodologic improvements in terms of the collection of family data have strengthened this approach, they do not directly address what is perhaps the most important issue, the problem of determining what is the appropriate specification of the phenotype.

One approach to this dilemma is to conduct multiple analyses for the same data sets using different criteria for defining the phenotype. Of course, those groups of disorders for which results were significant would need to be cross-validated on other samples. This type of exploratory strategy has been used in a few studies but the "right" group of disorders has still not clearly emerged. It may be that mathematical modeling studies will not be conclusive until a highly reliable and valid diagnosis of mood disorders becomes available.

It is crucial to remember that modeling studies are limited by the assumption that all families examined exhibit the same genetic disorder. If mood disorders are genetically heterogeneous, then the results of modeling studies are meaningless. Fortunately, the problem of heterogeneity can be somewhat mitigated by studies of genetic linkage.

Chapter Six

Linkage and Association Studies

The structure of human chromosomes and the well-described series of genetic events involved in human reproduction have enabled geneticists to develop experimental tests to detect the single genes that contribute to psychiatric and other disorders. To understand fully how tests of linkage and association can detect major genes, it is necessary to review basic facts of human cytogenetics.

At the molecular level, a gene is a sequence of the deoxyribonucleic acids (DNA). DNA consists of a sequence of deoxyribose sugar-phosphate groups each attached to one of four nitrogen bases: adenine (A), thymine (T), guanine (G), and cytosine (C). The sequence of base pairs in a gene determines the sequence of amino acids and hence the protein it will create. Although gene size is highly variable, the number of bases contained in a single gene is of the order of 1,000 for a typical gene (Morton, 1982). Individual genes are arranged sequentially on linear structures called chromosomes. Thus, a chromosome is a large strand of DNA containing many individual genes. Humans have 23 pairs of chromosomes. One pair consists of sex chromosomes. For females, this pair contains two X chromosomes, and for males, one X and one Y chromosome. The other 22 pairs are called autosomes. The location of a gene on a chromosome is called its locus. The different variants of a gene that may be found at that locus are called alleles.

Genetic transmission occurs because all individuals inherit one member of each pair of chromosomes from their father and one from their mother. However, the inherited chromosomes are not identical to any of the original parental chromosomes. This is due to the phenomenon known as crossing over, which occurs during meiosis. Meiosis is the process whereby gametes (sperm and egg) are created. Unlike other cells, gametes contain single chromosomes, not pairs. These single chromosomes are not simply one of the chromosomes from the original pair. Each chromosome in a gamete consists of a combination of genes, some from one member of the original pair, others from the other member of the original pair. This is the result of crossing over between the original pair during meiosis. We represent crossing over schematically in figure 6.1.

In the figure, the original pair of chromosomes is represented as one dark strand and one light strand. Three different genes are highlighted with uppercase and lowercase letters signifying different alleles at the same locus. During meiosis these two chromosomes will literally cross over each other and exchange portions of their DNA. In figure 6.1 we demonstrate the result of a single crossover. In reality, multiple crossovers will occur, resulting in a new pair of chromosomes in which each member of the pair is a complicated combination of genes from the original pair. This phenomenon we show schematically in figure 6.2.

When meiosis is complete, one chromosome from each new pair will be found in each gamete. Thus, the chromosome transmitted from parent to child contains a mixture of genes from the parents' original pair.

Linkage Studies

With figures 6.1 and 6.2 we illustrate genetic linkage and its relationship to crossing over. Linkage occurs when two loci on the same original chromosome are so close to each other that crossing over rarely occurs between them. Closely linked genes usually remain together on the same chromosome, in the same gamete, after meiosis has been completed. In figures 6.1 and 6.2, the A (or a) and the B

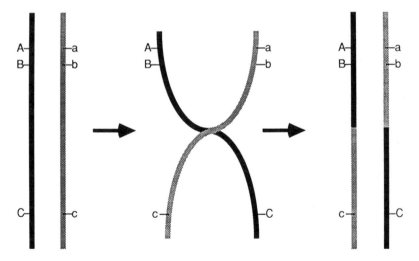

Figure 6.1.   Schematic representation of a single crossover

Figure 6.2. New chromosome pair created by multiple crossovers

(or *b*) locus are close to each other but distant from the *C* (or *c*) locus. Crossing over is unlikely to occur between the *A* and *B* loci. Therefore, it is very likely that, after meiosis, the rearranged chromosomes will contain either alleles *A* and *B* or alleles *a* and *b*. It is highly unlikely that a child will receive a chromosome containing either *A* and *b* or *a* and *B*. In contrast, because the *C* locus is far from the *A* locus, it is more possible that these two loci will exhibit recombination. That is, one would expect crossing over to occur between the *C* and *A* loci, resulting in new, recombinant chromosomes containing the pairs *Ac* and *aC*. Two loci will recombine if an odd number of crossovers occur between them, otherwise they will not recombine. If two loci are very far apart, the probability of an odd number of crossovers is equal to that for an even number, so the probability of recombination is 50 percent. Thus, genes on the same chromosome that are distant from one another are transmitted independently, as is the case for genes on different chromosomes.

To demonstrate that a single gene is involved in the etiology of a disease, one can show that the putative disease locus is linked to a known genetic marker. To be useful for linkage analysis, a genetic marker must be a measurable human trait controlled by a single gene with a known chromosomal location. In addition, the mode of inheritance of the marker must be known and the marker must be polymorphic (i.e., more than one version of the gene exists with a substantial frequency). Commonly used marker loci include blood groups, enzymes, proteins, and systems that control immune response. Linkage between a disease locus and a marker locus is demonstrated by showing that the genes at the two loci are not transmitted independently. This is done by estimating the recombination fraction, the probability that the disease and marker genes will recombine during meiosis.

Consider a hypothetical genetic marker locus such that individuals with genotypes *Mm* and *mm* are marker positive, whereas individuals with genotype *MM* are marker negative—that is, individuals with at least one *m* gene exhibit the trait. Next, consider a disease that is assumed to be autosomal dominant such that individuals with genotypes *Dd* and *dd* become ill, whereas those with the genotype *DD* are healthy. To demonstrate linkage between the marker locus and the disease locus, the investigator collects a series of families where one parent is marker negative (*MM*) and healthy (*DD*) while the other parent is a double heterozygote and therefore is marker positive (*Mm*) and is afflicted with the disease (*Dd*). If the afflicted parent is known to have genotype *MD/md* (i.e., *M* and *D* are on the same chromosome and *m* and *d* are on the other chromosome), then the expected distribution of children is given in table 6.1.

As column 1 indicates, the child always inherits an *MD* haplotype from the doubly homozygous parent. Four possible haplotypes can be inherited from the doubly heterozygous parent. The first two child genotypes will occur when the marker and disease loci do not recombine and are therefore called nonrecombinants. The last two genotypes in the table are recombinants; their second haplotype is a recombination of the ill parent's original haplotypes. Column 2 gives the probability of observing each genotype expressed in terms of the recombination fraction, θ. The recombination fraction ranges from 0 to 0.5. Low values indicate that the disease and marker loci

Table 6.1. The Distribution of Child Genotypes from *MD/md* × *MD/MD* Mating

Child Genotype	Probability of Genotype	Marker Status	Disease Status
MD/MD	$\dfrac{1 - \theta}{2}$	negative	well
MD/md	$\dfrac{1 - \theta}{2}$	positive	ill
MD/Md	$\dfrac{\theta}{2}$	negative	ill
MD/mD	$\dfrac{\theta}{2}$	positive	well

Note: θ = recombination fraction.

are tightly linked together on the same chromosome. A value of 0.5 means that the two loci either are on different chromosomes or are very distant on the same chromosome. When the two loci are tightly linked (i.e., $\theta = 0$), the two recombinant genotypes should be very rare in matings of the type given in table 6.1. The two nonrecombinant genotypes should be equally common. In this example, nonrecombinants can be distinguished from recombinants at the phenotypic level; nonrecombinants will be either marker negative and well or marker positive and ill, whereas recombinants will be either marker negative and ill or marker positive and well. Thus, in this example, linkage means that positive marker status and affliction with the disease will tend to travel together within a given family.

In practice, the detection of linkage is more complicated than the preceding example, because the genotypes and haplotypes at relevant loci may not be known with complete certainty. Thus, it is often not possible to determine from direct observation which children are recombinants and which are nonrecombinants. Fortunately, statistical techniques have been developed that allow one to estimate the recombination fraction in situations when genotypes and haplotypes are not well specified. A comprehensive and excellent review of these techniques is given by Ott (1985). The most common method of reporting linkage results is to compute a maximum likelihood estimate of the recombination fraction, the probability of observing an informative data set under the assumption that the recombination fraction is equal to the estimate and the probability of observing the data set under the assumption that the recombination fraction is equal to 0.5. The ratio of the second quantity to the third quantity is an odds ratio. It compares the probability that linkage is present ($\theta < 0.5$) with the probability of no linkage ($\theta = 0.5$). It has been customary for linkage results to be reported in terms of the logarithm to the base 10 of the odds ratio. The log of the odds ratio is called the lod score. Lod scores greater than 3 are considered to be evidence favoring linkage; lod scores less than -2 are considered to be evidence against linkage; lod scores greater than 2 but less than 3 are suggestive of linkage; lod scores in between -2 and 2 are considered to be uninformative (Ott, 1985). Thus, a linkage analysis will support the hypothesis of linkage if the statistical computations indicate that the odds favoring linkage are 1,000 to 1.

Although methods of linkage analysis have been available for some time, the ability to perform a linkage study has, until recently, been limited by the availability of genetic markers. Measurable traits, such as blood groups that are polymorphic enough to be suitable markers, are rare. That is, they cover only a very small proportion of the genome, making it, a priori, very unlikely that a known genetic trait could be mapped to a chromosomal locus. Fortunately, nature, in conjunction with the diligent and brilliant work of molecular geneticists, has provided a simple but powerful solution to this problem.

During evolution, bacteria developed a mechanism to protect themselves from the invasion of foreign DNA. At the core of this mechanism is a group of enzymes called restriction endonucleases. These enzymes neutralize foreign DNA by literally cutting it into pieces. The locations of the cuts are determined by the sequence of nucleotides in the foreign DNA. For example, the restriction endonuclease called AluI will cut DNA between nucleotides containing guanine and cytosine wherever the nucleotide sequence AGCT (i.e., four nucleotides sequentially containing the bases adenine, guanine, cytosine, and thymine) occurs. The enzyme EcoRI cleaves DNA between G and A within the nucleotide sequence GAATTC. Thus, if AluI is applied to the DNA sequence:

$$TACGGCCAGCTCGAAGT \qquad (1)$$

two fragments are produced:

$$TACGGCCAG \quad CTCGAAGT \qquad (2)$$

The application of EcoRI would not cut this sequence because it does not contain the recognition site GAATTC. If the DNA sequence given in (1) were to undergo a mutation deleting the nucleotides CAG, then the mutated sequence would be

$$TACGGCCTCGAAGT \qquad (3)$$

AluI would not cut this sequence because the recognition site AGCT no longer exists. The mutation is detected experimentally because AluI produces two short restriction fragments from the first DNA and one long restriction fragment from the second DNA.

For a variety of reasons, a large proportion of human DNA is highly polymorphic as regards the lengths of fragments produced by restriction enzymes. That is, if one extracts the same chromosomal segment from different individuals, the length and number of fragments produced from this segment by one or more restriction enzymes will vary substantially among individuals. Since restriction fragment lengths are highly polymorphic, they are known as restriction fragment length polymorphisms, or RFLPs (pronounced "riflips"). As of November 1988, 1,450 RFLP loci had been identified along the human genome (Howard Hughes Medical Institute, 1988). It is expected that most, if not all, genes will be within linkage distance of RFLP loci in the near future.

X-Linkage

In the previous chapter we showed that segregation analyses of large family-study data sets have failed to support the hypothesis of X-linked inheritance for bipolar disorder. However, these studies cannot rule out the involvement of an X-chromosomal locus for a subset of mood disorders, since the segregation analyses do not allow for genetic heterogeneity. Epidemiologic and family-study data are consistent with the hypothesis of X-linkage for some mood disorders. As Weissman and Boyd's (1984) comprehensive review indicates, epidemiologic studies have consistently found women to be at greater risk than men for mood disorders. The difference is primarily due to an excess of unipolar cases among women. For example, Robins et al. (1984) found women to be twice as likely to experience a major depressive episode but equally likely to have experienced a manic episode as men. The difference was consistent across three large samples from different American cities. Winokur and Crowe (1983) reviewed 14 family studies of bipolar probands and reported that among affected female relatives, the ratio of unipolar to bipolar disorder is approximately 2, whereas among affected male relatives, the ratio is approximately 1. An excess of mood disorder among women would be expected for a dominant, X-linked trait.

Also consistent with the X-linkage hypothesis is Winokur's (1970) report on the parent-child transmission of bipolar disorder in the families of 89 bipolar probands. He found 13 cases of father-daughter transmission, 17 cases of mother-daughter transmission, and 17 cases of mother-son transmission. No cases of father-son transmission were found. This is consistent with X-linkage, since fathers cannot transmit an X chromosome to their sons. Although father-son transmission has been reported in other studies, it is usually less than mother-son transmission. For example, Zerbin-Rudin (1982) reviewed 11 family studies of mood disorders and found 73 cases of father-son transmission. Mother-son transmission was twice as likely as father-son transmission. It is reasonable to hypothesize that the dearth of father-son transmission in family studies is due to the presence of an X-linked variant of mood disorder.

As we show in table 6.2, studies that have examined linkage between bipolar disorder and known X-chromosomal markers have been inconsistent. Mendlewicz, Fleiss, and Fieve (1972) studied nine pedigrees informative for mood disorder and color blindness. Both protan and deutan color blindness are recessive X-linked traits with known chromosomal location. All probands had bipolar disorder but relatives were considered ill if they had either unipolar or bipolar

Table 6.2.   Studies of X Linkage In Bipolar Disorder

Study	Marker	θ_{max}	Lod Score
Mendlewicz et al., 1972 Winokur, Clayton, and Reich, 1969	Protan CB	0.11	—
Reich, Clayton, and Winokur, 1969	Deutan CB	0.19	—
Fieve, Mendlewicz, and Fleiss, 1973	Xg	0.19	1.12
Winokur and Tanna, 1969 Mendlewicz and Fleiss, 1974	Deutan CB	0.07	4.50
	Protan CB	0.10	3.73
	Xg	0.19	1.82
Mendlewicz et al., 1975	Xg	0.19	1.82
Winokur and Tanna, 1969 Johnson and Leeman, 1977	Deutan CB	0.5	0.0
Baron, 1977	Deutan CB	0.09	2.33
Leckman et al., 1979	Xg	0.5	0.0
Gershon et al., 1980 ("Genetics of Plasma") and Gershon et al., 1979	Protan CB and Deutan CB	0.25	1.00
Mendlewicz et al., 1979 Mendlewicz et al., 1980	G6PD	0.05	4.32
Del Zompo et al., 1984	G6PD	0.0	0.97
	Protan CB	0.0	0.50
Kidd et al., 1984	CB	0.0	0.27
	Xg	0.0	0.36
Baron et al., 1987	Protan CB and Deutan CB	0.04	4.75
	G6PD	0.0	2.94
Mendlewicz et al., 1987	F9	0.11	3.10

Note: θ_{max} = recombination fraction at maximum lod score; CB = color blindness.

disorder. In addition to their own pedigrees, these authors used data from Winokur, Clayton, and Reich (1969) and Reich, Clayton, and Winokur (1969). Although they did not present a lod score analysis, their interpretation of the pedigrees suggested that among the five families informative for protan color blindness, there was one recombinant offspring and eight nonrecombinants, yielding a recombination fraction of 0.11. Among the four families informative for deutan color blindness, there were 3 recombinants and 14 nonrecombinants, suggesting a recombination fraction of 0.19. Since the estimates of the recombination fraction were less than 0.5, the authors concluded that their data supported the presence of a dominant X-linked gene in the transmission of mood disorders.

Fieve, Mendlewicz, and Fleiss (1973) tested for genetic linkage between mood disorder and the Xg blood group. This blood group is known to be controlled by a gene on the X chromosome. Six pedigrees ascertained through bipolar probands were studied; two of these had been previously described by Winokur and Tanna (1969). Their estimate of the recombination fraction, 0.19, was significantly less than 0.5. However, the associated lod score was 1.12, less than the score of 3 needed to assert linkage definitely. That is, the odds favoring linkage were only 13 to 1, as compared to the acceptance criterion of 1,000 to 1. Mendlewicz and Fleiss (1974) added six additional families to four previously studied pedigrees informative for deutan color blindness. The estimated recombination fraction was 0.07; this corresponded to a lod score of approximately 4.5, indicating the odds favoring linkage to be more than 30,000 to 1. An analysis of 15 bipolar pedigrees informative for protan color blindness produced similar results. Close linkage ($\theta = 0.10$) was supported with an odds ratio of 5,000 to 1. An analysis of 25 families informative for Xg-linkage was less conclusive. Although the odds favoring linkage were 920 to 1 for $\theta = 0.19$, the lod score of 2.96 fell short of the accepted threshold for statistical significance. The results for bipolar families differed markedly from studies of pedigrees containing unipolar, but no bipolar illness. In these latter pedigrees, linkage to protan color blindness was excluded with lod scores less than -2.3 for θ values less than 0.15. Linkage to Xg was excluded with lod scores less than -2.6 for θ values less than 0.20. Mendlewicz, Fleiss, and Fieve (1975) reported a linkage analysis using the Xg blood group that included some of the pedigrees studied by Fieve, Mendlewicz, and Fleiss (1973). A total of 12 families were studied. All probands were suffering from bipolar disorder and relatives were considered afflicted if they had either bipolar or unipolar disorders. The estimated recombination fraction of 0.19 was identical to that reported by Fieve, Mendlewicz, and Fleiss. This was significantly less than 0.5 but the lod score did not exceed 3.

Gershon and Bunney (1976) criticized the above-cited linkage analyses for several reasons. All the linkage studies used an analysis method that assumed the mood disorder phenotype to be unambiguously observable. The method did not take into account the issues of variable age of onset and incomplete penetrance. In addition, these authors pointed out that the assertion of linkage with both color blindness and Xg loci was inconsistent with the known chromosomal distance between Xg and color blindness on the X chromosome. That is, the Xg locus and the color blindness loci are so far apart that it would be impossible for any one gene to be linked to both Xg and color blindness.

A subsequent linkage analysis by Johnson and Leeman (1977) examined linkage to deutan color blindness in two pedigrees ascertained through bipolar probands. Relatives were considered ill if they had either unipolar or bipolar disorder. The linkage analysis, which did not correct for variable age of onset and incomplete penetrance, estimated the recombination fraction to be 0.5, suggesting no linkage. Linkage with deutan color blindness was studied by Baron (1977) in one large pedigree ascertained through a schizoaffective proband. Relatives were considered ill if they had either bipolar or unipolar disorder. The linkage analysis did not adjust for variable age of onset and incomplete penetrance. The recombination fraction, 0.09, was associated with a lod score of 2.33. Thus, the odds were more than 200 to 1 in favor of linkage. Leckman et al. (1979) examined linkage with Xg in six families ascertained through bipolar probands. Relatives were considered affected if they had either bipolar disorder, unipolar disorder, cyclothymic disorder, minor depression, or acute psychoses. Their analytic method, which corrected for variable age of onset and incomplete penetrance, estimated the recombination fraction to be 0.5. Therefore, the hypothesis of close linkage was not supported. Close linkage was definitively rejected because the lod scores for recombination fraction values lower than 0.1 were less than −2.

Gershon et al. (1980b) reported results from an international collaborative study of X-linkage under the auspices of the World Health Organization. Sixteen pedigrees ascertained through bipolar probands in the United States, Belgium, Switzerland, and Denmark were studied for linkage between color blindness and bipolar disorder. The method of analysis allowed for variable age of onset and incomplete penetrance. When all pedigrees were analyzed together, the recombination fraction was 0.25 at a lod score of 1.0. Thus, the overall sample could not definitively provide evidence for linkage. However, more detailed analyses indicated substantial differences between two large subsamples, six pedigrees from the United States and eight pedigrees from Belgium. The American data could definitively exclude close linkage because recombination fraction values less than 0.09 were associated with lod scores less than −2. In contrast, the Belgian data were more suggestive of linkage with a maximum lod score of 1.55 at $\theta = 0.15$. As these differing results would suggest, the entire series of pedigrees demonstrated significant linkage heterogeneity. The American subsample did not demonstrate linkage heterogeneity, but the Belgian subsample was significantly heterogeneous. This heterogeneity was accounted for by one Belgian family that had very high lod scores. The recombination fraction for this family was estimated to be 0, with a lod score of 2.3. Thus, for this family the odds favoring linkage were nearly 200 to 1. The authors concluded that one pedigree strongly suggested linkage, seven suggested nonlinkage, and eight were indeterminant. Their demonstration of linkage heterogeneity supported the hypothesis that mood disorders may be genetically heterogeneous.

More convincing evidence for X-linkage was provided by Mendlewicz, Linkowski, and Wilmotte (1980a), who examined one pedigree ascertained through a unipolar proband. The family was informative for both mood disorder and glucose-6-phosphate-dehydrogenase (G6PD) deficiency. Relatives were considered ill if they had either unipolar or bipolar disorder. G6PD is an enzyme known to be controlled by a gene on the X chromosome. Their method of analysis allowed for variable age of onset and incomplete penetrance. The estimated recombination fraction, 0.05, was highly significant with a lod score of 4.32. The odds favoring linkage were greater than 20,000 to 1. Linkage between G6PD and mood disorders was weakly suggested in a pedigree examined by Del Zompo et al. (1984). They used appropriate analytic techniques and estimated a recombination fraction of 0.0. However, the lod score was only 0.97. They also examined a second family that was informative for protan color blindness. Again, the estimated recombination fraction was 0.0 but the lod score was fairly low, 0.50.

Kidd et al. (1984a) examined one bipolar family informative for color blindness and three families informative for the Xg blood group. For color blindness, the linkage analysis was performed eight times, corresponding to four different definitions of color blindness and two different definitions of illness. The color blindness definitions varied the method of classification and the decision rules for classifying questionable subjects. The diagnostic definitions either included or excluded unipolar disorder as a variant of bipolar disorder. From these analyses, the only suggestion of linkage was an estimated recombination fraction of 0.0 associated with a lod score of only 0.27. Three Xg-linkage analyses were performed corresponding to three definitions of illness. The maximum lod scores from these analyses indicated a recombination fraction estimate of 0.0 associated with a lod score of 0.36.

Overall, the X-linkage studies discussed to this point provide weak evidence for X-chromosomal involvement in mood disorders.

The only study to find a statistically significant lod score was that of Mendlewicz, Linkowski, and Wilmotte (1980a), which found a close linkage between mood disorders and G6PD deficiency. The remaining studies are either weakly or not supportive of the X-linkage hypothesis. Fortunately, many of these studies have been reanalyzed in a single analysis using appropriate statistical methods. Risch and Baron (1982) reanalyzed data from Baron (1977), Gershon et al. (1979), Leckman et al. (1979), Mendlewicz and Fleiss (1974), Mendlewicz, Fleiss, and Fieve (1972), Mendlewicz et al. (1979), and Mendlewicz, Linkowski, and Wilmotte (1980a). The reanalysis assumed that bipolar disorder, unipolar disorder, and cyclothymic personality were phenotypic variants of the X-linked genotype. The 15 pedigrees informative for protan color blindness demonstrated close linkage ($\theta = 0.1$) with a statistically significant lod score of 3.74 (table 6.3).

Similarly, the 14 pedigrees displaying deutan color blindness yielded a recombination fraction estimate of 0.1 with a statistically significant lod score of 5.37. There was only one pedigree available for G6PD deficiency. The reanalysis of this pedigree supported the results of Mendlewicz, Linkowski, and Wilmotte (1980a) in finding close linkage ($\theta = 0$ at a lod score of 5.11). The reanalysis of 28 pedigrees informative for linkage with the Xg blood group could not demonstrate strong evidence for or against linkage ($\theta = 0.3$ at a lod score of 0.35).

Risch and Baron further clarified the controversial and inconsistent results of previous studies by demonstrating that the color blindness pedigrees exhibited significant linkage heterogeneity. That is, they estimated that approximately 60 percent of the pedigrees could be inferred to have an X-linked variant of mood disorder. This does not indicate the true proportion of the X-linked variant in the population because investigators exclude pedigrees with father-son transmission. Unfortunately, most of the positive linkage results are from pedigrees reported by one group of investigators (Mendlewicz et al.). Although Gershon et al. (1979) suggested that this may be due to systematic procedural errors on the part of these investigators, Risch and Baron argued that they are very likely due to genetic heterogeneity. Their heterogeneity hypothesis is supported by their analysis indicating that linkage heterogeneity is found even when analyses are limited to the pedigrees published by Mendlewicz et al.

Perhaps the most notable aspect of the reanalyses reported by Risch and Baron is that the results are consistent with current knowledge regarding the X-chromosome map. As Gershon and Bunney (1976) argued, mood disorders could not be linked to both the color

blindness loci and the Xg locus. Xg and color blindness are at opposite ends of the X chromosome and therefore should exhibit independent assortment (i.e., $\theta = 0.5$). These known chromosomal
locations are consistent with the results in table 6.3, indicating close
linkage to color blindness but no linkage to Xg. The two color blindness loci (protan and deutan) are known to be close to one another
and to the locus for G6PD deficiency. The results in table 6.3 are
consistent with this known clustering of genes, since each of the three
loci exhibit statistically significant linkage with mood disorder.

Risch and Baron found further support for their assertion of
X-linkage in an analysis of four Israeli families informative for color
blindness (Baron et al., 1987). All of the families were selected
through bipolar probands. Relatives were considered ill if they had
one of the following diagnoses: bipolar I, bipolar II, unipolar, schizoaffective (mainly affective), or cyclothymic disorder. The maximal
lod score of 4.75 for a recombination fraction of 0.04 indicates strong
support for X-linkage. Using similar diagnostic criteria, Baron et al.
(1987) examined one large Israeli pedigree informative for G6PD
deficiency. The maximal lod score was 2.94 at a recombination fraction of 0.0. Although the lod score falls short of the 3.0 significance
level, the results are strongly supportive of X-linkage.

The two families informative for protan color blindness had
maximal lod scores of 2.69 and 1.34, respectively; both were associated with a recombination fraction of 0.0. The two families informative for deutan color blindness had maximal lod scores of 0.0
at a recombination fraction of 0.5, and 2.31 at a recombination fraction of 0.0. Close linkage was definitively excluded in the latter
pedigree; lod scores fell well below -2 for very low recombination
fraction values (e.g., the lod score was -4.19 at $\theta = 0.0$). This
pedigree was also the only Ashkenazi pedigree. Linkage analysis of
the three non-Ashkenazi pedigrees resulted in a maximal lod score
of 6.34 at a recombination fraction of 0.0. The strong evidence for

Table 6.3. Reanalysis of Pooled Linkage Data

Marker	Number of Pedigrees	θ_{max}	Lod Score
Protan CB	15	0.1	3.74
Deutan CB	14	0.1	5.37
G6PD	1	0.0	5.11
Xg	28	0.3	0.35

Source: Risch and Baron, 1982.
Note: θ_{max} = recombination fraction at maximum lod score; CB = color blindness.

linkage in the non-Ashkenazi families, but not in the Ashkenazi, led the authors to speculate that X-linked inheritance of bipolar-related disorders could be more pronounced in this, and possibly other related ethnic groups. As they noted, however, rigorous comparison is not possible because there was only one Ashkenazi pedigree. Tests for linkage heterogeneity among the four pedigrees were, in fact, only marginally significant ($p < 0.10$). Nevertheless, these findings provide further support for the viability of the hypothesis of genetic heterogeneity among the mood disorders.

The results of Baron et al. supported the hypothesis of linkage for color blindness markers and G6PD deficiency. In addition to the analyses described above, they performed a multipoint analysis for the combined lod scores of both color blindness and G6PD. When only the non-Ashkenazi families were included in the analysis, the results suggested that the bipolar locus is extremely close to the color blindness locus. The maximal lod score of 9.17 occurred at the color blindness locus, indicating odds in favor of linkage of 10^9 to 1. The odds decreased rapidly as the distance from the color blindness locus increased in either direction. At 10 map units (equivalent to 10 percent recombination; $\theta = 0.1$, for example, there was a greater than tenfold reduction of the odds in favor of linkage.

When the Ashkenazi pedigree was included in the analysis, the maximal lod score occurred 5 map units from the color blindness locus, which was also 3 map units from the G6PD locus. The lod score was 7.52, indicating odds in favor of linkage of 3×10^7 to 1. Additional analyses using a more narrow definition of the phenotype in which relatives with cyclothymic disorder were considered to be unaffected resulted in smaller lod scores. These lod scores of 4.37 for color blindness and 2.02 for G6PD still are supportive of linkage. The authors concluded that the disease locus may be between these two marker loci.

Mendlewicz et al. (1987) used a DNA probe to demonstrate linkage between mood disorder and the F9 X-chromosomal locus in 10 Belgian pedigrees. The maximal lod score was 3.10 at a recombination fraction of 0.11. Since the F9 locus is itself closely linked to the G6PD deficiency and color blindness loci, these results are consistent with previous reports of X-linkage.

HLA-Linkage

On the short arm of chromosome 6 there is a tightly clustered group of genes known as the major histocompatibility complex (MHC). The MHC contains many genes involved in controlling the immune response to foreign antibodies. The MHC is often called the HLA region due to the role that human leukocyte antigens have played in establishing the chromosomal map of this area. Since the HLA loci control the immune response of leukocytes, it is relatively easy, via blood samples, to establish HLA antigen types in humans. Extensive international research has indicated that the antigens of the HLA system are primarily controlled by four genetic loci: HLA-A, HLA-B, HLA-C, and HLA-D.

The HLA system provides a very useful genetic marker for linkage studies. As previously noted, a genetic marker will be most useful for linkage analysis when it is easily measured, has a known mode of genetic transmission, and is highly polymorphic (i.e., more than one version of the gene exists with a substantial frequency). HLA antigens are easily measured and their mode of inheritance is well described. Furthermore, the A, B, C, and D loci are closely linked; recombination between any pair occurs less than 1 percent of the time. Additionally, each HLA locus is highly polymorphic. Thus, the HLA system should be a useful linkage marker for most families.

We have summarized studies of HLA linkage to mood disorders in table 6.4. The studies of Smeraldi et al. suggested linkage using the method of sibling pair analysis (Smeraldi et al., 1978a; Smeraldi and Bellodi, 1981). The sib pair method examines the distribution of HLA types among pairs of ill siblings. If the illness is not linked to HLA, this distribution should be significantly different from that predicted by simple Mendelian segregation. If the illness and HLA are linked, the observed distribution will deviate from the predicted such that pairs of ill siblings will be more likely than expected to have common HLA haplotypes. An HLA haplotype consists of the HLA genotypes at each HLA locus. Since the HLA loci are closely linked, the parental haplotypes are usually transmitted to the offspring without recombination. The high level of polymorphism at each HLA locus usually results in four unique parental haplotypes identifiable among the offspring.

The Smeraldi et al. studies examined 26 families with multiple cases of mood disorder among siblings. Illness was defined by the Research Diagnostic Criteria for unipolar disorder or bipolar disorder. Siblings concordant for mood disorder exhibited an excess of HLA similarity, whereas siblings discordant for mood disorder did not. This supports the hypothesis that a gene in the HLA region is mediating genetic susceptibility to mood disorders.

Targum et al. (1979) applied the lod score method to nine families of bipolar probands. Family members were considered ill if they exhibited either bipolar, unipolar, schizoaffective, or cyclothymic personality disorders. Lod scores were less than or equal to -2 for values of the recombination fraction, θ, less than 0.15. Thus, close linkage to the HLA region was significantly unlikely.

Different results for unipolar and bipolar disorders have been reported by Weitkamp and colleagues. Weitkamp, Pardue, and Huntzinger (1980) ascertained one large pedigree through a unipolar proband. Nineteen of the 36 pedigree members had a unipolar or schizoaffective disorder. Lod scores were less than -2 for values of the recombination fraction, θ, less than 0.20. Therefore, linkage between unipolar illness and the HLA region could be excluded in this pedigree. In contrast, Weitkamp et al. (1981) reported positive linkage results from a sib pair analysis of 30 sibships. Diagnoses were based on the Washington University criteria. Sibs were considered ill if they exhibited either unipolar, bipolar, or schizoaffective disorder. A sib pair analysis suggested linkage when these new data were pooled with the data from the three previously reported studies. However, linkage was indicated only by an analysis of sibships having only two affected members. The analysis of sibships having three or more ill members did not find evidence of linkage.

Johnson et al. (1981) studied seven families with a two-generational history of mood disorder. Psychiatric diagnoses were based upon the Washington University criteria. Four families were suitable for HLA linkage analysis. Family members were considered ill if they had either unipolar or cyclothymic disorder or if they were alcoholic. Lod scores were less than or equal to -1.9 for θ values less than 0.05. Thus, close linkage between mood disorder and the HLA system could be excluded in these families.

Goldin, Clergex-Darpoux, and Gershon (1982) expanded the sample of Targum et al. (1979) by adding 18 new families of bipolar probands. Relatives were considered ill if they exhibited either bipolar, unipolar, or schizoaffective disorder. A sib pair analysis of 21 sib pairs was not supportive of linkage. Similarly, a lod score analysis found lod scores less than -2 for values of θ close to zero, excluding close linkage to the HLA system.

Suarez and Croughan (1982) applied the sib pair method to 26 ill siblings from 10 families. The Research Diagnostic Criteria diagnoses of these siblings were either unipolar, bipolar, or schizoaffective disorder. The sib pair analysis could find no evidence for linkage. However, when their data were combined with those of Weitkamp, Targum, and Smeraldi (see table 6.4), the sib pair analysis did detect linkage at a statistically significant level. This reanalysis of previously collected data is particularly important because it used

Table 6.4.   Studies of HLA Linkage

Study	Results
Smeraldi et al., 1978 (HLA System)	Sib pair analysis suggests linkage
Smeraldi and Bellodi, 1981	
Targum et al., 1979	Lod scores ≤ -2 for $\theta < 0.15$, exclude close linkage
Weitkamp, Pardue, and Huntzinger, 1980	Lod scores < -2 for $\theta < 0.020$, exclude close linkage
Weitkamp et al., 1981	Sib pair analysis suggests linkage
Johnson et al., 1981	Lod scores ≤ -1.9 for $\theta < 0.05$ exclude close linkage
Goldin, Clergex-Darpoux, and Gershon, 1982	Sib pair analysis rejects linkage and lod scores < -2 for θ close to 0 exclude linkage
Suarez and Croughan, 1982	Sib pair analysis of new data rejects linkage, but pooling with old data suggests linkage
Turner and King, 1981, 1983	Lod score of 8.02 for $\theta = 0.15$ suggests linkage
Suarez and Reich, 1984	Sib pair analysis rejects linkage
Campbell et al., 1984	Lod scores ≤ -2 for $\theta < 0.10$ exclude close linkage
Kidd et al., 1984	Lod score of -2.6 for $\theta = 0$ excludes close linkage

a more appropriate analytic method. That is, the analysis of Suarez and Croughan accounted for the fact that many of the sib pairs in previous analyses came from the same family. Since previous studies had not accounted for this, the results may be called into question. Interestingly, although the pooled data were significant for linkage, none of the individual studies themselves exhibited significant linkage when the more appropriate method was applied. Thus, the authors conservatively concluded that their analyses could neither confirm nor reject linkage of mood disorder to the HLA region.

The strongest evidence supporting linkage between mood disorder and HLA was reported by Turner and King (1983). They examined seven pedigrees obtained through bipolar probands. Relatives were considered ill if they met *DSM III* criteria for major mood disorders, atypical major mood disorders, cyclothymic disorders, dysthymic disorders, agoraphobia, borderline personality, anorexia nervosa, hypochondria, psychogenic pain disorder, obsessionalism, schizotypal personality with depressive component, or childhood psychosis. A lod score analysis found a maximal lod score of 8.02 at the recombination fraction value of 0.15, highly suggestive of linkage between mood disorders and the HLA region. A sib pair analysis of these data also produced statistically significant results in favor of linkage.

Suarez and Reich (1984) studied 15 families each containing two or more siblings with a diagnosis of a major mood disorder. Relatives were considered ill if they exhibited either bipolar or unipolar disorder. A sib pair analysis, corrected for the presence of more than one sib pair from a single family, provided no evidence of linkage. Subsequent analyses redefined the illness by removing bipolar and alcoholic subjects; these also provided no evidence for linkage. Campbell et al. (1984) reported negative linkage results from a 37-member, five-generation family. Illness was defined as the presence of unipolar, bipolar, schizoaffective, or minor depressive disorder according to Research Diagnostic Criteria diagnoses. Lod scores less than -2 for θ values less than 0.10 indicated statistically significant evidence against close linkage. Kidd et al. (1984a) examined 59 individuals in two pedigrees. Individuals were considered ill if they had either unipolar, bipolar, or minor mood disorders based on Research Diagnostic Criteria diagnoses. The lod scores became increasingly negative with decreasing values of θ, with lod scores less than -2 for θ values close to 0. Thus, close linkage to the HLA region could be excluded in these pedigrees.

In summary, 11 studies have examined the hypothesis of linkage between mood disorder and the HLA region. Four of these provide statistically significant evidence for the presence of linkage; seven find no such evidence. There is no simple methodologic explanation for why some studies are positive and others negative. Although there are more negative results, the positive ones cannot be discounted. In particular, the large lod score of Turner and King (1983) is particularly impressive. Their results were further strengthened by a reanalysis (Kruger, Turner, and Kidd, 1982) using *DSM III* criteria and a more appropriate analytic method that allowed for corrections due to variable age of onset. This reanalysis, which included only two of seven pedigrees, found a significant maximal lod score of 3.9 at the recombination fraction value of 0.10. The variable results between the HLA studies are consistent with genetic heterogeneity with some cases of mood disorder being linked to HLA and others being unlinked. A more detailed examination of HLA-linked pedigrees is needed to determine how this possible form of mood disorder may differ from others.

Other Linkage Results

Fourteen research reports have studied a total of 47 other chromosomal markers. We have summarized these in table 6.5. Equivocal

Table 6.5. The Number of Positive (+), Negative (−), and Equivocal (?) Linkage Results for Forty-Seven Chromosomal Markers

Marker	+	−	?	Marker	+	−	?	Marker	+	−	?
ACP	0	3	0	GPT	0	3	1	Fy	0	5	2
JK	0	4	2	Se	0	2	1	Or	0	1	0
Gm	0	1	1	Inv	0	0	1	H6PD	0	0	1
Db	0	0	1	Pr	0	2	0	Pg	0	1	1
Bf	0	2	0	ABO	0	6	2	COMT	0	0	1
Rh	0	5	2	INS*	1	0	0	HRAS1*	0	2	1
MNS	0	4	1	P-1	0	2	2	Le	0	0	3
Yk	0	0	1	Cs	0	0	1	McC	0	0	1
Kn	0	0	1	GLO	0	2	2	MN	0	1	2
HBBC*	0	0	1	PTH*	0	0	1	Hp	2	3	2
Gc	0	4	2	C3	2	1	3	ESD	0	1	2
PGM-1	0	2	3	Ss	0	1	0	Lu	0	1	1
PGD	0	1	2	ADA	0	2	2	AK	0	2	2
Pep-A	0	1	0	PTC	0	0	2	AMY-2	0	2	0
GALT	0	2	0	Tc	0	1	0	Lp	0	1	0
Tf	0	1	0	K	0	4	1				

* Restriction fragment length polymorphism.

evidence for linkage has been found for three of these 47 markers. These markers are Hp, C3, and HRAS1. Only 2 of 7 studies report linkage between mood disorder and Hp (Tanna et al., 1976, 1977). Three studies could statistically reject linkage to Hp (Goldin et al., 1983; Johnson et al., 1981; Weitkamp, Pardue, and Huntzinger, 1980) and 2 were equivocal (Crowe et al., 1981; Tanna et al., 1979). A similar pattern of results is observed for linkage to C3. Two studies statistically support linkage (Tanna et al., 1976, 1977), one rejects linkage (Weitkamp, Pardue, and Huntzinger, 1980), and three are equivocal (Crowe et al., 1981; Goldin et al., 1983; Tanna et al., 1979). A further difficulty in interpreting these results is that the positive linkage findings for C3 and Hp were found in the same samples. That is, the sample of Tanna et al. (1976) was positive for both linkages, as was the sample of Tanna et al. (1977). These authors did note that linkage between Hp and C3 was unlikely. In fact, subsequent work has demonstrated them to be located on different chromosomes (McKusick, 1986). To complicate matters further, one of the studies that produced equivocal Hp and C3 results was based, in part, on the same sample as the positive results (Tanna et al., 1979). Whereas the two positive studies used the method of sib pair analysis, this latter, equivocal study applied the method of lod scores to 14 two-generation pedigrees overlapping with the original data sets. For C3, the maximal lod score was 0.06 for a recombination fraction of 0.33. For Hp, the maximal lod score was 1.03 for a recombination fraction of 0.15. Thus, although linkage to either C3 or Hp is possible, the available data are, as Tanna et al. (1976, 1977) indicated, only suggestive.

The linkage evidence for the HRAS1 locus on chromosome 11 was initially impressive. Egeland et al. (1987) examined a large pedigree from a study of the genetically isolated Old Order Amish population in Pennsylvania. All 12,000 members of this population are descended from 30 individuals who arrived in the United States from Europe in the eighteenth century. Since alcohol and drug use are strictly forbidden among the Amish, the ascertainment and diagnosis of mood disorders is facilitated in this population. In the 81-member pedigree examined, 14 were considered affected. The specific diagnoses were: bipolar I disorder (11), bipolar II disorder (1), schizoaffective-manic (1), atypical psychosis with prominent affective features (1), and major depression (5). The linkage analysis for HRAS1 reported maximal lod scores ranging from 3.07 to 4.32 for a recombination fraction of 0.0. The range of lod scores corresponded to genotype penetrances ranging from 0.55 to 0.95. A multipoint linkage analysis using both HRAS1 and the nearby INS locus produced a lod score of 4.90. Overall, the results of Egeland et al. initially suggested that a gene on chromosome 11 close to HRAS1 is involved in the etiology of bipolar disorders.

Unfortunately, a follow-up study of Egeland et al.'s Amish pedigree has rendered the original results more difficult to interpret (Kelsoe et al., 1989). This study extended the data from the original pedigree in several ways: (1) diagnoses of two members who had had an onset of mood disorder subsequent to the Egeland et al. report were updated; (2) additional genotypic data were collected from members of the original pedigree; (3) the pedigree was extended in one direction to include six additional subjects; and (4) the pedigree was extended in another direction to include thirty-one additional subjects. The net effect of items 1, 2, and 3 above was to reduce the evidence for linkage to a nonsignificant level. The effect of item 4 was to significantly *exclude* linkage to both the HRAS1 and INS loci with respective lod scores of -9.31 and -7.75 for $\theta = 0.0$. Tight linkage to these loci was also excluded when the additional thirty-one subjects were analyzed separately. As Kelsoe et al. remark, if mood disorders among the Amish are genetically homogeneous, then these results provide strong evidence against linkage to the HRAS1/INS region of chromosome 11. However, these investigators also leave open the possibility that this large pedigree may itself be genetically heterogeneous. Clearly, further work is needed to clarify the genetic etiology of mood disorders in this pedigree. The originally implicated region of chromosome 11 remains of interest, given the observed cosegregation of mood disorder and thalassemia in a single pedigree since the latter disorder is due to a mutation in the nearby beta-globin gene cluster of chromosome 11 (Joffe et al., 1986).

Linkage between HRAS1 and bipolar disorder has been ruled out for six other bipolar pedigrees. Detera-Wadleigh et al. (1987) reported lod scores less than -2.0 for each of three North American pedigrees. Family members were considered ill if they were diagnosed with any of the following disorders: bipolar I, bipolar II, major depression, schizoaffective, and anorexia. Close linkage between bipolar disorder and HRAS1 was also ruled out in three Icelandic pedigrees (Hodgkinson et al., 1987). Lod scores were consistently less than -2.0 for recombination fraction values less than 0.10 under a variety of genetic assumptions.

Although 44 of the 47 markers listed in table 6.5 have provided no positive evidence of linkage to mood disorder, linkage cannot be definitively excluded. Most of these markers have been examined in only one or two studies and, very often, results have been equivocal. Thus, further research is necessary to establish more definitively that no linkage exists. Six of the markers in table 6.5 are probably not linked to mood disorder, because linkage has been rejected by at least four studies. Five of these markers are blood groups (JK, Fy, Rh, MNS, and ABO). One is a serum protein group (Gc). The overrepresentation of blood groups here is probably due to methodologic reasons. The blood groups are highly polymorphic and easily measured. Therefore, they have received more intensive study than other genetic markers.

ASSOCIATION STUDIES

We have seen in figures 6.1 and 6.2 how crossing over and recombination result in the linkage of chromosomal loci within families. Although positive linkage results within families indicate that two genetic loci are linked, they do not indicate that the phenotypes produced by these loci are associated at the population level. For example, bipolar disorder may be linked to the X-chromosomal locus for color blindness. This does not mean that bipolar patients are more or less likely to be colorblind than healthy individuals. It only means that a colorblind bipolar mother is much more likely to have a colorblind bipolar son than a bipolar son with normal vision. Thus, although chromosomal linkage will produce phenotypic associations within families, these associations are not likely to be observed at the population level. However, there are three important exceptions to this conclusion.

First, if the same gene causes color blindness and bipolar disorder, one would expect to see a strong association between bipolar illness and color blindness in the general population. Second, a population association will occur between two phenotypes when they are mediated by genetic loci that are closely linked and are in linkage disequilibrium. Two loci are in linkage disequilibrium when the presence of a specific allele at one locus increases the likelihood a specific allele at the second locus. As Vogel and Motulsky (1979) indicated, linkage disequilibrium will occur if certain combinations of alleles at two closely linked loci offer a selective advantage to individuals (i.e., individuals with two loci are more likely to survive and reproduce than other individuals). Also linkage disequilibrium will occur when two loci are tightly linked but the relevant phenotypes have only recently been associated with one another. For example, if a mutation in the color blindness region of the X chromosome produced bipolar disorder in a colorblind individual 1,000 years ago, it is conceivable that the low rate of crossing over expected between two closely linked loci would not be sufficient to remove a population-level association by the twentieth century. In fact, it has been estimated that a population association due to this type of linkage disequilibrium could take as long as 5,000 years to disappear.

A third reason for an observed population level association is a methodologic artifact. Genetic markers are likely to have different frequencies among different racial and ethnic groups. For example, HLA antigen frequencies are known to differ between American Caucasians, American blacks, and African blacks (Payne, 1977). Such results are probably due to reduced mating between racial and ethnic populations. They can, however, lead to incorrect conclusions regarding disease associations with genetic markers. For instance, the HLA allele Bwl7 is nearly four times more common among American blacks than among American Caucasians. If one compared HLA antigens between a group of bipolars and a healthy comparison group, an artifactual relationship between Bwl7 and bipolar disorder would emerge if the proportion of black individuals in the two samples were substantially different.

HLA Associations

The HLA antigens have received considerable attention in genetic marker association studies for both empirical and theoretical reasons. From an empirical perspective, the HLA region has demonstrated numerous associations with a variety of diseases. Thomson (1981) listed 46 diseases known to be associated with specific HLA antigens. The most remarkable of these is ankylosing spondylitis.

The HLA B27 antigen is found in 90 percent of the patients with this disease but in only 8 percent of healthy individuals. The Bw2 antigen is found in 70 percent of patients' with multiple sclerosis; only 16 percent of healthy individuals have this antigen (Thomson, 1981).

Several theoretical reasons have been given to explain why so many disease genes may be linked to the HLA region (Amos and Ward, 1977). As discussed previously, the HLA region or major histocompatibility complex is believed to contain many immune response (Ir) genes. The Ir genes are probably responsible for mediating a variety of disease processes either through regulatory control of antibody synthesis or by coding for structural properties of receptors that mediate the antibody-antigen response. Structural properties of receptors may mediate the susceptibility of individuals to viral diseases due to the potential role of such receptors in transporting the virus across the cell membrane. Amos and Ward also discussed the possibility that specific antigens may produce abnormal differentiation during embryogenesis leading to disease. Thus, there are a number of theoretical reasons why genes in the HLA region could be responsible for a variety of diseases.

In table 6.6 we summarize studies that have looked for HLA

Table 6.6. Increased or Decreased HLA Antigens among Patients with Mood Disorder

	HLA Antigens	
Study	Increased	Decreased
Shapiro et al., 1977	Bw 16	None
Govaerts, Mendlewicz, and Verbanck, 1977	None	None
Stember and Fieve, 1977	A5, A13	A12
Bennahum et al., 1977	None	None
Johnson, 1978	None	None
Beckman, Perris, et al., 1978	A1, A10	B7
Majsky, Zvolsky, and Dvovakova, 1978	Bw4, Cw4	None
Smeraldi et al., 1978 (HLA Typing)	A29, Bw22	A10, Aw30
Temple et al., 1979	Bw22	A9
James et al., 1979	None	None
Targum et al., 1979	None	None
Johnson, 1978	None	None
Mendlewicz et al., 1981	None	None
Propert, Tait, and Davies, 1981	A28, Bw16	None
Wentzel, Roberts, and Whalley, 1982	A10, A31	B27, Cw5
Rosler et al., 1983	None	None
Maj et al., 1983	A11, A29	B18
Bersani et al., 1985	A10, B5, B37	A1

associations between mood disorder and HLA antigens. Out of 18 available studies, 8 report no evidence for an association. Studies providing some evidence for an association are inconsistent with one another. Three antigens have been shown to be increased among mood-disordered patients in two studies (Bwl6, A29, Bw22); one antigen, Al0, was elevated among patients in three different studies. However, this antigen was reported to be significantly decreased among patients in another study. These inconsistent results could be due to the fact that the reported investigations were performed in a variety of different countries with different ethnic groups. However, a closer examination of these studies suggests that this is not the case. For example, one of the studies finding a positive association with Bwl6 (Shapiro et al., 1977) was performed in Denmark, whereas the other (Propert, Tait, and Davies, 1981) used an Australian sample. The Swedish sample of Beckman et al. (1978c) and the Australian samples of Johnson (1978) and Johnson et al. (1981) found no such association. Similarly, the Bw22 antigen was associated with mood disorder in an Ashkenazi Jewish sample (Temple, Dupont, and Shopsin, 1979) and in an Italian sample (Smeraldi et al., 1978b) but not in other Italian samples (Bersani et al., 1985; Maj et al., 1983). Thus, it does not appear that differences in ethnicity can explain the conflicting pattern of results in table 6.6. The most conservative interpretation of these results is that mood disorder is not associated with HLA. If such an association exists, it is either very weak or limited to a subset of patients.

ABO Association

Like the HLA antigens, the ABO blood groups have been found to be associated with a variety of different diseases. There is a small but significant increase in the likelihood of developing a number of malignant diseases for individuals with blood group A. In contrast, blood group 0 appears to be associated with less serious diseases such as gastric and duodenal ulcers. As one would expect from these relationships, there is an increased frequency of blood group 0 among healthy, elderly people (Vogel and Motulsky, 1979).

In table 6.7 we summarize studies that have compared ABO blood groups between patients with mood disorders and healthy individuals. Nine of 16 studies found a significant increase in blood type O; one reported a significant decrease of blood type O among mood-disordered patients. Two studies found a significant increase in blood type B and one study found a significant increase in blood type A. Three studies found a significant decrease in blood type A.

The primary inference from these studies is the fairly strong suggestion that blood type O is found with greater frequency among patients with mood disorders in comparison to individuals from the general population. Lavori, Keller, and Roth (1984) reanalyzed data from nine individual studies. They concluded that there was overwhelming evidence for an increase in blood type O among bipolar patients as compared to controls. There was a smaller but statistically significant increase in type O in bipolar compared to unipolar patients. The comparison between unipolar patients and controls did not reach statistical significance. The association with type O is further strengthened by two observations. First, three of the studies that did not find increased type O (Johnson et al., 1981; Tanna and Winokur, 1968; Tanna et al., 1977) used the well relatives of ill probands as controls; the other studies used large samples from the general population as controls. The differences in methodology may account for the differences in findings, especially since the two negative studies had very small control groups. If these studies are discounted, only three of nine studies do not find an association between blood type O and affective disorders. There appears to be no simple way to account for these other discordant results except for noting that Beckman et al. (1978c) used a Swedish sample and Flemenbaum and Larson (1976) used a sample from Minnesota, a state known to have a high percentage of individuals with Scandinavian ancestry. None of the O-positive studies were from Scandinavian samples. Since genetic marker–disease associations are known to differ between ethnic groups, this may explain these discordant results (Thomson, 1981).

The reported ABO associations in table 6.7 are inconsistent with the negative ABO linkage results (table 6.5) of eight ABO linkage studies: six rejected linkage and two were equivocal. The association and linkage results are difficult to reconcile. If mood disorder is truly linked to the ABO locus, positive linkage results should be forthcoming. It is tempting to appeal to genetic heterogeneity to explain the negative linkage results. However, it seems unlikely that such heterogeneity would obscure the linkage analyses and not the association analyses. Since positive association results can be due to differential ethnicity in comparison samples, the positive association results must be seen as suggestive but not conclusive. It is, however, notable that the gene for dopamine-beta-hydroxylase (DBH) is strongly suspected to be closely linked to the ABO locus on chromosome 9 (Goldin et al., 1982; McKusick, 1986; Wilson et al., 1988). Since DBH is critical to the synthesis of catecholamines, it is a reasonable candidate as an etiologic gene for bipolar disorders.

Table 6.7. Increased or Decreased ABO Blood Types among Patients with Mood Disorder

Study	Blood Types	
	Increased	Decreased
Parker, Theilie, and Spielberger, 1961	0	None
Irvine and Miyashita, 1965	0	None
Masters, 1967	0	None
Tanna and Winokur, 1968	B	None
Mendlewicz et al., 1974	0	A
Flemenbaum and Larson, 1976	A	O
Tanna et al., 1977	None	None
Shapiro et al., 1977	0	None
Beckman, Beckman, Cedergren, et al., 1978	B	None
Retezeanu and Christodorescu, 1978	0	None
DelVecchio et al., 1979	None	None
James et al., 1979	None	None
Rinieris et al., 1979	0	A
Rihmer and Arato, 1981	0	A
Johnson et al., 1981	None	None
Lavori, Keller, and Roth, 1984	0	None

SUMMARY

In the near future most of the human genome will be mapped with RFLP markers. Thus, it will soon be possible to search exhaustively the chromosomes for single major genes responsible for mood disorders. Linkage studies to date have examined relatively few genetic loci. Specific locations on the X chromosome, chromosome 6, and chromosome 11 have been implicated in different studies. Only the X-linkage results have been replicated by different investigators. In other investigations, however, linkage to these chromosomal locations has been clearly rejected. One possibility is that varying assumptions in different linkage analyses result in different outcomes. Kruger, Turner, and Kidd (1982) showed that changing the assumptions for a given analysis can indeed change the results. In most cases, it does not appear that the inconsistencies can be explained simply on the basis of methodologic differences. Some investigators have, in fact, made a point of testing for linkage under a wide variety of assumptions to show that the results were not solely dependent upon a single set of prespecified parameters.

Nevertheless, the inconsistency does call for explanation. One can appeal to the notion of genetic heterogeneity, yet attempts to reduce heterogeneity have not resulted in greater consistency. In addition, there is a perplexing logical problem in the interpretation of results of multiple investigations of linkage. In some cases, the majority of studies reject linkage to a given locus. On the other hand, what is to be made of the few studies with positive linkage results showing odds so highly in favor of linkage that it would be extremely unlikely that these are chance findings? Take, for example, the findings of studies of HLA linkage. While the majority of studies exclude linkage, the lod score of 8.02 found by Turner and King (1981, 1983) suggests odds in favor of linkage that are so great as to make it unreasonable to consider this result to be a chance finding. Consequently, the hypothesis that major mood disorders are genetically heterogeneous is probably the most reasonable assumption under which to operate at the present time. The analyses of Risch and Baron (1982) strongly supported the heterogeneity hypothesis when studies from different investigators are pooled and when analyses are limited to a single investigator. Heterogeneity of linkage within a single study has also been demonstrated (Baron et al., 1987).

Since genetic heterogeneity is known to exist for certain disorders, it remains a viable hypothesis with regard to the variable results of genetic studies of mood disorders. Another clue to the genetic heterogeneity of mood disorders stems from the reasoning of Eliot Slater regarding the genetics of schizophrenia. Slater (1947/1971) argued that genetic heterogeneity was highly probable for schizophrenia because it is a disorder that is far more common than most single-gene disorders. The same reasoning is equally applicable to major mood disorders, which are even more common than schizophrenia. The point here is that all known single-gene disorders are exceedingly rare. The combined incidence of *all* known single-gene disorders is only 1 for every 100 live births (Emery, 1984). This is approximately the same as the population rate of bipolar disorder and is much lower than the population rate for unipolar disorder.

Propping and Friedl (1988) delineated the basic differences between single-gene and complex, common disorders in which there is genetic involvement (e.g., diabetes mellitus, atherosclerosis). The lifetime risk of single-gene disorders ranges from 1 in 500 to less than 1 in 1 million, whereas it may be as high as 20 percent for the more common disorders. These latter disorders may be caused by a multifactorial process and/or several distinct single-gene abnormalities. Small percentages of cases of a common disorder may be due primarily to specific, single-gene defects even if most cases are multifactorially determined. In either case, for complex common disorders the risks to relatives frequently do not follow Mendelian expectations. These and other differences enumerated by Propping and Friedl suggest that the patterns observed in major mood disorders are very likely to be indicative of genetic heterogeneity.

Another potentially significant dimension of the method of linkage analysis is the potential for dramatic improvement in our ability to make specific predictions regarding mood disorders. Linkage analysis would allow for positive identification of individuals within a pedigree who are marker positive and disease negative, but who have not yet passed through the period of risk for the illness. It would be predicted that these individuals would later manifest the disorder. If these predictors showed a high level of accuracy, the significance of the marker determined on the basis of linkage analysis would be strongly supported. Moreover, the ability to make such predictions would enable investigators to study the developmental and/or environmental factors that contribute to the onset of mood disorders. Thus, linkage analysis carries with it the promise of substantially increasing our understanding of etiology with hopes of providing leads toward primary prevention.

Chapter Seven

Biological Markers

To fully understand the genetics of mood disorders, we will need to develop a complete description of the chain of events that links the pathogenic genotype with the observed, psychiatric phenotype. As Cloninger, Reich, and Yokoyama (1983) noted, this chain may be long and complex for psychiatric disorders. In this chapter we consider studies that have attempted to delineate biological markers associated with links in the etiologic chain for mood disorders.

A biological marker is a measurable biological characteristic that meets the following criteria (Gershon and Goldin, 1986): (1) it is more prevalent among individuals with the disorder than among those without the disorder; (2) it is heritable; (3) it is observed in ill individuals whether or not the illness is in remission; and (4) within families, ill family members are more likely to manifest the marker than are well members. In practice, candidates for genetic marker studies are chosen based on previous research indicating that a biological factor meets criterion 1. This method of screening candidate markers is convenient in that it allows the psychiatric geneticist to develop a genetic hypothesis based on the nongenetic scientific literature. The demonstration of heritability (criterion 2) is straightforward; this can be accomplished through the traditional psychiatric methods of family, twin, and adoption studies. Criterion 3 requires the marker to be a trait, not a state phenomenon. This is accomplished most effectively by studying patients in both the active and remitted phases of their illness. The determination of criterion 4 is more complex and has led to the development of the four major psychiatric genetic experimental strategies (Gershon and Goldin, 1986).

The *cosegregation strategy* of Rieder and Gershon (1978) uses families ascertained through probands who exhibit both the illness and the genetic marker. Relatives of probands are examined both psychiatrically and biologically. Increased prevalence of the biological marker among ill relatives in comparison to well relatives provides support for cosegregation of the marker and the illness—that is, the biological marker and the psychiatric illness co-occur within families. The *familial/nonfamilial strategy* begins with a family study defining probands with and without a family history of the psychiatric illness under study. Since patients with a family history are more likely to have a genetic predisposition than are patients without a family history, one can compare the family history positive and family history negative proband groups with the biological marker. If these two groups differ on the biological marker, this can be interpreted as being indirectly supportive of criterion 4. This method is often easier to use, but is less definitive than the cosegregation strategy, since it is more sensitive to heterogeneity. In addition, negative results are difficult to interpret due to the difficulty in defining non-familial cases. The *high-risk strategy* compares the well relatives of ill probands with the well relatives of psychiatric and/or normal control probands. If a disorder is genetically mediated, then relatives of ill probands should be more likely to carry the pathogenic genotype than are relatives of control probands. Thus, the prevalence of a biological marker should be greater among relatives of ill probands. Since the high-risk approach studies well relatives, measurement of the biological marker cannot be biased in any way by effects that are secondary to the manifestation of the phenotype (e.g., side effects of medication). Thus, high-risk studies provide further support for criterion 3—that is, that the biological marker is a trait phenomenon. The high-risk method does not directly demonstrate cosegregation (criterion 4) because only the well relatives are examined. However, the method can be utilized prospectively to determine whether well relatives who carry the biological marker will eventually become ill.

Biological marker studies can be conveniently divided into two major categories. Neurobiological studies focus on markers whose biological functions are either directly or indirectly related to central nervous system functioning. Such markers are clearly of interest inasmuch as the etiology of mood disorders undoubtedly includes abnormalities in central nervous system functioning. Pharmacogenetic studies use drug response as a biological marker. The measurement of drug response may be either behavioral (e.g., symptomatic improvement with treatment) or biological (e.g., changes in a biological measure subsequent to drug administration).

NEUROBIOLOGICAL STUDIES

Neurobiological studies have focused primarily on neurochemical factors involved in the synthesis and degradation of neurotransmitters. Since neurotransmitters mediate neuron-to-neuron communication in the central nervous system, they are promising candidates for biological markers. To date, most studies of such markers have examined aspects of catecholaminergic or cholinergic pathways because both have been implicated in the etiology of mood disorders. Given the lack of direct access to the human central nervous system, measures of neurochemical functioning are necessarily indirect. That is, measures from blood and other peripheral samples are used to infer central nervous system activity. Thus, results must be interpreted with caution.

The most extensively studied neurobiological factor is monoamine oxidase (MAO), an enzyme involved in the metabolism of neurotransmitters. Twin studies indicate MAO to be under a substantial degree of genetic control (Nies et al., 1973; Sedvall et al., 1984; Winter et al., 1978). Leckman et al. (1977) studied platelet MAO activity in 32 bipolar probands and 89 of their first-degree relatives. The bipolar probands had significantly lower MAO activity in comparison to a normal control sample. The relatives of bipolar probands also had significantly lower MAO activity in comparison to controls. However, platelet MAO activity did not distinguish mood-disordered relatives and well relatives. These results suggest that platelet MAO is under genetic control within bipolar families. However, the association of low MAO and bipolar disorder is evident only for between-family comparisons.

Gershon et al. (1980a) performed a segregation analysis of platelet MAO in pedigrees of patients with mood disorders. Although no specific autosomal model could be fitted to these data, the hypothesis of no genetic transmission was rejected. MAO activity in bipolar and unipolar patients was significantly lower than MAO activity among normal controls. However, within the mood disorder pedigrees, MAO activity did not discriminate between ill and well relatives, consistent with the results of Leckman et al. (1977). Pandey et al. (1980) assessed platelet MAO activity in 31 bipolar probands and their 61 first-degree relatives. Control values from psychiatrically normal families were also obtained. The relatives of bipolar probands were divided into three categories: those with a history of bipolar disorder or alcoholism, those with a history of major or minor mood disorders, and those with no history of mood disorder. Relatives with a history of bipolar disorder or alcoholism had significantly lower MAO activity than did the other two relative groups. The bipolar/alcoholic relatives also had lower MAO activity than did the normal controls. These results are consistent with previous studies in suggesting an association between bipolar disorder and low MAO activity. However, they are somewhat discrepant in suggesting that low

MAO activity cosegregated with bipolar disorder and alcoholism within pedigrees of mood-disordered ill patients.

Further negative results were reported by Maubach et al. (1981) in their study of 26 psychotic mood-disordered probands and their 102 first-degree relatives. Each patient's relative was matched with a normal control subject based on sex and age. There were no differences in MAO activity between patients and normal controls or between relatives of patients and relatives of normal controls. These results are not consistent with the suggestion that MAO is a biological marker for mood disorders.

Buchsbaum, Coursey, and Murphy (1976) reversed the usual high-risk paradigm by defining risk groups based on MAO activity instead of psychiatric diagnosis. MAO activity was measured in 375 college students. Psychiatric interviews and family history data were obtained from individuals whose MAO activity was in the upper or lower 10 percent of this sample. The low-MAO probands had more psychiatric hospitalizations, suicide attempts, and problems with the law than did high-MAO probands. Furthermore, an increased prevalence of psychiatric hospitalization, suicide, and problems with the law were observed in relatives of the low-MAO probands in comparison to relatives of high-MAO probands. A two-year follow-up found that low-MAO students reported more job instability than did high-MAO students. The low-MAO subjects reported more medical problems and smoked significantly more than the high-MAO subjects. Although there was no apparent decline in the mental health status of the low-MAO probands during the two-year follow-up, they did report more mental health problems and mental health interventions among family members.

Another enzyme involved in neurotransmitter biosynthesis and degradation having a substantial degree of genetic determination is catechol-0-methyltransferase (COMT). The COMT correlation between monozygotic twins is significantly greater than the correlation between dizygotic twins (Winter et al., 1978), and the distribution of red blood cell COMT levels within pedigrees is consistent with autosomal models of genetic transmission (Goldin, 1985; Weinshilboum, 1979). The results of linkage analysis are supportive of the presence of a gene influencing COMT on chromosome 1 (Wilson et al., 1987). Gershon and Jonas (1975) examined red blood cell COMT levels in 53 unipolar and bipolar probands, their first-degree relatives, and 38 nonpsychiatric controls. Relative to the control group, patients had increased levels of COMT. Relatives with mood-related disorders had higher COMT levels than did relatives who were not ill. Thus, cosegregation of mood disorders and COMT was demonstrated in these families. Gershon et al. (1980a) examined COMT in 162 patients with mood disorder and their 1,125 first-degree relatives. A segregation analysis of COMT levels indicated that an autosomal codominant genetic hypothesis fit the data; all other genetic hypotheses could be rejected. However, the model predicted no significant differences in COMT genotypes between individuals with and without mood disorders. COMT levels did not differentiate patients with mood disorders from the control group. Egeland et al. (1984) examined COMT in the Amish pedigrees of bipolar probands. Four large pedigrees including 87 individuals were examined. COMT levels did not differentiate well and ill individuals.

Dopamine-beta-hydroxylase (DBH) is an enzyme involved in the biosynthesis of norepinephrine from dopamine. Correlations of serum DBH are consistently greater between monozygotic than dizygotic twins, suggesting a substantial degree of genetic control (Ross et al., 1973; Sedvall et al., 1984; Winter et al., 1978). The distribution of serum DBH within families is consistent with autosomal models of inheritance (Goldin, 1985; Weinshilboum, 1979) and linkage analyses indicate a locus of DBH near the ABO locus on chromosome 9. Levitt and Mendlewicz (1975) examined plasma DBH activity in 15 twin pairs and 21 sibling pairs. There were no differences in DBH activity between same-sex siblings discordant for mood disorder and between twins discordant for mood disorder. Four pairs of monozygotic twins discordant for mood disorder were concordant for DBH activity. Thus, no cosegregation of DBH activity and mood disorder was observed. Gershon et al. (1980a) studied plasma DBH activity in the pedigrees previously examined for MAO and COMT. Segregation analysis indicated that the hypothesis of nongenetic transmission could be rejected. Dominant and recessive autosomal transmissions were rejected, but codominant autosomal transmission could not be rejected. Predictions from the genetic model indicated that DBH genotypes were not differentially associated with mood disorders. The DBH measures did not differentiate patients from controls.

Sedvall et al. (1980) examined concentrations of monoamine metabolites in the cerebral spinal fluid of 60 mentally healthy individuals. Those with a family history of major depression exhibited a trend toward lower levels of 5-hydroxyindoleactic acid (5-HIAA) and homovanillic acid (HVA). These are metabolites of the neurotransmitters serotonin and dopamine, respectively. The number of individuals with a family history of depression was too small for meaningful statistical analyses.

It is possible to examine peripheral neurotransmitter receptors that are likely to have a genetic relationship to receptors in the central nervous system. Nadi, Nurnberger, and Gershon (1984) examined muscarinic cholinergic receptors from human skin fibroblasts of 18 unipolar and bipolar patients, their first-degree relatives, and 12 normal controls. All patients had a family history of major mood disorder and all unipolar patients had at least one bipolar relative. The 18 probands demonstrated increased receptor density in comparison to controls. Increased receptor density was also found for the ill relatives of probands but not for their well relatives. Thus, abnormal receptor density was shown to cosegregate with bipolar related mood disorders in these pedigrees.

Cholinergic mechanisms were examined by Sitaram et al. (1987) in a study of 34 depressed probands, 35 ill relatives, and 31 well relatives. In addition to their history of depression, probands were required to exhibit fast rapid eye movement (REM) sleep induction in response to the cholinergic agonist arecoline. This effect is consistent with the presence of increased cholinergic receptor density or other mechanisms that would produce a "supersensitive" cholinergic response.

The rate of fast REM sleep induction in response to arecoline was 63 percent among ill relatives and 22 percent among well relatives. These results suggest that this putative marker of cholinergic supersensitivity cosegregates with mood disorder in families known to have a depressed member who exhibits a positive response.

Beta-adrenoreceptor binding characteristics have been evaluated in five pedigrees with a two-generation history of mood disorder. Receptors were sampled from lymphoblast cell lines established from lymphocytes. In two of the five families, both ill and well individuals had no beta-adrenoreceptor binding defects. In the three other families, ill members manifested significant binding defects in comparison to well members. These results from a relatively small sample are equivocal but suggest that, for a subgroup of mood-disordered patients, beta-adrenoreceptor binding defects may constitute a genetic marker (Wright et al., 1984).

PHARMACOGENETIC STUDIES

The clinical use and experimental study of psychotropic medication have found that the therapeutic response to antidepressant and antimanic drugs can be highly variable, even in carefully diagnosed samples. The therapeutic effects of psychotropic drugs are probably due to their effects on central nervous system neurotransmitter systems. Since the enzymes and proteins involved in neurotransmission are known to be under a substantial degree of genetic control, it is reasonable to hypothesize that differential drug response is associated with genetic heterogeneity. That is, different genetic abnormalities are likely to correspond to different pathophysiologies, which, in turn, may be correctable by different medications.

Pharmacogenetic studies of mood disorder fall into two main categories, studies of the response to antidepressants in unipolar disorder and studies of the response to lithium in bipolar disorder. The pharmacokinetics and pharmacodynamics of these medications have been intensively studied. A full exposition of these properties is beyond the scope of this chapter. Pharmacogenetic studies have tended to focus on tricyclic antidepressants, MAO inhibitors, and lithium. The tricyclic antidepressants potentiate catecholaminergic and serotonergic neurotransmission while inhibiting cholinergic activity. As the name suggests, MAO inhibitors interfere with the activity of the enzyme monoamine oxidase. Thus, like the tricyclics, they facilitate catecholaminergic and serotonergic transmission by slowing the degradation of neurotransmitters in these systems. In contrast to the antidepressants, lithium has the effect of decreasing catecholaminergic transmission and serotonergic transmission.

The Pharmacogenetics of Antidepressants

Angst (1961) studied the effects of the tricyclic antidepressant imipramine in 105 cases of endogenous depression. The proportions of unipolar and bipolar patients in this sample cannot be determined from the report. The therapeutic response to imipramine did not differentiate patients having a family history positive for endogenous depression from those having no psychiatric family history. There was a tendency for first-degree relatives with endogenous depression to have an imipramine response that was similar to that of the probands. That is, probands who responded well to imipramine tended to have relatives who responded well; probands who responded poorly tended to have relatives who responded poorly.

Pare, Rees, and Sainsbury (1962) reported on the effects of tricyclic antidepressants and MAO inhibitors in seven depressed probands who had a first-degree relative treated for depression. For each of the 12 relatives examined, the response to medication was identical to the response in the proband. That is, the observed responses to tricyclics and MAO inhibitors were the same for probands and relatives. This work was extended by Pare (1970; Pare and Mack, 1971) in a study of 12 depressed probands and depressed first-degree relatives. Again, probands and relatives had significantly similar responses to medication. Probands who responded well to MAO inhibitors tended to have relatives who responded well to MAO inhibitors but poorly to tricyclics. Probands who responded well to tricyclics tended to have relatives who responded well to tricyclics and poorly to MAO inhibitors.

Deykin and DiMascio (1972) examined the therapeutic response to the tricyclic antidepressant amitriptyline in 163 depressed females. Patients having mothers with a history of depression had a significantly poorer response to this medication than did patients without depressed mothers. The presence of mental illness in fathers and siblings did not differentiate responders and nonresponders. Fahndrich (1983) examined the response to antidepressants in 30 patients receiving clomipramine and 30 receiving maprotiline. There were no statistically significant differences in family psychiatric history between responders and nonresponders for both drugs. However, there was a tendency for maprotiline responders to have more relatives with psychiatric illness than did maprotiline nonresponders. In contrast, there was a tendency for clomipramine nonresponders to have more relatives with a history of suicide attempts than did clomipramine responders.

The Therapeutic Response to Lithium

Mendlewicz et al. (1972) examined the response to lithium in 22 bipolar patients. Lithium responders were significantly more likely to have a family history of bipolar disorder than were lithium nonresponders. Similar results were reported by Mendlewicz, Fieve, and Stallone (1973) in a sample of 72 bipolar patients. Again, the presence of bipolar disorder among first-degree relatives was predictive of a good response to lithium. However, the presence of unipolar disorder among relatives was not predictive of lithium response.

Mendlewicz and Stallone (1975) enlarged the sample of Mendlewicz, Fieve, and Stallone (1973) to 89 bipolar patients. As with their previous research, lithium responders were significantly more likely to have a bipolar relative than were lithium nonresponders; the presence of unipolar disorder in the family did not differentiate responders and nonresponders.

Prien, Caffey, and Klett (1974) evaluated the results of lithium therapy in 205 patients with bipolar disorder. The 12 patients with a bipolar first-degree relative had a higher proportion of lithium responders (88 percent) than did the other patients (49 percent). However, the difference was not statistically significant probably due to the small sample size of family history positive patients. Zvolsky et al. (1974) examined lithium response in 14 patients with unipolar disorder and 26 patients with bipolar disorder. The morbidity risk for psychiatric disorders was greater among lithium responders than among nonresponders.

The antidepressant response to lithium was evaluated in 9 bipolar patients and 14 unipolar patients by Baron et al. (1975). The presence of unipolar or bipolar disorder in the family was not predictive of the antidepressant response to lithium.

A twin study of lithium response in 25 monozygotic and 27 dizygotic twins was reported by Mendlewicz et al. (1978). Of the 14 monozygotic pairs concordant for bipolar disorder, 12 probands were lithium responsive and two were not. Of the 11 monozygotic twins discordant for bipolar disorder, only four of the bipolar probands were lithium responsive. Similar results were found for the dizygotic pairs. Thus, the twin study is consistent with other family studies suggesting that a family history of bipolar disorder is predictive of a good response to lithium.

The finding that lithium response in the proband is related to increased rates of illness among relatives does not necessarily mean that the therapeutic effect of lithium is genetically determined. This latter issue has not been systematically studied. There has been one report of lithium response in a single pair of monozygotic twins concordant for bipolar disorder (Hoffman, 1987). One twin showed a good lithium response to acute mania and the other did not, suggesting that environmental factors play an important role in the response to lithium.

The observed relationship between lithium response and family history has led some investigators to incorporate lithium response in attempts to model the mechanism of genetic transmission. In the single major locus segregation analyses of Goldin et al. (1983), a separate analysis was performed for families containing a lithium-responsive proband. The results of this analysis could not provide any evidence for the involvement of a single major locus. The lithium-responsive subsample did not produce results that were substantially different from the larger sample including nonresponsive patients.

Smeraldi et al. (1984b) applied mathematical genetic models to family data collected from 92 lithium-responsive probands and 53 lithium-nonresponsive probands. Neither subgroup of patients produced results that could differentiate between single major locus and multifactorial transmission models. There was no indication in these results that lithium responders and nonresponders corresponded to different modes of genetic transmission. Thus, although previous reports indicate lithium responders to be more likely to have a family history of psychiatric illness, the lithium response/nonresponse distinction has not been useful in resolving the heterogeneity of genetic transmission in bipolar related mood disorders.

The Transport of Lithium into Red Blood Cells

The transport of lithium into red blood cells (RBCs) has received much attention since Mendels and Frazer (1973) reported that the ratio of intracellular lithium to extracellular lithium was higher in treatment-responsive depressive patients than in nonresponders. An elevated lithium ratio has also been found in bipolar individuals compared with normal controls (Lyttkins, Soderberg, and Wetterberg, 1973). Although these results have not been consistently replicated (e.g., Casper et al., 1976), there is agreement that lithium transport as measured by the lithium ratio is under a substantial degree of genetic control. Concentrations of lithium ions in RBCs are highly correlated among monozygotic twins and less highly correlated among dizygotic twins, suggesting a heritability between 0.76 and 0.85 (Dorus et al., 1974; Dorus, Pandey, and Davis, 1975). The correlation between first-degree relatives is approximately 0.50 (Dorus et al., 1980) and segregation analyses suggest that the genetic control of the lithium ratio is due to a single autosomal major locus in combination with a multifactorial background—that is, the mixed model of genetic transmission (Dorus et al., 1983).

Rybakowski (1977) examined the lithium ratio in 20 bipolar patients and their first-degree relatives. Patients with a family history positive for mood disorders had higher lithium ratios than did patients with no family history. Pandey et al. (1977) examined the lithium ratio in a bipolar patient, his nine first-degree relatives, and normal controls. The bipolar patient and some of his relatives had an increased lithium ratio. Among relatives, the increased lithium ratio was not related to the presence of mood disorder. Thus, cosegregation of the lithium ratio abnormality and mood disorder could not be established in this small pedigree. Similar results were obtained from a sample of five bipolar patients, two schizoaffective patients, and one unipolar patient (Pandey et al., 1979a). As compared with controls, bipolar patients manifested abnormally high lithium ratios. However, abnormally high ratios were also found among the schizoaffective and unipolar patients and some bipolar patients had normal ratios. In all cases, patients with high lithium ratios tended to have relatives with high lithium ratios and patients with low lithium ratios tended to have relatives with low lithium ratios. Again, there was no indication that abnormality in the lithium ratio cosegregated with mood disorder within these families.

Dorus et al. (1979) examined the lithium ratio in 31 bipolar patients, their 66 relatives, and normal controls. Among the 66 relatives, there were 16 cases of major mood disorder, 28 cases of minor mood disorder, and 22 cases of no mood disorder. Relatives with a history of major or minor mood disorders had significantly higher lithium ratios than did relatives with no history of mood disorder. The lithium ratio of ill relatives was significantly greater than values reported for normal controls. Further evidence for such cosegregation is found in a twin study. If an abnormally high lithium ratio indicates genetic vulnerability to mood disorder, then one would expect to find higher ratios among concordant as compared with discordant twin pairs. Such results have been reported by Mendlewicz and Verbanck (1981).

Evidence against cosegregation of the lithium ratio in mood disorder has been reported based on data from 87 individuals from four large Amish pedigrees (Egeland et al., 1984). Within these pedigrees, family members with and without mood disorder did not have different lithium ratios. Since the study did not include a control group, it is difficult to say whether or not the levels observed were in the normal or abnormal range. However, the values reported are consistent with normal control values reported by Pandey et al. (1979a).

Possible biological mechanisms underlying abnormal lithium ratios have been described (Ehrlich and Diamond, 1980). A logical step in understanding the genetic marker status of the lithium ratio is to examine the genetic marker status of potentially defective mechanisms involved in the intracellular transport of lithium. Waters, Thakar, and Lapierre (1983) studied 73 individuals from 12 families in which there was more than one bipolar member. Using a variety of biochemical probes, they were able to examine the operation of four processes involved in the transport of lithium across red blood cell membranes: passive diffusion, Na^+-Li^+ countertransport, anion exchange transport, and the sodium-potassium pump. None of these mechanisms could be implicated as a genetic marker. Thus, although the lithium ratio has been implicated as a genetic marker for bipolar disorder, the relationship between biological mechanisms underlying this marker and the disorder's pathophysiology is poorly understood.

SUMMARY

The study of biological markers is still in its infancy. Thus, it would be premature to conclude from the sometimes conflicting research in this area that further genetic marker studies would be unproductive. In fact, some consistencies emerge from the limited data already available. Neurobiological studies have found platelet monoamine oxidase to be decreased among some patients with mood disorder. However, there is scant evidence supporting the hypothesis that low MAO and mood disorder cosegregate within pedigrees. A similar pattern of results has been observed for peripheral measures of catechol-O-methyltransferase and dopamine-beta-hydroxylase. In contrast, measures of cholinergic supersensitivity and the transport of lithium into red blood cells have been shown to cosegregate within families. These latter findings remain tentative pending replication by other laboratories.

Results of pharmacogenetic studies indicate that the response to specific antidepressants is correlated between ill relatives. This suggests that the activity of these drugs at therapeutically relevant sites in the central nervous system points to a link in the chain from genotype to phenotype. A positive response to lithium has consistently been associated with bipolar illness among first-degree relatives; this suggests that lithium-nonresponsive bipolar patients may have a nongenetic form of the disorder.

Given the likely complex etiology of mood disorders, it is likely that future biological genetic studies will be most effective if multivariate strategies are employed. If the genetic etiology of mood disorders involves interactions among different genotype-phenotype pathways, then the examination of single markers may be uninformative. For example, the combination of high lithium ratio and low MAO activity may cosegregate with mood disorder more strongly than does either marker alone. Dorus et al. (1979) found support for this in a study of 61 first-degree relatives of bipolar patients. All 13 relatives who had both low MAO activity and a high lithium ratio also had a mood disorder. Biological markers will also benefit from the new molecular genetic technologies (see Chap. 6). As these methods continue to isolate suspected genes, more appropriate neurobiological markers will be suggested. The discovery of biological markers may suggest the examination of specific genes. For example, the studies of MAO suggest that it may be fruitful to locate and characterize the MAO gene or genes. In fact, recent work indicates that genes controlling MAO may lie on the short arm of the X chromosome, a vicinity already implicated in bipolar disorder through linkage studies (Ozelius et al., 1988). Thus, it is probable that converging evidence from molecular genetic studies, linkage studies, and biological marker studies will lead to a clearer understanding of the genotype-phenotype pathways involved in mood disorders.

Chapter Eight

Summary and Conclusions

Any inquiry into the genetics of mood disorders would be incomplete without some attempt to distill the basic facts that have emerged from the scientific literature. These we present below as empirical generalizations; although each point may have been contradicted in some studies, the weight of the evidence suggests these generalizations to be valid. Thus, they provide a firm foundation for future research.

1. The risk for mood disorders increases with the proportion of genes shared with a mood-disordered patient. The risk to relatives is greater than the risk to the general population determined by epidemiologic studies. It is also greater than the risk to relatives of well individuals as determined by double-blind case-controlled studies.

2. The concordance rate for mood disorder among monozygotic twins is approximately three times the rate observed among dizygotic twins.

3. The monozygotic twin concordance rate is approximately 0.70 for bipolar disorder and 0.50 for unipolar disorder. Since concordance is not perfect, nonfamilial environmental factors must play a role in the etiology of mood disorders. These factors appear to be less prominent for bipolar than for unipolar disorder.

4. The genetic relationship between unipolar and bipolar disorders is poorly understood. Further research into this area must distinguish recurrent unipolar cases that are not likely to have a subsequent manic episode from nonrecurrent cases that may be bipolar. It is *probably* true that cases of unipolar disorder within families that manifest bipolar disorder are genetic variants of bipolar disorder. The clearest and most consistent difference between the two forms of mood disorder is that relatives of bipolar probands are at greater risk for both unipolar and bipolar disorder than are relatives of unipolar probands. This is supported by evidence from both family and twin studies. Thus, it is likely that bipolar disorder has a greater familial component than does unipolar disorder; unipolar

disorder appears to be more greatly affected by nonfamilial, environmental factors.

5. Women are at greater risk for unipolar disorder, and the transmission of bipolar disorder from fathers to sons is less frequent than expected. Both phenomena suggest that a dominant locus on the X chromosome is involved in bipolar-related mood disorders.

6. The risk for mood disorders to siblings of the same sex as the proband is greater than the risk to opposite-sex siblings. Such a pattern is not consistent with X-chromosome linkage and raises the question of cultural transmission.

7. An earlier age of onset among probands confers an increased risk for mood disorders to their relatives. This effect is independent of the genders of both proband and relative.

8. Two methodologically strong adoption studies *suggest* that biological relationships are better predictors for the risk of mood disorders than are adoptive relationships. However, more adoption studies are needed to provide convergent support for these results.

9. Mathematical modeling studies do not consistently support a specific mode of genetic transmission.

10. The results of linkage studies have been inconsistent. Specific locations on three chromosomes (the X chromosome, chromosome 6, and chromosome 11) have been implicated by different investigators. Other investigators have rejected linkage to these chromosomal locations. Independent replication of the chromosome 6 and 11 linkages is required. The specific pathogenic genes and their gene products have not yet been identified.

11. Although linkage studies have not implicated the region of the ABO locus on chromosome 9, population studies have found an increased prevalence of blood type O among bipolar mood-disordered patients. This suggests that a disease-predisposing gene may be in linkage disequilibrium with the ABO locus.

12. Neurobiological genetic studies have implicated measures of cholinergic supersensitivity and the transport of lithium into red blood cells as biological markers that cosegregate with mood disorders within pedigrees. Further work is needed to confirm these findings and establish their relationship to genetic variation.

13. Pharmacogenetic studies have uncovered two reasonably consistent findings. First, the therapeutic response to specific antidepressants is correlated between ill relatives. It may be that the activity of these drugs at therapeutically relevant sites in the central nervous system counteracts a genetic defect that predisposes to major depression. Second, a good therapeutic response to lithium is more common among patients who have cases of bipolar illness among

their biological relatives. Thus, lithium response may be a marker of etiologic heterogeneity; poor response may indicate a nonfamilial form of the disorder.

Perhaps the most basic fact of all is that what is known about the genetics of mood disorder is far less than what is yet to be discovered. Nevertheless, the preliminary facts that have emerged from psychiatric genetic research are substantial enough to have implications for future research, clinical practice, and genetic counseling.

IMPLICATIONS FOR FUTURE RESEARCH

The inconsistent and sometimes conflicting results of mathematical modeling, linkage analysis, and genetic marker studies have often been interpreted to indicate that the mood disorders are genetically and phenotypically heterogenous. Genetic heterogeneity means that more than one genotype can cause mood disorder. Phenotypic heterogeneity suggests that a given pathogenic genotype can be expressed as one of several phenotypes. Research methodology must directly address these issues if future studies are to provide insight into genetic mechanisms.

Genetic Heterogeneity

The hypothesis of genetic heterogeneity is appealing; it explains inconsistent results with a genetic hypothesis that has been substantiated in other areas of medical genetics. For example, Morton (1956) demonstrated that linkage between elliptocytosis and the Rhesus blood group could be conclusively demonstrated in some families and clearly rejected in others. Ott (1985) discussed the case of Charcot-Marie-Tooth disease, a hereditary motor and sensory neuropathy. Although this disease appears clinically homogeneous, some families demonstrate linkage to the Duffy blood group while others do not. Glycogen storage diseases result in abnormal amounts of glycogen deposited in one or more organs. Ten different forms of the disease have been isolated, each corresponding to a different enzyme defect. Although the clinical manifestations of the 10 subtypes are similar, each can be considered to be a different single major locus disorder (Vogel and Motulsky, 1979).

The existence of genetic heterogeneity requires research designs capable of isolating genetically homogeneous samples. Homogeneity of clinical symptomatology will not guarantee genetic homogeneity. Creating samples that are homogeneous based upon biological marker criteria may be successful if these markers are under a substantial amount of genetic control and are known to be etiologically involved in the disorder. For example, the heterogeneity of the glycogen storage diseases is revealed if one studies the activity of relevant enzymes instead of the overt clinical manifestations. A more commonly used method to maximize genetic homogeneity is to study ill individuals from a single large pedigree. Although genetic homogeneity may be compromised by assortative mating, individuals from the same pedigree are more likely to have the same genetic disorder than are individuals from different pedigrees. When large pedigrees are not available, linkage studies can use statistical tests of homogeneity to test the hypothesis that some families demonstrate linkage to the marker locus while others do not (Ott, 1985).

Phenotypic Heterogeneity

It is not uncommon for a single gene to have different phenotypic effects in different individuals; this is known as pleiotropy. Matthysse (1985) discussed the example of neurofibromatosis. Although this autosomal dominant disease is almost completely penetrant, the manifestations range from the relatively mild appearance of café-au-lait spots to severe cases with peripheral nerve tumors, bony deformities, and mental retardation. GM2 gangliosidosis is an incompletely penetrant single gene disease. When the disorder is manifest, the clinical picture may include dementia, motor neuron disease, tremors, or psychosis (Gurling, 1985).

The combination of genetic and phenotypic heterogeneity results in the situation diagrammed in figure 8.1. This diagram indicates that a pathogenic genotype can lead to a specific clinical phenotype (e.g., bipolar disorder), a spectrum disorder (e.g., unipolar disorder), or no clinical symptomatology. Furthermore, there are individuals called phenocopies who manifest the clinical phenotype but do not have the specific genotype. They may have another pathogenic genotype or they may have nonfamilial forms of the disorder; both of these situations correspond to genetic heterogeneity. Clearly, if one studies only the clinical phenotype, many genotypically abnormal individuals will be considered normal. This will make the mode of inheritance more difficult to detect. In statistical analyses, this problem is accounted for by allowing genes to be incompletely penetrant. It must be emphasized, however, that "penetrance" is a descriptive term, not an explanation. Studying a phenotype with very low penetrance will require larger samples to discriminate between modes of inheritance. As we suggest in figure 8.1, progress in psychiatric

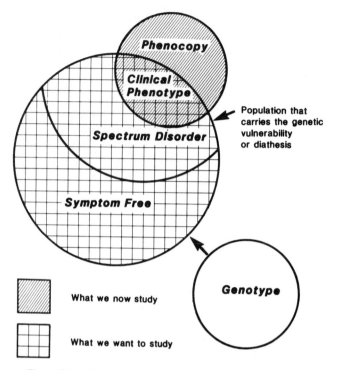

Figure 8.1. Genetic and phenotypic heterogeneity model

genetics would greatly benefit from a more rigorous and comprehensive description of phenotypes related to pathogenic genotypes.

The validation of spectrum disorder phenotypes is relatively straightforward. The basic experimental designs of psychiatric genetics, family, twin, and adoption studies, can indicate whether a specific disorder is more common among relatives of probands manifesting the clinical phenotype than among relatives of normal control probands. Comprehensive examination of potential mood spectrum disorders is beyond the scope of this volume. A number of disorders have been implicated as potential spectrum disorders. These include some personality disorders, cyclothymic disorder, dysthymic disorder, anorexia nervosa, substance abuse and dependence, chronic pain, and anxiety disorders.

The identification of symptom-free individuals who carry the pathogenic genotype is not an easy task. Ideally, biological marker research will supply us with some biological abnormality that is expressed in symptom-free individuals who have the pathogenic genotype. Studies of discordant monozygotic twins would be most useful in this regard. If the afflicted member of a discordant pair is expressing a genetically determined disorder, than one would expect that the unaffected twin might manifest an associated biological abnormality. The existence of symptom-free individuals with a pathogenic genotype may be one reason why biological marker studies have produced inconsistent results. It will be difficult to demonstrate cosegregation between a marker and a disorder if all individuals with the genotype display the marker but only some manifest the disorder.

Psychiatric genetics has reached a point where the sophistication of available experimental tools such as molecular genetic technologies and statistical procedures has surpassed the ability to describe relevant phenotypes. This would suggest that genetic analyses should have an exploratory component in which phenotypes are redefined according to clinical and biochemical criteria to search for a definition that fits a genetic model. The importance of exploratory data analysis is well recognized among statisticians (e.g., Tukey, 1978) and cannot be ignored. Of course, the results of such analyses require cross-validation from additional samples. The systematic application of such an approach combined with the examination of multiple marker loci could lead to spurious results.

For the mood disorders, polarity, gender, and age of onset appear to be the most robust, clinically evident indices of heterogeneity. Furthermore, there is a large literature, beyond the scope of this volume, that implicates familial relationships with other disorders as a significant index of genetic heterogeneity (Carey, 1987; Kendler et al., 1987; Leckman et al., 1983a). For example, it has been suggested that early-onset cases of major depression associated with panic disorder may define an etiologically homogeneous subgroup (Price, Kidd, and Weissman, 1987). Familial relationships between major depression, antisocial disorders, and attention-deficit disorders have also been reported (Biederman et al., 1986, 1989).

Perhaps the most comprehensive and heavily researched description of genetic heterogeneity for mood disorders is Winokur's distinction between pure depression, depressive spectrum disorders, and nonfamilial depression (Andreason and Winokur, 1979; Winokur et al., 1971; Winokur, 1979a,b). These categories arose initially from the observation that depressives having an age of onset less than 40 were more likely to be females. Their male relatives had a higher risk for antisocial personality and alcoholism. On the other hand, depressives having an age of onset greater than 40 were more likely to be males having a family history of depression only. The early-onset cases have been called depressive spectrum disorders. The late-onset cases were termed pure depression. Andreason and

Winokur (1979) suggested a third subtype, nonfamilial depression, which includes depressives having no family history of psychotic disorders. Although there is a good deal of overlap among these subtypes in terms of the expression of clinical signs and symptoms (Behar et al., 1981), there is some evidence, albeit equivocal, that they may be differentiable on the basis of biological parameters such as the electroencephalogram (Kupfer, Karg, and Stack, 1982), tritiated imipramine binding (Lewis and McChesney, 1985), and the dexamethasone suppression test (Zimmerman, Coryell, and Pfohl, 1985). More work is needed to establish genetic mechanisms that may account for these subgroups. Nonetheless, the approach of Winokur and colleagues does exemplify a useful paradigm for dissecting genetic and phenotypic heterogeneity.

IMPLICATIONS FOR CLINICAL PRACTICE

Meehl (1962, 1973) provided discussion of how the demonstration of a specific genetic etiology may influence perceptions of the potential efficacy of a therapeutic procedure. The isolation of a pathogenic gene points to the beginning of a chain of events leading to the disease. For psychiatric disorders, this chain of events is likely to be long and complex; the events probably include both biological and psychosocial processes. Although the gene itself may suggest a specific somatic therapy, its discovery does not rule out the possibility that interventions further along the chain of events will be useful. For example, an individual in an episode of major depression known to carry a "depression gene" may be a good candidate for cognitive-behavioral therapy. In Meehl's terms, the demonstration of a specific genetic etiology should not create an atmosphere of therapeutic nihilism. Finding the beginning of a pathophysiological pathway does *not* mean that interventions elsewhere along the pathway will be useless.

It is, of course, tempting to speculate about the possibilities of a "one gene, one treatment" therapy protocol for mood disorders in the future. For example, if future research indicates that the gene controlling tyrosine hydroxylase on chromosome 11 is a pathogenic bipolar gene, then some cases may respond well to treatments that correct the relevant abnormalities. Other treatments may be appropriate for HLA-linked mood disorders and so forth. On the other hand, it is also possible that genetic defects will not be easily corrected at the early stages of the genotype-phenotype chain. It is likely that mental health treatment in the twenty-first century will involve multiple treatments along the pathophysiologic pathway.

The pharmacogenetic literature has more immediate implications for psychiatric treatment. Since the response to antidepressants is similar between ill first-degree relatives, knowledge of treatment response in relatives will facilitate a psychiatrist's choice of medication for depressed patients. The use of lithium will be strongly indicated for patients with bipolar first-degree relatives. A comprehensive psychiatric family history will also facilitate treatment by improving the accuracy of diagnosis. Clinicians must deal with the fact that many psychotic patients do not easily fit into *DSM III-R* categories. If a patient manifests signs that are suggestive of both bipolar disorder and schizophrenia, the knowledge that the sibling is a lithium-responsive bipolar case has obvious implications. The field of psychopharmacogenetics is still in its infancy; more research is needed to discover the treatment implications of psychiatric disorders among relatives of mood-disorder patients.

IMPLICATIONS FOR GENETIC COUNSELING

The overall goal of genetic counseling is to reduce the adverse impact or possible recurrence of a genetically influenced disorder. Depending upon the level of genetic knowledge regarding a disease, genetic counseling may lead to medical interventions, reproductive choices, prenatal diagnosis, or predictions about the probability of disease onset (Fletcher, 1984). Given the current state of knowledge for mood disorders, genetic counseling is unlikely to lead to medical interventions or prenatal diagnosis at the present time. Patients with mood disorders will be concerned with the health of potential children and the well relatives of these patients will be concerned about their probability of developing the disorder.

In preparing an individual for genetic counseling, one should dispel common erroneous beliefs about mental disorders and genetic etiology in general and about genetic counseling in particular. Three points are particularly important (Tsuang, 1978). Many laypeople believe that if a disorder is genetic it must occur in those who possess the harmful genes. At the outset, the counselee must understand that genetic factors do not account 100 percent for mood disorders. The counselee may also believe that if a disorder is genetic it must be untreatable. As we discussed in the previous section, this attitude of therapeutic nihilism is incorrect. In practice, these two points may be difficult to communicate because many counselees expect simple answers to the complex problem of genetic risk prediction. A third misconception that can create a good deal of anxiety is the association of genetic counseling with eugenics and genocide. It is useful to clarify to the counselee that contemporary genetic counseling stresses autonomy in decision making and is in no way coercive. By correcting these common misconceptions, the counselor will alleviate unnecessary anxiety and allow the counselee to receive information in a more realistic fashion.

The process of genetic counseling can be divided into seven stages (Tsuang, 1978). The genetic counselee may be an identified patient or the relative of such an individual. In either case, the first step in the counseling process is to obtain an accurate diagnosis of the ill individual. The diagnosis should be based on a personal interview with the patient and a review of available medical records. Information from relatives should be incorporated as well. The difficulties in obtaining diagnoses of mood disorder have been discussed (see chap. 1) and must be rigorously taken into consideration. In diagnosing unipolar disorder, the clinician should supplement standard *DSM III-R* diagnoses with the recurrent/nonrecurrent classification of Perris (1966), since this distinction is known to have genetic implications. If the diagnostician is uncertain about the diagnosis, this must be communicated to the counselee along with the implications for genetic risk prediction.

The second stage of counseling is the formulation of a comprehensive family psychiatric history. The problems of collecting family history data from informants have been well described (see chap. 1). When possible, personal interviews with relatives should be used to resolve diagnostic uncertainties. Available medical records will also facilitate this process. Although the family psychiatric history often focuses on first-degree relatives, information on more distant relatives should be collected whenever possible. When interpreting diagnostic data from informants, the diagnostician must apply the general principle that diagnoses based on information from informants have low sensitivity and high specificity. That is, this method has a low probability of accurately identifying ill individuals and a high probability of accurately identifying well individuals. The use of relatively loose diagnostic criteria will improve the sensitivity without greatly hurting the specificity. Data from informants will also be more accurate if multiple informants are utilized and if at least one informant has lived for a substantial period of time with the individual being diagnosed.

With the information collected in steps one and two, along with a thorough knowledge of the genetics of mood disorder, the counselor can proceed to make an estimate of the risk of recurrence. In doing so, the counselor must determine whether the situation calls for the formulation of empirical risks or exact risks. Empirical risks ignore genetic mechanisms and are based solely on morbidity risks that have been determined by psychiatric genetic research. Unfortunately, as the data in tables 2.6–2.11 indicate, the variability between studies suggests that precise statements of risk will not be possible. Instead, the range of risks suggested by previous research must be communicated. Ideally, figures on empirical risks would take into account the multiple occurrence of mood disorders within a family. Such figures, however, are not available. One exception to this is the risk for mood disorders among siblings of patients when the status of their parents is known. Several researchers have examined this family constellation (table 8.1). All of the available studies indicate that the risk to a sibling is substantially increased if one of the parents is also ill.

The computation of an exact risk requires unambiguous knowledge of the mode of inheritance along with accurate psychiatric diagnoses. The precision of an exact risk can be further increased if a chromosomal marker for the disorder is available. Given the current state of knowledge, exact genetic risks cannot be computed for the

Table 8.1. The Risk of Major Mood Disorder among Siblings of Probands by the Status of the Parents

Study	Proband Diagnosis	Sibling Diagnosis	Risk to Sibling (%) Affective Diagnosis in Parents	
			Well	Ill
Rudin (1920s)[a,b]	MD	MD	7.4	23.8
Schulz (1930s)[a,c]	MD	MD	14.3	26.1
Luxenburger (1930s)[a,b]	MD	MD	3.4	16.1
Pollock, Malzberg, and Fuller, 1939[a]	MD	MD	1.3	3.8
Stenstedt, 1952[d]	MD	MD	13.5	17.9
Reich, Clayton, and Winokur, 1969[e]	BP	MD	10.0	21.0
Johnson and Leeman, 1977[d]	BP	MD	18.4	23.2
Angst et al., 1980[d,f]	BP	BP	1.2	5.6
	BP	UP	4.1	8.4

Note: MD = mood disorder, BP = bipolar disorder, UP = unipolar disorder.
[a]Age of onset correction not stated.
[b]From Rosenthal, 1970.
[c]From Kallmann, 1954.
[d]Strömgren method of age correction.
[e]Weinberg method of age correction.
[f]Includes risk to children of probands having ill and well parents.

mood disorders. Before communicating results to the counselee, the clinician must have a clear understanding of the counselee's intentions, intellectual level, and current emotional state. These factors will determine the manner in which results can be most effectively communicated.

After learning about risk, it is essential that the counselee understand the burdens and benefits associated with the disorder. Burden includes such unquantifiable elements as the physical and emotional pain caused by mental illness. Financial burdens include the direct medical costs associated with the potential illness and indirect costs, such as loss of employment. Benefit refers not to the benefits of being ill but to the benefits of choosing to have a child. These will be influenced by religious convictions, political ideology, the current size of the family, social expectations, economic conditions, perceptions of parenthood, and the potential joy that a child may bring to the family. Unlike the burden of illness, which the counselor can communicate based on a thorough understanding of the course and outcome of mood disorders, the benefit of parenthood cannot be scientifically formulated. The counselor must be an empathic and sensitive listener to help the counselee understand the benefits involved in choosing to have children. It is useful to conceptualize burden and benefit as weights at the opposite end of the balance; the recurrence risk is the fulcrum. As the risk increases from zero to 100 percent, the fulcrum moves from the burden side of the balance to the benefit side. With lower risks, the benefits are more heavily weighed; as the risk increases, the burdens take on more and more weight in arriving at a decision.

After the benefits and burdens have been considered in the context of the recurrence risk, the counselor must help the counselee form a reasonable plan of action if reproductive choices are involved. The final stage of counseling is the follow-up. This is sometimes done in person, over the telephone, or through the mail. The length of the follow-up period will depend upon the specific circumstances of the counselee. The goal of the counselor is to determine that the counselee has remembered and understood the information imparted. The counselee is also given a second opportunity to ask questions that may have arisen since the original visits or to discuss new information relative to recurrence risk estimation.

References

Ablon SL, Carlson GA and Goodman FK. 1974. Ego Defense Patterns in Manic-Depressive Illness. *Am J Psychiatry* 131:803–807.

Abrams R and Taylor MA. 1974. Unipolar Mania: A Preliminary Report. *Arch Gen Psychiatry* 30:441–443.

Abrams R and Taylor MA. 1980. A Comparison of Unipolar and Bipolar Depressive Illness. *Am J Psychiatry* 137:1084–1087.

Abrams R and Taylor MA. 1983. The Importance of Mood-Incongruent Psychotic Symptoms in Melancholia. *J Affective Disorders* 5:179–181.

Achenheil M. 1982. Hormonal Response to Stress in Mental Illness. In *Biological Psychiatry: Part III Brain Mechanism and Abnormal Behavior-Gender and Neuroendocrinology,* Van Praag HM, Lader MH, Rafaelson OJ and Sachar EF, Eds. New York: M Dekker, 195–215.

Aden GC. 1976. Lithium Carbonate Versus ECT in the Treatment of the Manic State of Identical Twins with Bipolar Affective Disease. *Dis Nerv Syst* 37:393–397.

Allen G. 1979. Holzinger's Hc Revised. *Acta Genet Med Gemellol* 28:161–164.

Allen MG, Cohen S, Pollin W and Greenspan SI. 1974. Affective Illness in Veteran Twins: A Diagnostic Review. *Am J Psychiatry* 131:1234–1239.

American Psychiatric Association, Committee on Nomenclature and Statistics. 1987. In *Diagnostic and Statistical Manual of Mental Disorders,* 3rd Ed., Revised. Washington, D.C.: American Psychiatric Assoc.

Amos DB and Ward FE. 1977. Theoretical Considerations in the Association between HLA and Disease. In *HLA and Disease,* Dausset J and Svejaard A, Eds. Copenhagen: Munksgaard, 268–279.

Andreasen NC. 1986. The Family History Approach to Diagnosis: How Useful Is It? *Arch Gen Psychiatry* 43:421–429.

Andreasen NC, Endicott J, Spitzer RL and Winokur G. 1977. The Family History Method Using Diagnostic Criteria. *Arch Gen Psychiatry* 34:1229–1235.

Andreasen NC and Grove WM. 1982. The Classification of Depression: Traditional versus Mathematical Approaches. *Am J Psychiatry* 139:45–52.

Andreasen NC, Rice J, Endicott J, Coryell W., Grove WM and Reich T. 1987. Familial Rates of Affective Disorder: A Report from the National Institute of Mental Health Collaborative Study. *Arch Gen Psychiatry* 44:461–469.

Andreasen NC, Scheftner W, Reich T, Hirschfeld RMA, Endicott J and Keller MB. 1986. The Validation of the Concept of Endogenous Depression: A Family Study Approach. *Arch Gen Psychiatry* 43:246–251.

✳ Andreasen NC and Winokur G. 1979. Newer Experimental Methods of Classifying Depression. *Arch Gen Psychiatry* 36:447–452.

Angst J. 1961. A Clinical Analysis of the Effects of Tofranil in Depression: Longitudinal and Follow-Up Studies, Treatment of Blood-Relations. *Psychopharmacologia* 2:381–407.

Angst J. 1966. Zur Atiologie Und Nosologie Endogener Depressiver Psychosen. In *Monographien Aus Der Neurologie Und Psychiatrie, no.* 112. Berlin: Springer-Verlag, 1–118.

Angst J, Baastrup P, Hippius H, Poldinger W and Weis P. 1973. The Course of Monopolar Depression and Bipolar Psychoses. *Psychiatrica, Neurologica, et Neurochirurgia* 76:489–500.

Angst J, Fedler W and Lohmeyer B. 1979a. Are Schizoaffective Psychoses Heterogeneous?: Results of a Genetic Investigation, II. *J Affect Disorders* 1:155–165.

Angst J, Fedler W and Lohmeyer B. 1979b. Schizoaffective Disorders: Results of a Genetic Investigation, I. *J Affect Disorders* 1:139–155.

Angst J, Frey R, Lohmeyer B and Zerbin-Rudin E. 1980. Bipolar Manic-Depressive Psychoses: Results of a Genetic Investigation. *Hum Genet* 55:237–254.

Asmussen MA. 1985. The Use of Incompletely Linked Markers in Genetic Counseling: Accuracy versus Linkage. *Hum Hered* 35:73–88.

Asmussen MA and Clegg MT. 1982. Use of Restriction Fragment Length Polymorphisms for Genetic Counseling: Population Genetic Considerations. *Am J Hum Genet* 34:369–380.

Avery DH, Osgood TB, Ishiki DM, Wilson LG, Kenney M and Dunner DL. 1985. The DST in Psychiatric Outpatients with Generalized Anxiety Disorder, Panic Disorder, or Primary Affective Disorder. *Am J Psychiatry* 142:844–849.

Baker M, Dorzab J, Winokur G and Cadoret R. 1972. Depressive Disease: Evidence Favoring Polygenic Inheritance Based on an Analysis of Ancestral Cases. *Arch Gen Psychiatry* 27:320–327.

Banse J. 1929. Zur Problem Der Erbprognosebestimmung: Die Erkrankung-Aussichten Der Vettern Und Basen Von Manisch-Depressiven. *Z Ges Neurol* 119.

Barber TX and Silver MJ. 1968. Fact, Fiction, and the Experimenter Bias Effect. *Psychological Bulletin Monograph Supplement* 70:1–29.

Baron M. 1977. Linkage between an X-Chromosome Marker (Deutan Color Blindness) and Bipolar Affective Illness: Occurrence in the Family of a Lithium Carbonate-Responsive Schizoaffective Proband. *Arch Gen Psychiatry* 34:721–725.

Baron M. 1980. Genetic Models of Affective Disorder: Application to Twin Data. *Acta Genet Med Gemllol* 29:289–294.

Baron M. 1981. Genetic Heterogeneity in Affective Disorders: Implications for Psychobiological Research. *Acta Psychiat Scand* 64:431–441.

Baron M. 1983. Polarity and Sex Effect in Genetic Transmission of Affective Disorders: The Single Major Locus Hypothesis. *Hum Hered* 33:112–118.

Baron M, Gershon ES, Rudy V, Jonas WZ and Buchsbaum M. 1975. Lithium Carbonate Response in Depression. *Arch Gen Psychiatry* 32:1107–1111.

Baron M, Gruen R, Asnis L and Kane J. 1982. Schizoaffective Illness, Schizophrenia and Affective Disorders: Morbidity Risk and Genetic Transmission. *Acta Psychiat Scand* 65:253–262.

Baron M, Mendlewicz J, Gruen R, Asnis L and Fieve RRL. 1981. Assortative Mating in Affective Disorders. *J Affect Disorders* 3:167–171.

Baron M, Rainer JD and Risch N. 1981. X-Linkage in Bipolar Affective Illness: Perspectives on Genetic Heterogeneity, Pedigree Analysis and the X-Chromosome Map. *J Affect Disorders* 3:141–157.

Baron M and Risch N. 1983. X-Linkage in Affective and Schizoaffective Disorders: Genetic and Diagnostic Implications. In *Neuropsychobiology*, Mendlewicz J, Ed. Basel: S Karger, 8:304–311.

Baron M, Risch N, Hamburger R, Mandel B, Kushner S, Newman M, Drumer D and Belmaker RH. 1987. Genetic Linkage between X-Chromosome Markers and Bipolar Affective Illness. *Nature* 326:289–292.

Baron M, Risch N, Levitt M and Gruen R. 1985. Genetic Analysis of Plasma Amine Oxidase Activity in Schizophrenia. *Psychiatr Res* 15:121–132.

Beckman G, Beckman L, Cedergren B, Perris C and Strandman E. 1978a. Serum Protein and Red Cell Enzyme Polymorphisms in Affective Disorders. *Hum Genet* 28:41–47.

Beckman G, Beckman L, Perris C and Strandman E. 1978b. Short Communications: No Association of Red Cell Adenylate Kinase Phenotypes with Affective Disorders. *Hum Genet* 41:355–357.

Beckman L, Perris C, Strandman E and Wahlby L. 1978c. HLA Antigens and Affective Disorders. *Hum Hered* 28:96–99.

Behar D, Winokur G, Van Valkenburg C, Lowry M, and Lachenbruch PA. 1981. Clinical Overlap among Familial Subtypes of Unipolar Depression. *Neuropsychobiology* 7:179–184. ✳

Beigel A, and Murphy DL. 1971. Unipolar and Bipolar Affective Illness: Differences in Clinical Characteristics Accompanying Depression. *Arch Gen Psychiatry* 24:215–220.

Benirschke K and Kim CK. 1973. Multiple Pregnancy. *N Engl J Med* 288:1276–1284; 1329–1336.

Bennahum DA, Troup GM, Rada RT and Kellner R. 1977. Human Leukocyte Antigens (HL-A) in Psychiatric Illness. *Clinical Research* 23, 387.

Bersani G, Valeri M, Cavallari S, Piazza A, Ciani N, and Casciani CU. 1985. The HLA system as a Genetic Marker of Affective Disorders: Reports on a Population from Central Italy, with Comments on Methodology. *Biol Psychiatry* 20:1328–1331.

Bertelsen A. 1985. A Danish Twin Study of Manic-Depressive Disorders. In *Genetic Aspects of Human Behavior,* Sakai T and Tsubsi T, Eds. New York: Igaku-Shoin, 97–102.

Bertelsen A, Harvald B and Hauge M. 1977. A Danish Twin Study of Manic-Depressive Disorders. *Brit J Psychiat* 130:330–351.

Biederman J, Faraone SV, Keenan K and Tsuang MT. 1989. Family-Genetic and Psychosocial Risk Factors in Attention Deficit Disorder. (Abstract) *Biological Psychiatry* Suppl. 25:145A.

Biederman J, Munir K, Knee D, Habelow W, Armentano M, Autor S, Hoge SK and Waternaux C. 1986. A Family Study of Patients with Attention Deficit Disorder and Normal Controls. *J Psychiat Res* 20:263–274.

Bielski RJ and Fiedel RO. 1976. Prediction of Tricyclic Antidepressant Response: A Critical Review. *Arch Gen Psychiatry* 33:1479–1489.

Blumer D, Zorick F, Heilbronn M and Roth T. 1982. Biological Markers for Depression in Chronic Pain. *J Nerv and Ment Disease* 170:425–528.

Bodmer WF. 1984. The HLA System, 1984. In *Histocompatibility Testing,* Albert ED et al., Eds. Berlin: Springer-Verlag, 11–22.

Bohman M. 1978. Some Genetic Aspects of Alcoholism and Criminality: A Population of Adoptees. Alcoholism and Criminality, *Arch Gen Psychiatry* 35:269–276.

Bohman M. 1981. The Interaction of Heredity and Childhood Environment: Some Adoption Studies. *J Child Psychol Psychiat* 22:195–200.

Bohman M, Cloninger CR, Sigvardsson S and Von Knorring AL. 1982. Predisposition to Petty Criminality in Swedish Adoptees: Genetic and Environmental Heterogeneity. Criminality in Adoptees. *Arch Gen Psychiatry* 39:1233–1241.

Bohman M and Sigvardsson S. 1980. A Prospective, Longitudinal Study of Children Registered for Adoption: A 15-Year Follow-Up. *Acta Psychiat Scand* 61:339–355.

Bohman M, Sigvardsson S and Cloninger CR. 1981. Maternal Inheritance of Alcohol Abuse: Cross-Fostering Analysis of Adopted Women. Maternal Inheritance. *Arch Gen Psychiatry* 38:965–969.

Bond TC, Rothschild AJ, Lerbinger J and Schatzberg AF. 1986. Delusional Depression, Family History and DST Response: A Pilot Study. *Biol Psychiatry* 21:1239–1246.

Bonner TI, Young A, Buckley N, Brann M, Modi W and O'Brien S. 1987. Molecular Genetics of the Muscarinic Acetylcholine Receptor Gene Family. *American College of Neuropsychopharmacology, 26th Annual Meeting,* 1:62 (Abstract).

Botstein D, White RL, Skolnick M and Davis RW. 1980. Construction of a Genetic Linkage Map in Man Using Restriction Fragment Length Polymorphisms. *Am J Hum Genet* 32:314–331.

Bowers M and Astrachan B. 1967. Depression in Acute Schizophrenic Psychosis. *Am J Psychiatry* 123:976–979.

Boyd JH, Burke JD, Jr., Gruenberg E, Holzer CE III, Rae DS, George LK, Karno M, Stoltzman R, McEvoy L, and Nestadt G. 1984. Exclusion Criteria of DSM-III: A Study of Co-occurrence of Hierarchy-free Syndromes. *Arch Gen Psychiatry* 41:983–989.

Boyd JH and Weissman MM. 1981. Epidemiology of Affective Disorders: A Reexamination and Future Directions. *Arch Gen Psychiatry* 38:1039–1046.

Breborowicz G and Trzebiatowska-Trzeciak O. 1976. A Method for Testing Differences in Morbidity Risk for Affective Psychoses. *Acta Psychiatr Scand* 54:353–358.

Breslow RE, DeMuth GW and Weiss C. 1985. Lithium Incorporation in the Fibroblasts of Manic-Depressives. *Biol Psychiatry* 20:58–65.

Brim J, Wetzel RD, Reich T, Wood D, Viesselman J and Rutt C. 1984. Primary and Secondary Affective Disorder: III. Longitudinal Differences in Depression Symptoms. *J Clinical Psychiatry* 45:64–69.

Brockington I, Kendall R, Wainwright S, Hiller V and Walker J. 1979. The Distinction between the Affective Psychoses and Schizophrenia. *Brit J Psychiatry* 135:243–248.

Brodie HKH and Leff MJ. 1971. Bipolar Depression: A Comparative Study of Patient Characteristics. *Am J Psychiatry* 127:1086–1090.

Brown WA and Shuey I. 1980. Response to Dexamethasone and Subtype of Depression. *Arch Gen Psychiatry* 37:747–751.

Bucher KD, Elston RC, Green R, Whybrow P, Helzer J, Reich T, Clayton P and Winokur G. 1981. The Transmission of Manic Depressive Illness: II. Segregation Analysis of Three Sets of Family Data. *J Psychiat Res* 16:65–78.

Buchsbaum MS. 1974. Average Evoked Response and Stimulus Intensity in Identical and Fraternal Twins. *Physiological Psychology* 2:365–370.

Buchsbaum MS, Coursey R and Murphy DL. 1976. The Biochemical High-Risk Paradigm: Behavioral and Familial Correlates of Low Platelet Monamine Oxidase and the Average Evoked Response. *Acta Psychiatr Scand* 56:69–79.

Bunney WE, Jr., and Murphy DL. 1973. The Behavioral Switch Process and Psychopathology. In *Biol Psychiatry,* J Mendels, Ed. New York: Wiley-Interscience.

Cadoret RJ. 1978. Evidence for Genetic Inheritance of Primary Affective Disorder in Adoptees. *Am J Psychiatry* 135:463–466.

Cadoret RJ, Baker M, Dorzab J and Winokur G. 1971. Depressive Disease: Personality Factors in Patients and Their Relatives. *Biol Psychiatry* 3:85–93.

Cadoret RJ, Cunningham L, Loftus R and Edwards J. 1976. Studies of Adoptees from Psychiatrically Disturbed Biological Parents: III. Medical Symptoms and Illnesses in Childhood and Adolescence. *Am J Psychiatry* 133:1316–1318.

Cadoret RJ, O'Gorman TW, Heywood E and Troughton E. 1985. Genetic and Environmental Factors in Major Depression. *J Affect Disorders* 9:155–164.

Campbell J, Crowe RR, Goeken N, Pfohl B, Pauls D and Palmer D. 1984. Affective Disorder Not Linked to HLA in a Large Bipolar Kindred. *J Affect Disorders* 7:45–51.

Carey G. 1987. Big Genes, Little Genes, Affective Disorder, and Anxiety: A Commentary. *Arch Gen Psychiatry* 44:486–491.

Carpenter W and Stephens J. 1979. An Attempted Integration of Information Relevant to Schizophrenic Subtypes. *Schizophrenia Bulletin* 5:490–506.

Carroll BJ. 1984. Problems with Diagnostic Criteria for Depression: Diagnostic Criteria. *J Clin Psychiatry* 45:14–18.

Carroll BJ, Greden JF, Feinberg M, James NM, Haskett RF, Steiner M and Tarika J. 1980. Neuroendocrine Dysfunction in Genetic Subtypes of Primary Unipolar Depression. *Psychiatry Res* 2:251–258.

Casper RC, Pandey G, Gosenfeld L et al. 1976. Intracellular Lithium and Clinical Response. *Lancet* 2:418–419.

Cavalli-Sforza LL and Bodmer WF. 1971. *The Genetics of Human Populations*. San Francisco: Freeman.

Cederlof R, Friberg L, Jonsson E and Kay L. 1961. Studies on Similarity Diagnosis in Twins with the Aid of Mailed Questionnaires. *Acta Genet* 11:338–362.

Charney ES and Nelson JC. 1981. Delusional and Non-Delusional Unipolar Depression: Further Evidence for Distinct Subtypes. *Am J Psychiatry* 138:328–333.

Clark J and Mallet B. 1963. A Follow-Up Study of Schizophrenia and Depression in Young Adults. *Brit J Psychiatry* 109:491–499.

Clayton PJ, Rodin L and Winokur G. 1968. Family History Studies: III. Schizoaffective Disorder, Clinical and Genetic Factors including a One to Two Year Follow-Up. *Comprehensive Psychiatry* 9:31–49.

Clifford CA, Hopper JL, Fulker DW and Murray RM. 1984. A Genetic and Environmental Analysis of a Twin Family Study of Alcohol Use, Anxiety and Depression. *Genetic Epidemiology* 1:63–79.

Cloninger CR, Reich T and Yokoyama S. 1983. Genetic Diversity, Genome Organization and Investigation of the Etiology of Psychiatric Diseases. *Psychiatric Developments* 3:775–796.

Comings DE. 1979. PC 1 Duarte, A Common Polymorphism of a Human Brain Protein, and Its Relationship to Depressive Disease and Multiple Sclerosis. *Nature* 28–32.

Copeland JRM. 1983. Psychotic and Neurotic Depression: Discriminant Function Analysis and Five-Year Outcome. *Psychological Medicine* 13:373–383.

Copeland JRM. 1984. Reactive and Endogenous Depressive Illness and Five Year Outcome. *J Affect Disorders* 6:153–162.

Coppen A, Cowie V and Slater E. 1965. Familial Aspects of "Neuroticism" and "Extraversion." *Brit J Psychiat* 3:70–83.

Coryell W, Gaffney G and Burkhardt PE. 1982. The Dexamethasone Suppression Test and Familial Subtypes of Depression: A Naturalistic Replication. *Biol Psychiatry* 17:33–40.

Coryell W, Pfohl B and Zimmerman M. 1984. The Clinical and Neuroendocrine Features of Psychotic Depression. *J Nerv and Ment Disease* 172:521–528.

Coryell W and Tsuang MT. 1982. Primary Unipolar Depression and the Prognostic Significance of Delusions. *Arch Gen Psychiatry* 39:1181–1184.

Coryell W and Tsuang MT. 1985. Major Depression with Mood-Congruent or Mood-Incongruent Psychotic Features: Outcome after 40 Years. *Am J Psychiatry* 142:479–482.

Coryell W, Tsuang MT and McDaniel J. 1982. Psychotic Features in Major Depression: Is Mood Congruence Important? *J Affect Disorders* 4:227–236.

Coursey RD, Buchsbaum MS and Murphy DL. 1979. Platelet MAO Activity and Evoked Potentials in the Identification of Subjects Biologically at Risk for Psychiatric Disorders. *Brit J Psychiat* 134:372–381.

Coursey RD, Buchsbaum MS and Murphy DL. 1982. Two-Year Follow-Up of Subjects and their Families Defined as at Risk for Psychopathology on the Basis of Platelet MAO Activities. *Neuropsychobiology* 8:51–56.

Crowe RR. 1974. An Adoption Study of Antisocial Personality. *Arch Gen Psychiatry* 31:785–791.

Crowe RR, Namboodiri KK, Ashby HB and Elston RC. 1981. Segregation and Linkage Analysis of a Large Kindred of Unipolar Depression. *Neuropsychobiology* 7:20–25.

Crowe RR, Paulo DL, Slymen DJ and Noyes R. 1980. A Family Study of Anxiety Neurosis: Morbidity Risk in Families of Patients with and without Mitral Valve Prolapse. *Arch Gen Psychiatry* 37:77–79.

Crowe RR and Smouse RE. 1977. The Genetic Implications of Age-Dependent Penetrance in Manic-Depressive Illness. *J Psychiat Res* 13:273–285.

Cummings JL and Mendez MF. 1984. Secondary Mania with Focal Cerebrovascular Lesions. *Am J Psychiatry* 141:1084–1087.

Cunningham L, Cadoret RJ, Loftus R and Edwards JE. 1975. Studies of Adoptees from Psychiatrically Disturbed Biological Parents: Psychiatric Conditions in Childhood and Adolescence. *Brit J Psychiat* 126:534–549.

Da Fonseca A. 1959. Analise Heredo-Clinca das Perturbacoes Afectivas (Estudio de 60 pares de gemeos, e sues conganguin neos), Impresna Protuguesa, Proto.

Da Fonseca AF. 1963. Affective Equivalents. *Brit J Psychiat* 109:464–469.

Davidson JRT, McLeod MN, Kurland AA and White HL. 1977. Antidepressant Drug Therapy in Psychotic Depression. *Brit J Psychiat* 131:351–360.

D'Elia G and Perris C. 1971. Childhood Environment and Bipolar and Unipolar Recurrent Depressive Psychosis. In *Depressive States in Childhood and Adolescence,* Annell AL, Ed. Proceedings of the Fourth Union of European Child Psychiatrists Congress. Stockholm: Almqvist & Wiksell, 55–62.

D'Elia G, von Knorring L and Perris C. 1974. Non-Psychotic Depressive Disorders: A Ten-Year Follow-Up. *Acta Psychiatr Scand* Suppl, 255:173–186.

Del Vecchio M, Famiglietti LA and Amati A. 1979. Subgroups of Manic-Depressive Patients in Relation to the ABO System. *Acta Neurologica* 34:150.

Del Zompo M, Bocchetta, A, Goldin LR and Corsini GU. 1984. Linkage between X-Chromosome Markers and Manic-Depressive Illness. *Acta Psychiatr Scand* 70:282–287.

Depue RA and Monroe SM. 1978. The Unipolar-Bipolar Distinction in the Depressive Disorders. *Psychological Bull* 85:1001–1029.

Depue RA and Monroe SM. 1979. The Unipolar-Bipolar Distinction in the Depressive Disorders: Implications for Stress-Onset Interaction. In *The Psychobiology of the Depressive Disorders: Implications of the Effects of Stress.* New York: Academic Press, 23–53.

Detera-Wadleigh SD, Berrettini H, Goldin LR, Boorman D, Anderson CM and Gershon ES. 1987. Close Linkage of c-Harvey-ras-1 and the Insulin Gene to Affective Disorder Is Ruled Out in Three North American Pedigrees. *Nature* 325:806–808.

Detre T, Himmelhoch J, Swartzburgh M, Anderson CM, Byck R and Kupfer DJ. 1972. Hypersomnia and Manic-Depressive Disease. *Am J Psychiatry* 128:1303–1305.

Deutsch CK, Swanson JM, Bruell JH, Cantwell DP, Weinberg F and Baren M. 1982. Short Communication: Overrepresentation of Adoptees in Children with the Attention Deficit Disorder. *Behavior Genetics* 12:231–238.

Deykin AY and DiMascio A. 1972. Relationship of Patient Background Characteristics to Efficacy of Pharmacotherapy in Depression. *J Nerv and Ment Disorders* 155:209–215.

Dorus E, Cox NJ, Gibbons RD, Shaughnessy R, Pandey GN and Cloninger R. 1983. Lithium Ion Transport and Affective Disorders within Families of Bipolar Patients: Identification of a Major Gene Locus. *Arch Gen Psychiatry* 40:545–552.

Dorus E, Pandey GN and Davis JM. 1974. Genetic Determinant of Lithium Ion Distribution: An In-Vitro Monozygotic-Dizygotic Twin Study. *Arch Gen Psychiatry* 31:463–465.

Dorus E, Pandey GN and Davis JM. 1975. Genetic Determinant of Lithium Ion Distribution: An In-Vitro Monozygotic-Dizygotic Twin Study. *Arch Gen Psychiatry* 32:1097–1102.

Dorus E, Pandey GN, Shaughnessy R, and Davis JM. 1979. Low Platelet Monoamine Oxidase Activity, High Red Blood Cell Lithium Ratio and Affective Disorders: A Multivariate Assessment of Genetic Vulnerability to Affective Disorders. *Biol Psychiatry* 14:989–993.

Dorus E, Pandey GN, Shaughnessy R and Davis JM. 1980. Lithium Transport across the RBC Membrane: A Study of Genetic Factors. *Arch Gen Psychiatry* 37:80–81.

Dorus E, Pandey GN, Shaughnessy R, Gaviria M, Val E, Ericksen S and Davis JM. 1985. Lithium Transport across Red Blood Cell Membrane Abnormality in Manic-Depressive Illness. *Science* 230:753–758.

Drayna D and White R. 1985. The Genetic Linkage Map of the Human X-Chromosome. *Science* 230:753–758.

Dunner DL, Gershon ES and Goodwin FK. 1976. Heritable Factors in the Severity of Affective Illness. *Biol Psychiatry* 11:31–42.

Egeland JA, Gerhard DS, Pauls DL, Sussex JN, Kidd KK, Allen CR, Hostetter AM and Housman DE. 1987. Bipolar Affective Disorders Linked to DNA Markers on Chromosome 11. *Nature* 325:783–787.

Egeland JA and Hostetter AM. 1983. Amish Study: I. Affective Disorders among the Amish. *Am J Psychiatry* 140:56–61.

Egeland JA, Kidd JR, Frazer A, Kidd KK and Neuhauser VI. 1984. Amish Study: V. Lithium-Sodium Countertransport and Catechol O-Methyltransferase in Pedigrees of Bipolar Probands. *Am J Psychiatry* 141:1049–1054.

Ehrlich BE and Diamond JM. 1980. Lithium, Membranes and Manic-Depressive Illness. *J Membrane Biol* 52:187–200.

Elston RC. 1981. Segregation Analysis. In *Advances in Human Genetics*, Harris H and Hirschorn K, Eds. New York: Plenum, 2:63–120.

Elston RC, Kringlen E and Namboodiri KK. 1973. Possible Linkage Relationships between Certain Blood Groups and Schizophrenia or Other Psychoses. *Behavior Genetics* 3:101–106.

Elston RC and Namboodiri KK. 1980. Types of Disease and Models for Their Genetic Analysis. *Schizophrenia Bull* 6:368–374.

Elston RC and Yelverton KC. 1975. General Models for Segregation Analysis. *Am J Hum Genet* 27:31–45.

Emery AEH. 1984. *An Introduction to Recombinant DNA*. New York: Wiley.

Endicott J, Nee J, Andreasen N, Clayton P, Keller M and Coryell W. 1985. Bipolar II: Combine or Keep Separate? *J Affective Disorders* 8:17–28.

Endicott J and Spitzer RL. 1978. A Diagnostic Interview: The Schedule for Affective Disorders and Schizophrenia. *Arch Gen Psychiatry* 35:837–844.

Essen-Moller E. 1963. Twin Research and Psychiatry. *Acta Psychiatr Scand* 39:65–77.

Essen-Moller E and Hagnell O. 1961. The Frequency and Risk of Depression within a Rural Population Group in Scandinavia. *Acta Psychiatr Scand* Suppl., 162:28–32.

Everitt GA and Kendall R. 1971. An Attempt at Validation of Traditional Psychiatric Syndromes by Cluster Analysis. *Brit J Psychiat* 119:399–412.

Fahndrich E. 1983. Clinical and Biological Parameters as Predictors for Antidepressant Drug Responses in Depressed Patients. *Pharmacopsychiat* 16:179–185.

Falconer DS. 1965. The Inheritance of Liability to Certain Diseases Estimated from the Incidence among Relatives. *Annals of Hum Genetics* 29:51–76.

Faraone SV, Lyons MJ, Pepple J and Tsuang MT. 1988. Twin Studies of Affective Disorders. Manuscript.

Faraone SV, Lyons MJ and Tsuang MT. 1987. Sex Differences in Affective Disorder: Genetic Transmission. *Genetic Epidemiology* 4:331–343.

Faraone SV and Tsuang MT. In Press. The Genetics of Affective Disorders: An Overview. In *Hereditary Aspects of Neurological and Psychiatric Disorders,* Abuelo D, Ed. New York: Ware.

Farber SL. 1981. *Identical Twins Reared Apart: A Reanalysis.* New York: Basic Books.

Feder J, Gurling HMD, Darby J and Cavalli-Sforza LL. 1985. DNA Restriction Fragment Analysis of the Propiomelanocortin Gene in Schizophrenia and Bipolar Disorders. *Am J Hum Genet* 37:286–294.

Feighner JP, Robins E, Guze SB, Woodruff RA, Winokur G, Munzo R. 1972. Diagnostic Criteria for Use in Psychiatric Research. *Arch Gen Psychiatry* 26:57–73.

Feinberg M and Carroll BJ. 1982. Separation of Subtypes of Depression Using Discriminant Analysis: I. Separation of Unipolar Endogenous Depression from Non-Endogenous Depression. *Brit J Psychiat* 140:384–391.

Feinberg M and Carroll BJ. 1983. Separation of Subtypes of Depression Using Discriminant Analysis: Separation of Bipolar Endogenous Depression from Nonendogenous ("Neurotic") Depression. *J Affect Disorders* 5:129–139.

Fieve RR, Mendlewicz J and Fleiss JL. 1973. Manic-Depressive Illness: Linkage with the Xg Blood Group. *Am J Psychiatry* 130:1355–1359.

Fieve RR, Mendlewicz J, Rainer and Fleiss JL. 1975. A Dominant X-Linked Factor in Manic-Depressive Illness: Studies with Color Blindness. In *Genetic Research in Psychiatry,* Fieve RR, Rosenthal D and Brill H, Eds. Baltimore: Johns Hopkins, 241–255.

Flemenbaum A and Larson JW. 1976. ABO-RH Blood Groups and Psychiatric Diagnosis: A Critical Review. *Dis Nerv Syst* 37:581.

Fletcher JC. 1984. Ethical and Social Aspects of Risk Predictions. *Clinical Genetic* 25:25–31.

Floderus-Myrhed B, Pedersen N and Rasmusson I. 1980. Assessment of Heritability for Personality, Based on a Short Form of the Eysenck Personality Inventory: A Study of 12,898 Twin Pairs. *Behavior Genetics* 10(2):153–162.

Fowles DC and Gersh F. 1979. Neurotic Depression: The Endogenous-Neurotic Distinction. In *The Psychobiology of the Depressive Disorders: Implications for the Effect of Stress*, Depue RA, Ed. New York: Academic Press, 55–80.

Frances A, Brown RE and Cocsis JH, et al. 1981. Psychotic Depression: A Separate Entity? *Am J Psychiatry* 138:831–833.

Frances RJ, Bucky S and Alexopoulos GS. 1984. Outcome Study of Familial and Nonfamilial Alcoholism. *Am J Psychiatry* 141:1469–1471.

Frangos E, Athanassenas G, and Tsitourides S et al. 1983. Psychotic Depressive Disorder: A Separate Entity. *J Affect Disorders* 5:259–265.

Freedman DX. 1984. Psychiatric Epidemiology Counts. *Arch Gen Psychiatry* 41:931–933.

Fremming GH. 1951. *The Expectation of Mental Infirmity in a Sample of the Danish Population*. London: Cassell.

Fremming K. 1947. *Morbid Risk of Mental Diseases and Other Abnormal Psychic States among Average Danish Population*. Copenhagen: Munksgaard.

Gaffney GR, Lurie SF and Berlin FS. 1984. Is There Familial Transmission of Pedophilia? *J Nerv and Mental Disease* 172:546–548.

Garfinkel PE, Moldofsky H and Garner DM. 1980. The Heterogeneity of Anorexia Nervosa. *Arch Gen Psychiatry* 37:1036–1040.

Garvey MJ, Tuason VB, and Johnson RA et al. 1982. RDC Depressive Subtypes: Are They Valid? *J Clin Psychiatry* 43:442–444.

Gerner RH and Gwirtsman HE. 1981. Abnormalities of Dexamethasone Suppression Test and Urinary MHPG in Anorexia Nervosa. *Am J Psychiatry* 138:650–653.

Gersh FS and Fowles DC. 1979. Neurotic Depression: The Concept of Anxious Depression. In *The Depressive Disorders: Implications for the Effects of Stress*, Depue RA, Ed. New York: Academic Press, 81–104.

Gershon ES. 1983. Genetics of the Major Psychoses. In *Genetics of Neurological and Psychiatric Disorders,* Kety SS, Rowland LP, Sidman RL and Matthysse SW. New York: Raven Press, 121–144.

Gershon ES, Baron M and Leckman JF. 1975. Genetic Models of the Transmission of Affective Disorders. *J Psychiat Res* 12:301–317.

Gershon ES and Buchsbaum M. 1977. A Genetic Study of Average Evoked Response Augmentation/Reduction in Affective Disorders. In *Psychopathology and Brain Dysfunction*, Shagass C, Gershon ES and Friedhoff AJ, Eds. New York: Raven Press, 279–290.

Gershon ES and Bunney WE, Jr. 1976. The Question of X-Linkage in Bipolar Manic-Depressive Illness. *J Psychiat Res* 13:99–117.

Gershon ES, Bunney WE, Jr., Leckman JF, Van Eerdewegh M and DeBauche BA. 1976. The Inheritance of Affective Disorders: A Review of Data and of Hypotheses. *Behavior Genetics* 6:227–261.

Gershon ES, Dunner DL, Sturt L and Goodwin FK. 1973. Assortative Mating in the Affective Disorder. *Biol Psychiatry* 7:63–74.

Gershon ES and Goldin LR. 1986. Clinical Methods in Psychiatric Genetics: I. Robustness of Genetic Marker Investigative Strategies. *Acta Psychiatr Scand* 74:113–118.

Gershon ES, Goldin LR, Lake CR, Murphy DL and Guroff JJ. 1980a. Genetics of Plasma Dopamine-B-Hydorxylase (DBH), Erythrocyte Catechol-O-Methyltransferase (COMT), and Platelet Monoamine Oxidase (MAO) in Pedigrees of Patients with Affective Disorders. In *Enzymes and Neurotransmitters in Mental Disease,* Usdin E, Sourkes L and Young MBH, Eds. New York: Wiley, 281–299.

Gershon ES and Guroff JJ. 1984. Information from Relatives: Diagnosis of Affective Disorders. *Arch Gen Psychiatry* 41:173–179.

Gershon ES, Hamovit J, Guroff JJ, Dibble E, Leckman JF, Sceery W, Targum SD, Nurnberger JI, Jr., Goldin LR and Bunney WE, Jr. 1982. A Family Study of Schizoaffective Bipolar I, Bipolar II, Unipolar and Normal Control Probands. *Arch Gen Psychiatry* 39:1157–1167.

Gershon ES, Hamovit JH, Guroff JJ and Nurnberger JI. 1987. Birth-Cohort Changes in Manic and Depressive Disorders in Relatives of Bipolar and Schizoaffective Patients. *Arch Gen Psychiatry* 44:314–319.

Gershon ES and Jonas WZ. 1975. Erythrocyte Soluble Catechol-O-Methyl Transferase Activity in Primary Affective Disorder: A Clinical and Genetic Study. *Arch Gen Psychiatry* 32:1351–1356.

Gershon ES, Mark A, Cohen N, Belizon N, Baron M and Knobe KE. 1975. Transmitted Factors in the Morbid Risk of Affective Disorders: A Controlled Study. *J Psychiat Res* 12:283–299.

Gershon ES, Mendlewicz J, Gastpar M, Bech P, Goldin LR, Kielholz P, Rafaelsen OJ, Vartanian F and Bunney WE, Jr. 1980b. A Collaborative Study of Genetic Linkage of Bipolar Manic-Depressive Illness and Red/Green Colorblindness. *Acta Psychiat Scand* 61:319–338.

Gershon ES, Schreiber JL, Hamovit JR, Dibble ED, Kaye W, Nurnberger JI, Jr., Andersen AE and Ebert M. 1984. Clinical Findings in Patients with Anorexia Nervosa and Affective Illness in Their Relatives. *Am J Psychiatry* 141:1419–1422.

Gershon ES, Targum SD, Matthysse S and Bunney WE, Jr. 1979. Color Blindness Not Closely Linked to Bipolar Illness: Report of a New Pedigree Series. *Arch Gen Psychiatry* 36:1423–1430.

Gillin J, Sitaram N, Wehr T, Duncan W, Post R, Murphy DL, Mendelson WB, Wyatt RJ and Bunney WE, Jr. 1984. Sleep and Affective Illness. In *Neurobiology of Mood Disorders,* Post RM and Ballenger JC, Eds. Baltimore: Williams & Wilkins.

Glassman AH, Kantor SJ and Shostak M. 1975. Depression, Delusions and Drug Response. *Am J Psychiatry* 132:716–718.

Glassman AH, Perel JM, Shostak M, Kantor SJ and Fleiss JL. 1977. Clinical Implications of Imipramine Plasma Levels for Depressive Illness. *Arch Gen Psychiatry* 34:197–204.

Glassman AH and Roose SP. 1981. Delusional Depression. *Arch Gen Psychiatry* 38:424–427.

Goetzl U, Green R, Whybrow P and Jackson R. 1974. X-Linkage Revisited: A Further Family Study of Manic Depressive Illness. *Arch Gen Psychiatry* 31:665.

Goldin LR. 1985. Segregation Analysis of Dopamine-Beta-Hydroxylase (DBH) and Catechol-O-Methyltransferase (COMT): Identification of Major Locus and Polygenic Components. *Genetic Epidemiology* 2:317–325.

Goldin LR, Clergex-Darpoux F and Gershon ES. 1982. Relationship of HLA to Major Affective Disorder Not Supported. *Psychiatry Research* 7:29–45.

Goldin LR and Gershon ES. 1983. Association and Linkage Studies of Genetic Marker Loci in Major Psychiatric Disorders. *Psychiatric Developments* 4:387–418.

Goldin LR, Gershon ES, Lake CR, Murphy DL, McGinniss M, and Sparkes RS. 1982. Segregation and Linkage Studies of Plasma Dopamine-Beta-Hydroxylase (DBH), Erythrocyte Catechol-O-Methyltransferase (COMT), and Platelet Monoamine Oxidase (MAO): Possible Linkage between the ABO Locus and a Gene Controlling DBH Activity. *Am J Hum Genet* 34:250–262.

Goldin LR, Gershon ES, Targum SD, Sparkes RS and McGinniss M. 1983. Segregation and Linkage Analyses in Families of Patients with Bipolar, Unipolar, and Schizoaffective Mood Disorders. *Am J Genetics* 35:274–287.

Goldin LR, Nurnberger JI, Jr., and Gershon ES. 1986. Clinical Methods in Psychiatric Genetics: II. The High Risk Approach. *Acta Psychiatr Scand* 74:119–128.

Goodwin FK, Murphy DL and Bunney WE, Jr. 1969. Lithium-Carbonate Treatment in Depression and Mania. *Arch Gen Psychiatry* 21:486–496.

Goodwin FK, Murphy DL and Dunner DL and Bunney WE, Jr. 1972. Lithium Response in Unipolar versus Bipolar Depression. *Am J Psychiatry* 129:44–47.

Gottesman II. 1963. Heritability of Personality: A Demonstration. *Psychol Monogr* 77:whole no. 572.

Gottesman II. 1965. Personality and Natural Selection. In *Methods and Goals in Human-Behavior Genetics,* Vandenberg SG, Ed. New York: Academic Press, 253–296.

Govaerts A, Mendlewicz J and Verbanck P. 1977. Manic-Depressive Illness and HLA. In *Tissue Antigens.* Copenhagen: Munksgaard, 19:60–62.

Greenberg DB and Brown GL. 1985. Single Case Study: Mania Resulting from Brain Stem Tumor. *J Nerv and Mental Disease* 173:434–436.

Growe G, Crayton J, Klass D, Evans H and Struzich M. 1979. Lithium in Chronic Schizophrenia. *Am J Psychiatry* 136:454–455.

Gurling H. 1985. Application of Molecular Biology to Mental Illness: Analysis of Genomic DNA and Brain mRNA. *Psychiatric Developments* 3:257–273.

Gusella JF. 1986. DNA Polymorphism and Human Disease. *Ann Rev Biochem* 55:831–854.

Guze SB, Woodruff RA and Clayton PJ. 1971. Secondary Affective Disorder: A Study of 95 Cases. *Psychol Med* 1:426–428.

Guze SB, Woodruff RA and Clayton PJ. 1975. The Significance of Psychotic Affective Disorders. *Arch Gen Psychiatry* 32:1147–1150.

Gwirtsman HE and Gerner RH. 1981. Neurochemical Abnormalities in Anorexia Nervosa: Similarities to Affective Disorders. *Biological Psychiatry* 16:991–995.

Hagnell O and Kreitman N. 1974. Mental Illness in Married Pairs in a Total Population. *Brit J Psychiat* 125:293–302.

Hagnell O, Lanke J, Rorsman B and Ojesio L. 1982. Are We Entering an Age of Melancholy? Depressive Illnesses in a Prospective Epidemiological Study over 25 Years: Lundby Study. *Psychological Medicine* 12:122–129.

Hall RL, Hesselbrock VM and Stabenau JR. 1983. Familial Distribution of Alcohol Use: I. Assortative Mating in the Parents of Alcoholics. *Behavior Genetics* 13:361–383.

Hare E. 1981. The Two Manias: A Study of the Evolution of the Modern Concept of Mania. *Brit J Psychiat* 138:89–99.

Harris EL, Noyes R Jr., Crowe RR and Chaudhry DR. 1983. Family Study of Agoraphobia: Report of a Pilot Study. *Arch Gen Psychiatry* 40:1061–1064.

Harvald B and Hauge M. 1965. Hereditary Factors Elucidated by Twin Studies. In *Genetics and the Epidemiology of Chronic Diseases*, Neel JV, Ed. Public Health Services Publication 1163. Washington, D.C.: U.S. Government Printing Office, 61–75.

Hedlund JL and Vieweg BG. 1981. Structured Psychiatric Interviews: A Comparative Review. *J Operational Psychiatry* 12:40–67.

Helgason T. 1961. Frequency of Depressive States within Geographically Delimited Population Groups: The Frequency of Depressive States in Iceland as Compared with the Other Scandinavian Countries. *Acta Psychiatr Scand* Suppl., 162:81–90.

Helgason T. 1979. Epidemiological Investigations concerning Affective Disorders. In *Origin Prevention and Treatment of Affective Disorders*, Schou M and Stromgren E, Eds. New York: Academic Press.

Helzer JE. 1975. Bipolar Affective Disorder in Black and White Men. *Arch Gen Psychiatry* 32:1140.

Helzer JE and Winokur G. 1974. A Family Interview Study of Male Manic Depressives. *Arch Gen Psychiatry* 31:73–76.

Hoffmann WF. 1987. Identical Twins' Nonidentical Responses to Lithium. *Am J Psychiatry* 144:1240–1241.

Holzinger KJ. 1929. The relative effect of nature and nurture on twin differences. *J Educ Psych* 20:241–248.

Hope K. 1969. Review of *The Classification of Depressive Illness* by R. E. Kendell. *Brit J Psychiatry* 115:731–741.

Hopkinson G. 1964. A Genetic Study of Affective Illness in Patients over 50. *Brit J Psychiatry* 110:244–254.

Hopkinson G and Ley P. 1969. A Genetic Study of Affective Disorder. *Brit J Psychiatry* 115:917–922.

Howard Hughes Medical Institute. 1988. New Haven Gene Mapping Library Chromosome Plots (no. 4). New Haven: HHMI.

Howarth BG and Grace MGA. 1985. Depression, Drugs, and Delusions. *Arch Gen Psychiatry* 42:1145–1147.

Hudson JI, Hudson MS, Pliner LF, Goldenberg DL and Pope HG, Jr. 1985. Fibromyalgia and Major Affective Disorder: A Controlled Phenomenology and Family History Study. *Am J Psychiatry* 142:441–446.

Hudson JI, Laffer PS and Pope HG, Jr. 1982. Bulimia Related to Affective Disorder by Family History and Response to the Dexamethasone Suppression Test. *Am J Psychiatry* 139:685–687.

Hudson JI, Pope HG, Jr., Jonas JM and Yurgelun-Todd D. 1983. Family History Study of Anorexia Nervosa and Bulimia. *Brit J Psychiat* 142:133–138.

Hudson JI, Pope HG, Jr., Jonas JM and Yurgelun-Todd D. 1986. Phenomenologic Relationship of Eating Disorders to Major Affective Disorder. *Psychiatry Research* 9:345–354.

Humm DG. 1932. Mental Disorders in Siblings. *Am J Psychiatry* 89:239–284.

Irvine DG and Miyashita H. 1965. Blood Groups in Relation to Depressions and Schizophrenia. *Can Med Assoc J* 92:551.

Jakimow-Venulet B. 1981. Hereditary Factors in the Pathogenesis of Affective Disorder. *Am J Psychiatry* 139:450–456.

James NM. 1977. Early- and Late-Onset Bipolar Affective Disorder: A Genetic Study. *Arch Gen Psychiatry* 34:715–717.

James NM, Carroll BJ, Haines RF and Smouse PE. 1979. Genetic Markers in Affective Disorders: ABO and HLA. In *Genetic Aspects of Affective Disorders,* Mendlewicz J and Shopsin B, Eds. New York: SP Medical Spectrum Publications, 35–44.

James NM and Chapman CJ. 1975. A Genetic Study of Bipolar Affective Disorder. *Am J Psychiatry* 126:449–456.

James NM, Smouse PE, Carroll BJ and Haines RF. 1980. Affective Illness and HLA Frequencies: No Compelling Association. *Neuropsychobiology* 6:208–216.

Jamieson RC and Wells CE. 1979. Manic Psychosis in a Patient with Multiple Metastatic Brain Tumors. *J Clin Psychiatry* 40:280–282.

Jardine R, Martin NG and Henderson AS. 1984. Genetic Covariation between Neuroticism and the Symptoms of Anxiety and Depression. *Genetic Epidemiology* 1:89–107.

Joffe RT, Horvath Z and Tarvydas I. 1986. Bipolar Affective Disorder and Thalassemia Minor. *Am J Psychiatry* 143:933.

Johnson GFS. 1978. HLA Antigens and Manic-Depressive Disorders. *Biol Psychiatry* 13:409–412.

Johnson GFS, Hunt GE, Robertson S and Doran TJ. 1981. A Linkage Study of Manic-Depressive Disorders with HLA Antigens, Blood Groups, Serum Proteins, and Red Cell Enzymes. *J Affective Disorder* 3:43–58.

Johnson GFS and Leeman MM. 1977. Analysis of Familial Factors in Bipolar Affective Illness. *Arch Gen Psychiatry* 34:1074–1083.

Jorgensen P. 1985. Manic-Depressive Patients with Delusions: Clinical and Diagnostic Course. *Acta Psychiatr Scand* 72:364–368.

Joyce PR. 1984. Age of Onset in Bipolar Affective Disorder and Misdiagnosis as Schizophrenia. *Psychological Medicine* 14:145–149.

Juel-Nielsen N. 1965. *Individual and Environment: A Psychiatric-Psychological Investigation of Monozygotic Twins Reared Apart.* Copenhagen: Munksgaard.

Juel-Nielsen N and Videbech T. 1970. A Twin Study of Suicide. *Acta Genet Med Gemellol* 19:307–310.

Kallmann FJ. 1953. *Heredity in Health and Mental Disorder.* New York: Norton.

Kallmann FJ. 1954. Genetic Principles in Manic-Depressive Psychosis. In *Depression,* Hoch PH and Zubin J, Eds. New York: Grune and Stratton.

Kasriel J and Eaves L. 1976. The Zygosity of Twins: Further Evidence on the Agreement between Diagnosis by Blood Groups and Written Questionnaires. *J Biosocial Science* 8:263–266.

Kathol RG and Petty F. 1981. Relationship of Depression to Medical Illness: A Critical Review. *J Affect Disorder* 3:111–121.

Kay DWK. 1978. Assessment of Familial Risks in the Functional Psychoses and Their Application in Genetic Counselling. *Brit J Psychiat* 133:385–403.

Kelsoe JR, Ginns EE, Egeland JA, Gerhard DS, Goldstein AM, Bale SJ, Pauls DL, Long RT, Kidd KK, Conte G, Housman DE and Paul S. 1989. Re-evaluation of the Linkage Relationship between Chromosome 11p Loci and the Gene for Bipolar Affective Disorder in the Old Order Amish. *Nature* 342:16, 238–243.

Kendall R and Gourlay J. 1970. The Clinical Distinction between the Affective Psychoses and Schizophrenia. *Brit J Psychiatry* 117:261–266.

Kendell RE and Brockington IF. 1980. The Identification of Disease Entities and the Relationship between Schizophrenic and Affective Psychoses. *Brit J Psychiat* 137:324–31.

Kendler KS. 1983. Overview: A Current Perspective on Twin Studies of Schizophrenia. *Am J Psychiatry* 140:1413–1425.

Kendler KS, Gruenberg AM and Tsuang MT. 1986. A DSM-III Family Study of the Nonschizophrenic Psychotic Disorders. *Am J Psychiatry* 143:1098–1105.

Kendler KS, Heath A, Martin NG and Eaves LJ. 1986. Symptoms of Anxiety and Depression in a Volunteer Twin Population: The Etiologic Role of Genetic and Environmental Factors. *Arch Gen Psychiatry* 43:213–221.

Kendler KS, Heath AC, Martin NG and Eaves LJ. 1987. Symptoms of Anxiety and Symptoms of Depression: Same Genes, Different Environments? *Arch Gen Psychiatry* 44:451–457.

Kendler KS and Tsuang MT. 1982. Identical Twins Concordant for the Progression of Affective Illness to Schizophrenia. *Brit J Psychiat* 141:563–566.

Kety S. 1979. Disorders of the Human Brain. *Sci Am* (Sept. 8), 202–214.

Kety SS, Rosenthal D, Wender PH, Schulsinger F and Jacobson B. 1975. Mental Illness in the Biological and Adoptive Families of Adopted Individuals Who Have Become Schizophrenic: A Preliminary Report Based on Psychiatric Interviews. In *Genetic Research in Psychiatry,* Fieve RR, Rosenthal D and Brill H, Eds. Baltimore: Johns Hopkins, 1975, 147–165.

Kety SS, Rosenthal D, Wender PH, Schulsinger F and Jacobson B. 1978. The Biological and Adoptive Families of Adopted Individuals Who Become Schizophrenic: Prevalence of Mental Illness and Other Characteristics. In *The Nature of Schizophrenia: New Approaches to Research and Treatment,* Wynne LC, Cromwell RL and Matthysse S, Eds. New York: Wiley, 25–37.

Kidd KK. 1981. Genetic Models for Psychiatric Disorders. In *Genetic Research Strategies for Psychobiology and Psychiatry,* Gershon ES, Matthysse S, Breakefield XO and Ciaranello RD, Eds. New York: Boxwood, 369–382.

Kidd KK. 1985. New Genetic Strategies for Studying Psychiatric Disorders. In *Genetic Aspects of Human Behavior,* Sakai T and Tsuboi T, Eds. New York: Igaku-Shoin, 235–246.

Kidd KK and Cavalli-Sforza LL. 1973. An Analysis of the Genetics of Schizophrenia. *Social Biology* 20:254–265.

Kidd KK, Egeland JA, Molthan L, Pauls DL, Kruger SD and Messner KH. 1984a. Amish Study: IV. Genetic Linkage Study of Pedigrees of Bipolar Probands. *Am J Psychiatry* 141:1042–1048.

Kidd KK, Gerhard DS, Kidd JR, Houseman D and Egeland JA. 1984b. Recombinant DNA Methods in Genetic Studies of Affective Disorders. *Clinical Neuropharmacology* 7:198–199.

Klein DF. 1974. Endogenomorphic Depression: A Conceptual and Terminological Revision. *Arch Gen Psychiatry* 31:477–454.

Klerman GL. 1976. Age and Clinical Depression: Today's Youth in the Twenty-First Century. *J Geront* 31:318–323.

Klerman GL. 1981. The Spectrum of Mania. *Comprehensive Psychiatry* 22:11–20.

Klerman GL, Lavori PW, Rice J, Reich T, Endicott J, Andreasen NC, Keller MB and Hirschfield RMA. 1985. Birth-Cohort Trends in Rates of Major Depressive Disorder among Relatives of Patients with Affective Disorder. *Arch Gen Psychiatry* 42:689–693.

Knott V, Waters B, Lapierre Y and Gray R. 1985. Neurophysiological Correlates of Sibling Pairs Discordant for Bipolar Affective Disorder. *Am J Psychiatry* 1442:248–250.

Koch HL. 1966. *Twins and Twin Relations*. Chicago: University of Chicago Press.

Kringlen E. 1967. *Heredity and Environment in the Functional Psychoses*. Oslo: Universitetsforlaget, 1:27–47.

Krauthammer C and Klerman GL. 1978. Secondary Mania: Manic Syndromes Associated with Antecedent Physical Illness or Drugs. *Arch Gen Psychiatry* 35:1333–1339.

Kruger SD, Turner WS and Kidd KK. 1982. The Effects of Requisite Assumptions of Linkage Analysis of Manic-Depressive Illness with HLA. *Biological Psychiatry* 17:1081–1099.

Kupfer DJ, Himmelhoch JM, Swartzburg M, Anderson C, Byck R and Detre TP. 1972. Hypersomnia in Manic-Depressive Disease. *Disorders of the Nervous System* 33:720–724.

Kupfer DJ, Pickar D, Himmelhoch JM and Detre TP. 1975. Are There Two Types of Unipolar Depression? *Arch Gen Psychiatry* 32:866–870.

Kupfer DJ, Targ E and Stack J. 1982. Electroencephalographic Sleep in Unipolar Depressives Subtypes: Support for a Biological and Familial Classification. *J Nerv and Mental Disease* 170:494–498.

Kupfer DJ, Weiss BL, Foster G, Detre TP, Delgado J and McPhartland R. 1974. Psychomotor Activity in Affective States. *Arch Gen Psychiatry* 30:765–786.

Lake CR, Tenglin R, Chernow B and Holoway HC. 1983. Psychomotor Stimulant-Induced Mania in a Genetically Predisposed Patient: A Review of the Literature and Report of a Case. *J Clinical Psychopharmacology* 3:97–100.

Larson I and Sjogren T. 1954. A Methodological, Psychiatric and Statistical Study of a Large Swedish Rural Population. *Acta Psychiat Neurol Scand* 89:40–54.

Lathrop GM, Huntsman JW, Hooper AB and Ward RH. 1983. Evaluating Pedigree Data: II. Identifying the Case of Error in Families with Inconsistencies. *Hum Hered* 33:377–389.

Lavori PW, Keller MB and Roth SL. 1984. Affective Disorders and ABO Blood Groups: New Data and a Reanalysis of the Literature Using the Logistic Transformation of Proportions. *J Psychiat Res* 18:119–129.

Lavori PW, Klerman GL, Keller MB, Reich T, Rice J and Endicott J. 1986. Age-Period-Cohort Analysis of Secular Trends in Onset of Major Depression: Findings in Siblings of Patients with Major Affective Disorder. *J Psychiat Res* 21:23–35.

Leckman JF, Caruso KA, Prusoff BA, Weissman MM, Merikangas KR and Pauls DL. 1984a. Appetite Disturbance and Excessive Guilt in Major Depression: Use of Family Study Data to Define Depressive Subtypes. *Arch Gen Psychiatry* 41:839–844.

Leckman JF and Gershon ES. 1977. Autosomal Models of Sex Effect in Bipolar-Related Major Affective Illness. *J Psychiat Res* 13:237–246.

Leckman JF, Gershon ES, McGinniss MH, Targum SD and Dibble ED. 1979. New Data Do Not Suggest Linkage between the Xg Blood

Group and Bipolar Illness. *Arch Gen Psychiatry* 36:1435–1441.

Leckman JF, Gershon ES, Nichols AS and Murphy DL. 1977. Reduced MAO Activity in First-Degree Relatives of Individuals with Bipolar Affective Disorders: A Preliminary Report. *Arch Gen Psychiatry* 34:601–606.

Leckman JF, Merikangas KR, Pauls DL, Prusoff BA and Weissman MM. 1983a. Anxiety Disorders and Depression: Contradictions between Family Study Data and DSM-III Conventions. *Am J Psychiatry* 140:880–882.

Leckman JF, Sholomska D, Thompsom WD, Belanger A, Weissman MM. 1982. Best Estimate of Lifetime Psychiatric Diagnosis: A Methodological Study. *Arch Gen Psychiatry* 39:879–883.

Leckman JF, Weissman MM, Merikangas KR, Pauls DL and Prusoff BA. 1983b. Panic Disorder and Major Depression: Increased Risk of Depression, Alcoholism, Panic, and Phobic Disorders in Families of Depressed Probands with Panic Disorder. *Arch Gen Psychiatry* 40:1055–1060.

Leckman JF, Weissman MM, Prusoff BA, Caruso KA, Merikangas KR, Pauls DL and Kidd KK. 1984b. Subtypes of Depression: A Family Study Perspective. *Arch Gen Psychiatry* 41:833–838.

Levitt JJ and Tsuang MT. 1988. The Heterogeneity of Schizoaffective Disorder: Implications for Treatment. *Am J Psychiatry* 145:926–936.

Levitt M and Mendlewicz J. 1975. A Genetic Study of Plasma Dopamine B-Hydroxylase in Affective Disorder. *Mod Prob Pharmacopsych* 10:89–90.

Lewis A. 1933. Inheritance of Mental Disorders. An Address to the Society at the Annual General Meeting. *Eugenics Reviews* 25:79–84.

Lewis DA and McChesney C. 1985. Tritiated Imipramine binding Distinguishes among Subtypes of Depression. *Arch Gen Psychiatry* 42:485–488.

Liebowitz MR, Klein DF, Quitkin FM, Stewart JW and McGrath PJ. 1984. Clinical Implications of Diagnostic Subtypes of Depression. In *Neurobiology of Mood Disorders*, Post RM and Ballenger JC, Eds. Baltimore: Williams & Wilkins.

Loehlin JC. 1973. *Personality: The Genes and What Environment?* Paper presented at the Prospects in Behavior Genetics Conference, University of Texas, 15–17.

Loehlin JC, Horn JM and Willerman L. 1981. Personality Resemblance in Adoptive Families. *Behavior Genetics* 11:309–330.

Loehlin JC and Nichols RC. 1976. *Heredity, Environment, and Personality: A Study of 850 Sets of Twins.* Austin and London: University of Texas Press.

Loranger AW and Tulis EH. 1985. Family History of Alcoholism in Borderline Personality Disorder. *Arch Gen Psychiatry* 42:153–157.

Lowry M, Van Valkenburg C, Winokur G and Cadoret R. 1978. Baseline Characteristics of Pure Depressive Disease. *Neuropsychobiology* 4:333–343.

Luxenberger H. 1928. Vorlaufiger bericht uber psychiatrische serinumter-suchungen an zwillinger. *Zeitschrift fur die gesamte Neurologie and Psychiatrie* 116:297–326.

Luxenberger H. 1930. Psychiatrisch-neurologisch zwillingspathologie. *Zentralblat fur die gesamte Neurologie and Psychiatrie* 56:145–180.

Lyttkens L, Soderberg U and Wetterberg L. 1973. Increased Lithium Erythrocyte-Plasma Ratio in Manic-Depressive Psychosis. *Lancet* 1:40.

Maj M and Perris. 1985. An Approach to the Diagnosis and Classification of Schizoaffective Disorders for Research Purposes. *Acta Psychiatr Scand* 72:405–413.

Maj M, Reese M, Minucci P, Guida L, Pirozzi R and Salvati A. 1983. HLA Antigens in Patients with Major Affective Disorders. *Clinica Psichiatrica* 5:198–204.

Majsky A, Zvolsky P and Dvorakova M. 1978. Primary Affective Disorders and HLA Antigens. *Tissue Antigens* 11:190–191.

Manshadi M, Lippmann S, Daniel R and Blackman A. 1983. Alcohol Abuse and Attention Deficit Disorder. *J Clin Psychiatry* 44:379–380.

Marks IM. 1986. Genetics of Fear and Anxiety Disorders. *Brit J Psychiatry* 149:406–418.

Marneros A and Tsuang MT. 1986. *Schizoaffective Psychoses*. Berlin: Springer-Verlag.

Marten SA, Cadoret RJ, Winokur G and Ora E. 1972. Unipolar Depression: A Family History Study. *Biological Psychiatry* 4(3):205–213.

Martin NG and Wilson SR. 1982. Bias in the Estimation of Heritability from Truncated Samples of Twins. *Behavior Genetics* 12:467–472.

Masters A. 1967. The Distribution of Blood Groups in Psychiatric Illness. *Brit J Psychiatry* 113:1309.

Matheny AP, Jr., Wilson SR and Dolan AB. 1976. Relations between Twins Similarity of Appearance and Behavioral Similarity: Testing an Assumption. *Behavior Genetics* 6:343–351.

Mathsuyana SS and Joseph J. 1984. Haptoglobin Types and Unipolar Depression. *Hum Hered* 34:65–68.

Matthysse S. 1985. Genetic Latent Structure Analysis. In *Genetic Aspects of Human Behavior*, Sakai T and Tsuboi T, Eds. Tokyo: Igaku-Shoin.

Matthysse SW and Kidd KK. 1976. Estimating and Genetic Contribution to Schizophrenia. *Am J Psychiatry* 133:185–191.

Matthysse SW and Kidd KK. 1981. Evidence of HLA Linkage in Depressive Disorders. *New England J Medicine* 305:1340–1341.

Maubach M, Diebold K, Fried W and Propping P. 1981. Platelet MAO Activity in Patients with Affective Psychosis and Their First-Degree Relatives. *Pharmacopsychiat* 14:87–93.

Mazure C and Gershon ES. 1979 Blindness and Reliability in Lifetime Psychiatric Diagnosis. *Arch Gen Psychiatry* 36:521–525.

McDonald-Scott P and Endicott J. 1984. Informed versus Blind: The Reliability of Cross-Sectional Ratings of Psychopathology. *Psychiat Res* 12:207–217.

McGlashan T and Carpenter W. 1976a. An Investigation of the Postpsychotic Depressive Syndrome. *Am J Psychiatry* 133:14–19.

McGlashan T and Carpenter W. 1976b. Postpsychotic Depression in Schizoenia. *Arch Gen Psychiatry* 33:231–239.

McGuffin P, Katz R and Bebbington P. 1987. Hazard, Heredity and Depression: A Family Study. *J Psychiat Res* 21:365–375.

McKusick V. 1986. *Mendelian Inheritance in Man,* 7th Ed. Baltimore: Johns Hopkins.

Meehl PE. 1962. Schizotaxia, Schizotypy, Schizophrenia. *Am Psychologist* 17:827–838.

Meehl PE. 1973. *Psychodiagnosis Selected Papers.* New York: Norton.

Meltzer HY, Cho HW and Carroll BJ. 1976. Serum Dopamine-B-Hydroxylase Activity in the Affective Psychoses and Schizophrenia. *Arch Gen Psychiatry* 33:585.

Mendels J. 1976. Lithium in the Treatment of Depression. *Am J Psychiatry* 133:373–378.

Mendels J and Cochrane C. 1968. The Nosology of Depression: The Endogenous-Reactive Concept. *Am J Psychiatry* 124:1–11.

Mendels J and Frazer A. 1973. Intracellular Lithium Concentration and Clinical Response: Towards a Membrane Theory of Depression. *Am J Psychiatry* 10:9–18.

Mendlewicz J. 1979. Perspectives and Practical Applications of Psychopharmacogenetics. *Prog Neuropsychopharmacol* 3:155–163.

Mendlewicz J and Baron M. 1981. Morbidity Risks in Subtypes of Unipolar Depressive Illness: Differences between Early and Late Onset Forms. *Brit J Psychiatry* 139:463–466.

Mendlewicz J, Fieve RR, Rainer JD and Cataldo M. 1973. Affective Disorder on Paternal and Maternal Sides: Observations in Bipolar (Manic-Depressive) Patients with and without a Family History. *Brit J Psychiat* 122:31–34.

Mendlewicz J, Fieve RR and Stallone F. 1973. Relationship between the Effectiveness of Lithium Therapy and Family History. *Am J Psychiatry* 130:1011–1013.

Mendlewicz J, Fieve RR, Stallone F and Fleiss JL. 1972. Genetic History as a Predictor of Lithium Response in Manic-Depressive Illness. *Lancet* 599–600.

Mendlewicz J and Fleiss JL. 1974. Linkage Studies with X-Chromosome Markers in Bipolar (Manic-Depressive) and Unipolar (Depressive) Illness. *Biological Psychiatry* 9:261–294.

Mendlewicz J, Fleiss JL, Cataldo M and Rainer JD. 1975. Accuracy of the Family History Method in Affective Illness. *Arch Gen Psychiatry* 32:309–314.

Mendlewicz J, Fleiss JL and Fieve RR. 1972. Evidence for X-Linkage in the Transmission of Manic-Depressive Illness. *JAMA* 222:1624–1627.

Mendlewicz J, Fleiss JL and Fieve RR. 1975. Linkage Studies in Affective Disorders: The Xg Blood Group and Manic-Depressive Illness. In

Genetic Research in Psychiatry, Fieve RR, Rosenthal K and Brill H, Eds. Baltimore: Johns Hopkins, 221–232.

Mendlewicz J, Linkowski P, Guroff JJ and Van Praag HM. 1979. Color Blindness Linkage to Bipolar Manic-Depressive Illness: New Evidence. *Arch Gen Psychiatry* 36:1442–1447.

Mendlewicz J, Linkowski P and Wilmotte J. 1980a. Linkage between Glucose-6-Phosphate Dehydrogenase Deficiency and Manic-Depressive Psychosis. *Brit J Psychiat* 137:337–342.

Mendlewicz J, Linkowski P and Wilmotte J. 1980b. Relationships between Schizoaffective Illness and Affective Disorders or Schizophrenia. *J Affect Disorders* 2:289–302.

Mendlewicz J, Massart-Guiot T, Wilmotte J et al. 1974. Blood Groups in Manic-Depressive Illness and Schizophrenia. *Diseases Nervous System* 35:39.

Mendlewicz J and Rainer JD. 1974. Morbidity Risk and Genetic Transmission in Manic-Depressive Illness. *Am J Hum Genet* 26:692–701.

Mendlewicz J and Rainer JD. 1977. Adoption Study Supporting Genetic Transmission in Manic-Depressive Illness. *Nature* 268:327–329.

Mendlewicz J, Simon P, Sevy S, Charon F, Brocas H, Legros S and Vassart G. 1987. Polymorphic DNA Marker on X Chromosome and Manic Depression. *Lancet* 1230–1231.

Mendlewicz J and Stallone F. 1975. Genetic Factors and Lithium Response in Manic-Depressive Illness. *Genetics and Psycho-Pharmacology of Probl Pharmacopsych* 10:23–29.

Mendlewicz J and Verbanck PMP. 1981. Cell Membrane Anomaly as a Genetic Marker for Manic-Depressive Illness. *Am J Psychiatry* 138:119.

Mendlewicz J, Verbanck P, Linkowski P and Goaverts A. 1981. HLA Antigens in Affective Disorders and Schizophrenia. *J Affect Disorders* 3:17–24.

Mendlewicz J, Verbanck P, Linkowski P and Wilmotte J. 1978. Lithium Accumulation in Erythrocytes of Manic-Depressive Patients: An in Vitro Twin Study. *Brit J Psychiat* 133:436–444.

Merikangas KR. 1984. Divorce and Assortative Mating among Depressed Patients. *Am J Psychiatry* 141:74–76.

Merikangas KR, Bromet EJ and Spiker DG. 1983. Assortative Mating, Social Adjustment, and Course of Illness in Primary Affective Disorder. *Arch Gen Psychiatry* 40:795–800.

Merikangas KR, Leckman JF, Prusoff VA, Pauls DL and Weissman MM. 1985. Familial Transmission of Depression and Alcoholism. *Arch Gen Psychiatry* 42:367–372.

Merikangas KR and Spiker DG. 1982. Assortative Mating among In-Patients with Primary Affective Disorder. *Psychological Medicine* 12:753–764.

Merikangas KR, Weissman MM and Pauls DL. 1985. Genetic Factors in the Sex Ratio of Major Depression. *Psychological Medicine* 15:63–69.

Meyers BS, Kalayam B and Nei-Tal V. 1984. Late-Onset Delusional Depression: A Distinct Clinical Entity? *Clin Psychiatry* 45:347–349.

Mezzich JE, Evanczuk KJ, Mathias RJ and Coffamn GA. 1984. Admission Decisions and Multiaxial Diagnosis. *Arch Gen Psychiatry* 41:1001–1004.

Moran C and Andrews G. 1985. The Familial Occurrence of Agoraphobia. *Brit J Psychiat* 146:262–267.

Morrison J. 1980. Adult Psychiatric Disorders in Parents of Hyperactive Children. *Am J Psychiatry* 137:825–827.

Morrison J and Stewart MA. 1971. A Family Study of the Hyperactive child Syndrome. *Biological Psychiatry* 3:189–195.

Morrison J and Stewart MA. 1973. The Psychiatric Status of the Legal Families of Adopted Hyperactive Children. *Arch Gen Psychiatry* 28:888–891.

Morton NE. 1956. The Detection and Estimation of Linkage between the Genes for Elliptocytosis and the Rh Blood Type. *Am J Hum Genet* 8:80–96.

Morton NE. 1982. *Outline of Genetic Epidemiology*. Basel: S. Karger.

Morton LA, Kidd KK, Matthysse SW and Richards RL. 1979. Recurrence Risks in Schizophrenia: Are They Model Dependent? *Behavior Genetics* 9:389–406.

Morton NE and MacLean CJ. 1974. Analysis of Family Resemblance: III. Complex Segregation Analysis of Quantitative Traits. *Am J Hum Genet* 26:489–503.

Munjack DJ and Moss HB. 1981. Affective Disorder and Alcoholism in Families of Agoraphobics. *Arch Gen Psychiatry* 38:869–871.

Munsinger H and Douglass A II. 1976. The Syntactic Abilities of Identical Twins, Fraternal Twins and Their Siblings. *Child Development* 47:40–50.

Myers JK, Weissman MM, Tischler GL, Holzer CE III, Leaf PJ, Orvaschel H, Anthony JC, Boyd JH, Surke JD, Kramer M and Stoltzman R. 1984. Six-Month Prevalence of Psychiatric Disorders in Three Communities, 1980–1982. *Arch Gen Psychiatry* 41:959–967.

Nadi NS, Nurnberger JI Jr and Gershon ES. 1984. Muscarinic Cholinergic Receptors on Skin Fibroblasts in Familial Affective Disorder. *New England J Medicine* 311:225–230.

Negri F, Melica AM, Zuliani R, Gasperine M, Macciardi F and Smeraldi E. 1981. Genetic Implications in Assortative Mating of Affective Disorders. *Brit J Psychiat* 138:236–239.

Nelson JC and Bowers MB. 1978. Delusional Unipolar Depression: Description and Drug Response. *Arch Gen Psychiatry* 35:1321–1328.

Nelson JC and Charney DS. 1980. Primary Affective Disorder Criteria and the Endogenous-Reactive Distinction. *Arch Gen Psychiatry* 37:787–793.

Nelson JC and Charney DS. 1981. The Symptoms of Major Depressive Illness. *Am J Psychiatry* 138:1–13.

Nelson WH, Khan A and Orr WW, Jr. 1984. Delusional Depression: Pheno-menology, Neuroendocrine Function, and Tricyclic Antidepressant Response. *J Affective Disorders* 6:297–306.

Nichols RC and Bilbro WC, Jr. 1966. The Diagnosis of Twin Zygosity. *Acta Genet* 16:265–275.

Nies A, Robinson DS, Harris LS and Lamborn KR. 1974. Comparison of Monoamine Oxidase Substrate Activities in Twins, Schizophrenics, Depressives and Controls. *Biochem Psychopharm* 59–70.

Nies A, Robinson DS, Lamborn KR and Lampert RP. 1973. Genetic Con-trol of Platelet and Plasma Monoamine Oxidase Activity. *Arch Gen Psychiatry* 28:834–838.

Noble P and Lader M. 1972. A Physiological Comparison of "Endogenous" and "Reactive" Depression. *Brit J Psychiat* 120:541–542.

Noyes R, Dempsey CM, Blum A and Chavanaugh GL. 1974. Lithium Treatment of Depression. *Comprehensive Psychiatry* 15:187–193.

Nunn C. 1979. Mixed Affective States and the Natural History of Manic Depressive Psychosis. *Brit J Psychiatry* 134:153–160.

Nurnberger JI, Jr. 1987. Pharmacogenetics of Psychoactive Drugs. *J Psychiat Res* 21:499–505.

Nurnberger J, Jr., and Gershon ES. 1982. Genetics. In *Handbook of Af-fective Disorders,* Paykel E, Ed. New York: Guilford Press, 126–145.

Nurnberger J, Jr., Gershon ES, Murphy DL, Buchsbaum MS, Goodwin FK, Post RM, Lake CR, Guroff JJ and McGinnis MH. *Biological and Clinical Predictors of Lithium Response in Depression,* 241–256.

Nurnberger J, Jr., Roose SP, Dunner DL and Fieve RR. 1979. Unipolar Mania: A Distinct Clinical Entity. *Am J Psychiatry* 136:1420.

Nurnberger J, Jr., Sitaram N, Gershon ES and Gillin JC. 1983. A Twin Study of Cholinergic REM Induction. *Biological Psychiatry* 18:1161–1165.

Ogihara T, Nugent CA, Shen SW and Goldfein S. 1975. Serum Dopamine-B-Hydroxylase Activity in Parents and Children. *J Lab Clin Med* 85:566–573.

Orvaschel H, Thompson WD, Belanger A, Prusoff BA and Kidd KK. 1982. Comparison of the Family History Method to Direct Interview: Fac-tors Affecting the Diagnosis of Depression. *J Affect Disorders* 4:49–59.

Ostrow DG, Pandey GN, Davis JM, Hurt SW and Tosteson DC. 1978. A Heritable Disorder of Lithium Transport in Erythrocytes of a Sub-population of Manic-Depressive Patients. *Am J Psychiatry* 135:1070–1078.

Ott J. 1985. *Analysis of Human Genetic Linkage.* Baltimore: Johns Hopkins.

Overall JE, Hollister LE, Johnson M et al. 1966. Nosology of Depression and Differential Response to Drugs. *JAMA* 195:946–948.

Ozelius L, Hsu YPP, Bruns G, Powell JF, Chen S, Weyler PM, Gusella JF and Breakefield XO. 1988. Human Monoamine Oxidase Gene *(MAOA)*: Chromosome Position (Xp21-p11) and DNA Polymorph-ism. *Genomics* 3:53–58.

Paluszny M and Abelson G. 1975. Twins in a Child Psychiatry Clinic. *Am J Psychiatry* 132:434–436.

Paluszny M, Selzer ML, Winokur A and Lewandowski L. 1977. Twin Relationships and Depression. *Am J Psychiatry* 134:988–990.

Pandey GN, Dorus E, Davis JM and Tosteson DC. 1979a. Lithium Transport in Human Red Blood Cells: Genetic and Clinical Aspects. *Arch Gen Psychiatry* 36:902–908.

Pandey GN, Dorus E, Shaughnessy R and Davis JM. 1979b. Genetic Control of Platelet Monoamine Oxidase Activity: Studies on Normal Families. *Life Sciences* 25:1173–1178.

Pandey GN, Dorus E, Shaughnessy R, Gaviria M, Val E and Davis JM. 1980. Reduced Platelet MAO Activity and Vulnerability to Psychiatric Disorders. *Psychiatry Research* 2:315–321.

Pandey GN, Ostrow DG, Haas M, Dorus E, Casper RC, Davis JM and Tosteson DC. 1977. Abnormal Lithium and Sodium Transport in Erythrocytes of a Manic Patient and Some Members of His Family. *Proc Natl Acad Sci* 74:3607–3611.

Pare CMB. 1970. Differentiation of Two Genetically Specific Types of Depression by the Response to Antidepressant Drugs. *Humangenetik* 9:199–210.

Pare CMB and Mack JW. 1971. Differentiation of Two Genetically Specific Types of Depression by the Response to Antidepressant Drugs. *J Medical Genetics* 8:306–309.

Pare CMB, Rees L and Sainsbury MJ. 1962. Differentiation of Two Genetically Specific Types of Depression by the Response to Antidepressants. *Lancet* 1340–1343.

Parisi HA, Lanara EC and Triantaphyllidis CD. 1980. Protein and Enzyme Polymorphisms in Affective Disorders in Northern Greece. *Hum Hered* 30:181–184.

Parker JB, Theilie A and Spielberger CD. 1961. Frequency of Blood Types in a Homogenous Group of Manic-Depressive Patients. *J Mental Science* 107:936.

Parsons PL. 1965. Mental Health of Swansea's Old Folk. *Br J Prev Soc Med* 19:43–47.

Pauls DL, Bucher KD, Crowe RR and Noyes R, Jr. 1980. A Genetic Study of Panic Disorder Pedigrees. *Am J Hum Genet* 32:639–644.

Pauls DL, Crowe RR and Noyes R, Jr. 1979. Distribution of Ancestral Secondary Cases in Anxiety Neurosis (Panic Disorders). *J Affect Disorders* 1:287–290.

Paykel ES. 1972. Depressive Typologies and Response to Amitriptyline. *Brit J Psychiatry* 120:147–156.

Payne R. 1977. The HLA Complex: Genetics and Implications in the Immune Response. In *HLA and Disease,* Dausset J and Svejgaard A, Eds. Baltimore: Williams and Wilkins.

Pederson AM, Barry DJ and Babigian HM. 1972. Epidemiological Considerations of Psychotic Depression. *Arch Gen Psychiatry* 27:193–197.

Pepper GM and Krieger DT. 1984. Hypothalmic-pituitary-adrenal Abnormalities in Depression: Their Possible Relation to Central Mechanisms Regulating ACTH Release. In *Neurobiology of Mood Disorders,* Post RM and Ballenger JC, Eds. Baltimore: Williams & Wilkins.

Perris C. 1966. A Study of Bipolar (Manic-Depressive) and Unipolar Recurrent Depressive Psychoses. *Acta Psychiatrica Scand* 42 (Suppl. 194), 1–188.

Perris C. 1971. Abnormality on Paternal and Maternal Sides: Observations in Bipolar (Manic-Depressive) and Unipolar Depressive Psychoses. *Brit J Psychiatry* 118:207–210.

Perris C. 1982. The Distinction between Bipolar and Unipolar Disorders. In *Handbook of Affective Disorders,* Paykel E, Ed. New York: Guilford Press, 45–58.

Perry PJ, Morgan DE, Smith RE, Tsuang MT. 1982. Treatment of Unipolar Depression Accompanied by Delusions. *J Affective Disorders* 4:195–200.

Petterson U. 1977. Manic-Depressive Illness: A Clinical, Social and Genetic Study. *Acta Psychiatrica Scand* Suppl. 269, 5–93.

Pfohl B, Vasquez N and Nasrallah H. 1981. The Mathematical Case against Unipolar Mania. *J Psychiat Res* 16:259–265.

Piran N, Kennedy S, Garfinkel PE and Ownes M. 1985. Affective Disturbance in Eating Disorders. *J Nerv and Mental Disease* 173:395–400.

Pollin W, Allen MG, Hoffer A, Stabenau JR and Hrubec Z. 1969. Psychopathology in 15,909 Pairs of Veteran Twins: Evidence for a Genetic Factor in the Pathogenesis of Schizophrenia and Its Relative Absence in Psychoneurosis. *Am J Psychiatry* 126:597–610.

Pollock HM, Malzberg B and Fuller RG. 1939. *Hereditary and Environmental Factors in the Causation of Manic-Depressive Psychoses and Dementia Praecox.* Utica: State Hospital Press.

Pope HG, Jr, Hudson JI, Jonas JM and Yurgelun-Todd D. 1983. Bulimia Treated with Imipramine: A Placebo-Controlled, Double-Blind Study. *Am J Psychiatry* 143:554–558.

Price J. 1968. The Genetics of Depressive Behaviour. *Brit J Psychiatry* Spec. Pub. #2, Coppen A and Walk A, Eds.

Price LH, Conwell Y and Nelson JC. 1983. Lithium Augmentation of Combined Neuroleptic-Tricyclic Treatment in Delusional Depression. *Am J Psychiatry* 140:318–322.

Price RA, Kidd KK, Pauls DL, Gershon ES, Prusoff BA, Weissman MM and Goldin LR. 1985. Multiple Threshold Models for the Affective Disorders: The Yale-NIMH Collaborative Family Study. *J Psychiat Res* 19:533–546.

Price RA, Kidd KK and Weissman MM. 1987. Early Onset (Under Age 30 Years) and Panic Disorder as Markers for Etiologic Homogeneity in Major Depression. *Arch Gen Psychiatry* 44:434–440.

Prien RF, Caffey EM, Jr., and Klett CJ. 1974. Factors Associated with Treatment Success in Lithium Carbonate Prophylaxis: Report of the Veterans Administration and National Institute of Mental Health Collaborative Study Group. *Arch Gen Psychiatry* 31:189–192.

Prien RF, Klett CJ and Caffey EM, Jr. 1973. Lithium Carbonate and Imipramine in the Prevention of Affective Episodes. *Arch Gen Psychiatry* 29:420–425.

Procci W. 1976. Schizoaffective Psychosis: Fact or Fiction? *Arch Gen Psychiatry* 33:1167–1178.

Propert DN, Tait BD and Davies B. 1981. HLA Antigens and Affective Illness. *Tissue Antigens* 18:335–340.

Propping P. 1978. Pharmacogenetics. *Res Physiol Biochem Pharmacol* 83:124–173.

Propping P and Friedl W. 1985. Pharmacogenetics in Psychiatry and Psychobiology. In *Genetic Aspects of Human Behavior,* Sakai T and Tsuboi T, Eds. New York: Igaku-Shoin, 219–233.

Propping P and Friedl W. 1988. Genetic Studies of Biochemical, Pathophysiological and Pharmacological Factors in Schizophrenia. In *Handbook of Schizophrenia: vol. 3, Nosology, Epidemiology and Genetics of Schizophrenia,* Tsuang MT and Simpson JC, Eds. Amsterdam: Elsevier, 579–608.

Propping P and Kopun M. 1973. Pharmacogenetic Aspects of Psychoactive Drugs: Facts and Fancy. *Humangenetik* 20:291–320.

Prusoff BA, Weissman MM, Klerman G and Rounsaville BJ. 1980. Research Diagnostic Criteria Subtypes of Depression: Their Role as Predictors of Differential Response to Psychotherapy and Drug Treatment. *Arch Gen Psychiatry* 37:796–801.

Prusoff BA, Weissman MM, Merikangas KR, Leckman JF and Kidd KK. 1985. Drug Response as a Predictor of Transmission of Non-Bipolar Major Depression within Families. *J Affect Disorders* 8:171–176.

Puchall LB, Coursey RD, Buchsbaum MS and Murphy DL. 1980. Parents of High Risk Subjects Defined by Levels of Monoamine Oxidase Activity. *Schizophrenia Bulletin* 6:338–346.

Quitkin F, Rifkin A and Klein D. 1978. Imipramine Response in Deluded Depressive Patients. *Am J Psychiatry* 135:806–811.

Reich T, Clayton PJ and Winokur G. 1969. Family History Studies: V. The Genetics of Mania. *Am J Psychiatry* 125:64–75.

Reich LH, Davies RK and Himmelhoch JM. 1974. Excessive Alcohol Use in Manic-Depressive Illness. *Am J Psychiatry* 131:83–89.

Reich T, James JW and Morris C. 1972. The Use of Multiple Thresholds in Determining the Mode of Transmission of Semi-continuous Traits. *Ann Hum Genet* 36:163–184.

Reich T, James JW and Morris C. 1979. The Use of Multiple Thresholds in Determining the Mode of Transmission of Semi-Continous Traits. *Ann Hum Genet* 42:371–389.

Reich T, Van Eerdewegh P, Rice J, Mullaney J, Endicott J and Klerman GL. 1987. The Familial Transmission of Primary Major Depressive Disorder. *J Psychiat Res* 21:613–624.

Reiser D and Brock A. 1976. A Favorable Response to Lithium Carbonate in a Schizoaffective Father and Son. *Am J Psychiatry* 133:824–827.

Retezeanu A and Christodorescu D. 1978. ABO Blood Groups in Affective and in Schizophrenic Psychosis. *(Rev Roum Med) Neurol Psychiat* 16(4):271.

Reveley A. 1985. Genetic Counselling for Schizophrenia. *Brit J Psychiat* 147:107–112.

Reveley AM and Reveley MA. 1981. The Distinction of Primary and Secondary Affective Disorders: Clinical Implications. *J Affective Disorders* 3:273–279.

Reznikoff M and Honeyman MS. 1967. MMPI Profiles of Monozygotic and Dizygotic Twin Pairs. *J Consult Psychol.* 31:100.

Rice J, Cloninger R and Reich T. 1980. General Causal Models for Sex Differences in the Familial Transmission of Multifactorial Traits: An Application to Human Spatial Visualizing Ability. *Social Biology* 27(1):36–47.

Rice JP, Endicott J, Knesevich MA and Rochberg N. 1987a. The Estimation of Diagnostic Sensitivity Using Stability Data: An Application to Major Depressive Disorder. *J Psychiat Res* 21:337–345.

Rice J, McGuffin P and Shaskan EG. 1982. A Commingling Analysis of Platelet Monoamine Oxidase Activity. *Psychiatry Research* 7:325–335.

Rice J, Reich T, Andreasen NC, Endicott J, Van Eerdewegh M, Fishman R, Hirschfeld RMA and Klerman GL. 1987. The Familial Transmission of Bipolar Illness. *Arch Gen Psychiatry* 44:441–447.

Rice J, Reich T, Andreasen NC, Lavori PW, Endicott J, Clayton PJ, Keller MB, Hirschfeld RMA and Klerman GL. 1984b. Sex-Related Differences in Depression: Familial Evidence. *J Affect Disorders* 7:199–210.

Rieder RO and Gershon ES. 1978. Genetic Strategies in Biological Psychiatry, *Arch Gen Psychiatry* 35:866–873.

Rihmer Z and Arato M. 1981. ABO Blood Groups in Manic-Depressive Patients. *J Affective Disorder* 3:1.

Rimmer J, and Chambers DS. 1969. Alcoholism: Methodological Considerations in the Study of Family Illness. *Am J Orthopsychiatry* 39:760–768.

Rinieris PM, Stefanis CN, Lykouras EP and Varsou EK. 1979. Affective Disorder and ABO Blood Types. *Acto Psychiatrica Scan* 60:272.

Risch N and Baron M. 1982. X-Linkage and Genetic Heterogeneity in Bipolar-Related Major Affective Illness: Reanalysis of Linkage Data. *Am J Hum Genet* 46:153–166.

Risch N, Baron M and Mendlewicz J. 1986. Assessing the Role of X-Linked Inheritance in Bipolar-Related Major Affective Disorder. *J Psychiatric Research* 20:275–288.

Rivinus TM, Biederman J, Herzog DB, Kemper K, Harper GP, Harmatz JS and Houseworth S. 1984. Anorexia Nervosa and Affective Disorders: A Controlled Family History Study. *Am J Psychiatry* 141:1414–1418.

Robins LN. 1985. Epidemiology: Reflections on Testing the Validity in Psychiatric Interviews. *Arch Gen Psychiatry* 42:918–924.

Robins E and Guze SB. 1970. Establishment of Diagnostic Validity in Psychiatric Illness: Its Application to Schizophrenia. *Am J Psychiatry* 126:107–111.

Robins LN, Helzer JE, Croughan J and Ratcliff KS. 1981. National Institute of Mental Health Diagnostic Interview Schedule: Its History, Characteristics and Validity. *Arch Gen Psychiatry* 38:381–389.

Robins LN, Helzer JE, Weissman MM, Orvaschel H, Gruenberg E, Burke JD Jr. and Regier DA. 1984. Lifetime Prevalence of Specific Psychiatric Disorders in Three Sites. *Arch Gen Psychiatry* 41:949–958.

Robinson DG and Spiker DG. 1985. Delusional Depression: A One Year Follow-Up. *J Affect Disorders* 9:79–83.

Roll A and Entres JL. 1936. Zum Problem Der Erbprognosebestimmung. *Z Ges Neurol Psychiat* 156:169–202.

Rosanoff AJ, Handy LM and Rosanoff Plesset I. 1935. The Etiology of Manic-Depressive Syndromes with Special Reference to Their Occurrence in Twins. *Am J Psychiatry* 91:725–762.

Rose RJ, Miller JZ, Pogue-Geile MF and Cardwell GF. 1981. Twin-Family Studies of Common Fears and Phobias. In *Twin Research 3: Intelligence, Personality and Development*. New York: Alan R. Liss, 169–174.

Rosenthal D. 1970. *Genetic Theory and Abnormal Behavior*. New York: McGraw-Hill.

Rosenthal R. 1966. *Experimenter Bias in Behavioral Research*. New York: Appleton-Century-Crofts.

Rosenthal D, Wender PH, Kety SS, Schulsinger F, Welner J and Ostergaard L. 1968. Schizophrenics' Offspring Reared in Adoptive Homes. In *The Transmission of Schizophrenia*, Rosenthal D and Kety SS, Eds. Oxford: Pergamon, 377–392.

Rosenthal D, Wender PH, Kety SS, Schulsinger F, Welner J and Reider R. 1975. Parent-Child Relationships and Psychopathological Disorder in the Child. *Arch Gen Psychiatry* 32:466–476.

Rosler M, Bellaire W, Gressnich N, Giannitisis D and Jarovici A. 1983. HLA Antigens in Schizophrenia, Major Depressive Disorder, and Schizoaffective Disorder. *Med Microbiol Immunol* 172:57–65.

Ross SB, Wetterberg L and Myrhed M. 1973. Genetic Control of Plasma Dopamine-B-Hydroxylase. *Life Sciences* 12:529–532.

Roth S. 1970. The Seemingly Ubiquitous Depression Following Acute Schizophrenic Episodes: A Neglected Area of Clinical Discussion. *Am J Psychiatry* 127:51–58.

Rudorfer MV, Hwu HG and Clayton PJ. 1982. Dexamethasone Suppression Test in Primary Depression: Significance of Family History and Psychosis. *Biological Psychiatry* 17:41–48.

Rundle A, Sudell B, Wood K and Coppen A. 1977. Red Cell Adenylate Kinase Phenotypes in the Affective Disorders. *Hum Genet* 36:161–166.

Rybakowski J. 1977. Pharmacogenetic Aspect of Red Blood Cell Lithium Index in Manic-Depressive Psychosis. *Biological Psychiatry* 12:425–429.

Sachar EJ.Endocrine Abnormalities in Depression. In *Handbook of Affective Disorders*, Paykel E, Ed. New York: Guilford Press, 191–201.

Sautter FJ, Hitzemann R, Griffin J and Garver DL. 1986. Lithium Ratio in Vitro: Familial Patterns of Illness. *Psychiatry Research* 18:257–266.

Scarr S. 1968. Environmental Bias in Twin Studies. *Eugenics Quarterly* 15:34–40.

Scarr S and Carter-Saltzman L. 1979. Twin Method: Defense of a Critical Assumption. *Behavior Genetics* 9:527–542.

Schaedler E. 1938. Eine Untersuchung Uber Die Nachfahren Von Manisch-Depressiven. Ph.D. diss., University of Wurzburg.

Schaffer CB, Donlon PT and Bittle RM. 1980. Chronic Pain and Depression: A Clinical and Family History Survey. *Am J Psychiatry* 137:118–120.

Scharfetter C. 1981. Subdividing the Functional Psychoses: A Family Hereditary Approach. *Psychological Med* 11:637–640.

Scharfetter C and Nusperli M. 1980. The Group of Schizophrenias, Schizoaffective Psychoses and Affective Disorders. *Schizophrenia Bulletin* 6:586–591.

Schiffer RB, Wineman NM and Weitkamp LR. 1986. Association between Bipolar Affective Disorder and Multiple Sclerosis. *Am J Psychiatry* 143:94–95.

Schuckit MA. 1982. The Importance of Family History of Affective Disorder in a Group of Young Men. *J Nerv and Mental Disease* 170:530–535.

Schultz B. 1937. Ubersicht Uber Auslesefreie Untersuchungen in Der Verwandtschaft Manisch-Depressiver. *Ztschr F Psych Hyg* 10:39.

Scriver CR. 1983. Genetic Screening: Implications for Preventive Medicine. *Am J Public Health* 73:243–245.

Sedvall G, Fyro B, Gullberg V, Nybacek H, Wiesel FA and Wode-Helgodt B. 1980. Relationships in Healthy Volunteers between Concentrations of Monoamine Metabolities in Cerebrospinal Fluid and Family History of Psychiatric Morbidity. *Brit J Psychiat* 136:366–374.

Sedvall G, Iselius L, Nyback H, Oreland L, Oxenstierna G, Ross SB and Wiesel FA. 1984. Genetic Studies of CSF Monoamine Metabolites. In *Frontiers in Biochemical and Pharmacological Research in Depression*, Usdin E, Ashberg M, Bertlisson L and Sjoquist F, Eds. New York: Raven Press, 79–85.

Shapiro RW. 1970. A Twin Study of Non-Endogenous Depression. *Acta Jutlandica* 42:1–179.

Shapiro RW, Bock E, Rafaelsen OJ, Ryder LP and Svejgaard A. 1976. Histocompatibility Antigens and Manic-Depressive Disorders. *Arch Gen Psychiatry* 33:823–825.

Shapiro RW, Ryder LP, Svejgaard A and Faraelsen OJ. 1977. HLA Antigens and Manic-Depressive Disorders: Further Evidence of an Association. *Psychological Medicine* 7:387–396.

Shaughnessy R, Greene SC, Pandey GN and Dorus E. 1985. Red-Cell Lithium Transport and Affective Disorders in a Multigeneration Pedigree: Evidence for Genetic Transmission of Affective Disorders. *Biol Psychiatry* 20:451–460.

Sheldrick C, Jablensky A, Sartorious N and Shepherd M. 1977. Schizophrenia Succeeded by Affective Illness: Catamnestic Study and Statistical Inquiry. *Psychological Medicine* 7:619–624.

Shields J. 1962. *Monozygotic Twins Brought Up Apart and Brought Up Together.* London: Oxford University Press.

Shields J. 1975. Genetic Factors in Neurosis. In *Research in Neurosis,* Van Praag HM, Ed. New York: Spectrum, 155–170.

Shopsin B, Mendlewicz J, Suslak L, Silbey and Gershon ES. 1976. Genetics of Affective Disorders: II. Morbidity Risk and Genetic Transmission. *Neuropsychobiology* 2:28–36.

Siever LJ and Davis KL. 1985. Overview: Toward a Dysregulation Hypothesis of Depression. *Am J Psychiatry* 142:1017–1031.

Sigvardsson S, Bohman M, Von Knorring AL and Cloninger CR. 1986. Symptom Patterns and Causes of Somatization in Men: I. Differentiation of Two Discrete Disorders. *Genetic Epidemiology* 3:153–169.

Sigvardsson S, Cloninger CR, Bohman M and Von Knorring AL. 1982. Predisposition to Petty Criminality in Swedish Adoptees: III. Sex Differences and Validation of the Male Typology. *Arch Gen Psychiatry* 39:1248–1253.

Sitaram N, Dube S, Keshavan M, Davies A and Reynal P. 1987. The Association of Supersensitive Cholinergic REM-Induction and Affective Illness within Pedigrees. *J Psychiat Res* 21:487–497.

Sjogren T. 1948. Genetic-Statistical and Psychiatric Investigations of a West Swedish Population. *Acta Psychiat et Neurol* Suppl., 52.

Slater E. 1936. The Inheritance of Manic-Depressive Insanity and Its Relation to Mental Defect. *J Ment Sci* 82:626–634.

Slater E. 1966. Expectation of Abnormality on Paternal and Maternal Sides: A Computational Model. *J Med Genet* 3:159.

Slater E. 1971. Schizophrenia: Problems of Heterogeneity. In *Man, Mind and Heredity,* Shields J and Gottesman II, Eds. Baltimore: Johns Hopkins, 84–87.

Slater E and Cowie V. 1971. *The Genetics of Mental Disorder.* London: Oxford University Press.

Slater E, Maxwell J and Price JS. 1971. Distribution of Ancestral Secondary Cases in Bipolar Affective Disorders. *Brit J Psychiatr* special pub. no. 1, 62–71.

Slater E and Shields J. 1953. Psychotic and Neurotic Illnesses in Twins. Medical Research Current Special Report, Series #ZN8. London: HMSO.

Slater E and Shields J. 1969. Genetic Aspects of Anxiety. In Studies of Anxiety, Lader M., Ed. *Brit J Psychiatr* spec. pub. no. 3. Ashford (Kent): Headley, 62–71.

Slater E and Tsuang MT. 1968. Abnormality on Paternal and Maternal Sides: Observations in Schizophrenia and Manic-Depression. *J Med Genet* 5:197–199.

Small J, Kellams J, Milstein V and Moore J. 1975. A Placebo-Controlled

Study of Lithium Combined with Neuroleptics in Chronic Schizophrenic Patients. *Am J Psychiatry* 132:1315–1319.

Smeraldi E and Bellodi L. 1981. Possible Linkage between Primary Affective Disorder Susceptibility Locus and HLA Halotypes. *Am J Psychiatry* 139:1232–1234.

Smeraldi E, Negri F, Heimbuch RC and Kidd KK. 1981. Familial Patterns and Possible Modes of Inheritance of Primary Affective Disorders. *J Affect Dis* 3:173–187.

Smeraldi E, Negri F and Melica AM. 1977. A Genetic Study of Affective Disorders. *Acta Psychiat Scand* 56:382–399.

Smeraldi E, Negri F, Melica AM and Scorza-Smeraldi R. 1978a. HLA System and Affective Disorders: A Sibship Genetic Study. *Tissue Antigens* 12:270–274.

Smeraldi E, Negri F, Melica AM, Scorza-Smeraldi R, Fabio G, Banara P, Bellodi L, Sacchetti E, Sabbadini-Villa MG, Cazzullo CL and Zanussi C. 1978b. HLA Typing and Affective Disorders: A Study in the Italian Population. *Neuropsychobiology* 4:344–352.

Smeraldi E, Petroccione A, Gasperini M, Macciardi F and Orsini A. 1984a. The Search for Genetic Homogeneity in Affective Disorders. *J Affect Disorders* 7:99–107.

Smeraldi E, Petroccione A, Gasperini M, Macciardi R, Orsini A and Kidd KK. 1984b. Outcomes on Lithium Treatment as a Tool for Genetic Studies in Affective Disorders. *J Affect Disorders* 6:139–151.

Smith C. 1974. Concordance in Twins: Methods and Interpretation. *Am J Hum Genet* 26:454–466.

Smith JC. 1925. Atypical Psychoses and Heterologous Hereditary Taints: Researches into the Effect of the Simultaneous Presence of Heterogenous Hereditary Conditions for Mental Diseases, Having Special Regard to the Question concerning the Origin of Atypical, Endogenous Psychoses. *J Nerv and Mental Disease* 62:1–32.

Smith RT. 1965. A Comparison of Socioenvironmental Factors in Monozygotic and Dizygotic Twins, Testing an Assumption. In *Methods and Goals in Human Behavior Genetics,* Vandenberg SG, Ed. New York, 45–61.

Snyder SH. 1984. Cholinergic Mechanisms in Affective Disorders. *New England J Medicine* 311:254–255.

Spitzer RL, Endicott J and Robins EL. 1975. Reliability of Clinical Criteria for Psychiatric Diagnosis. *Am J Psychiatry* 132:1187–1192.

Spitzer RL, Endicott J and Robins E. 1977. *Research Diagnostic Criteria RDC for a Selected Group of Functional Disorders,* 3rd Ed. New York: New York State Psychiatric Institute.

Spitzer RL, Fleiss JL and Endicott J. 1978. Problems of Classification: Reliability and Validity. In *Psychopharmacology: A Generation of Progress,* Lipton MA, DiMascio A and Killam KF, Eds. New York: Raven Press.

Sprock J. 1985. Classification of Depression. *Comprehensive Psychiatry* 26:404–420.

Srole L and Fischer A. 1980. The Midtown Manhattan Longitudinal Study vs the Mental Paradise Lost Doctrine. *Arch Gen Psychiatry* 37:209–221.

Stabenau JR. 1969. Schizophrenic and Affective Psychosis: Twin and Family Studies. In *Future of the Brain Sciences,* Bogoch S, Ed. Proceedings of the Third International Conference: Future of the Brain Sciences. New York: Plenum Press, 421–459.

Stangl B, Pfhol B, Zimmerman M, Bowers W and Corenthal C. 1985. A Structured Interview for the DSM-III Personality Disorders: A Preliminary Report. *Arch Gen Psychiatry* 42:591–596.

Stein G, Holmes J, Bradford JW and Kennedy L. 1980. HLA Antigens and Affective Disorder: A Family Case Report. *Psychological Medicine* 10:677–681.

Steinberg H, Green R and Durell J. 1967. Depression Occurring during the Course of Recovery from Schizophrenic Symptoms. *Am J Psychiatry* 124:679–702.

Steinhausen HC, Gobel D and Nestler V. 1984. Psychopathology in the Offspring of Alcoholic Parents. *J Am Academy Child Psychiatry* 23:465–471.

Stember RH and Fieve RR. 1977. Histocompatibility Antigens in Affective Disorders. *Clinical Immunology and Immunopathology* 7:10–14.

Stenstedt A. 1952. *A Study in Manic-Depressive Psychoses. Clinical, Social and Genetic Investigations.* Stockholm: Karolinska Institutet.

Stern SL, Dixon KN, Nemzer E, Lake MD, Sansone RA, Smeltzer DJ, Lantz S and Schrier SS. 1984. Affective Disorder in the Families of Women with Normal Weight Bulimia. *Am J Psychiatry* 141:1224–1227.

Stern M, Pillsbury J and Sonnenberg S. 1976. Postpsychotic Depression in Schizophrenics. *Comprehensive Psychiatry* 13:591–598.

Strober M and Carlson G. 1982. Bipolar Illness in Adolescents with Major Depression: Clinical, Genetic, and Psychopharmacologic Predictors in a Three-to-Four-Year Prospective Follow-Up Investigation. *Arch Gen Psychiatry* 39:549–555.

Suarez BK and Croughan J. 1982. Is the Major Histocompatibility Complex Linked to Genes that Increase Susceptibility to Affective Disorder? A Critical Appraisal. *Psychiatry Research* 7:19–27.

Suarez BK and Reich T. 1984. HLA and Major Affective Disorder. *Arch Gen Psychiatry* 41:22–27.

Suranji-Cadotte BE, Wood PL, Schwartz G and Nair NPV. 1983. Altered Platelet 3H-Imipramine Binding in Schizo-Affective and Depressive Disorders. *Biological Psychiatry* 18:923–927.

Sweeney D, Nelson C, Bowers M et al. 1978. Delusional versus Non-Delusional Depression: Neurochemical Differences. *Lancet* 2:100–101.

Tanna VL, Go RCP, Winokur G and Elston RC. 1977. Possible Linkage between Group-Specific Component (Gc Protein) and Pure Depressive Disease. *Acta Psychiat Scand* 55:111–115.

Tanna VL, Go RCP, Winokur G and Elston RC. 1979. Possible Linkage between X-Haptoglobin (Hp) and Depression Spectrum Disease. *Neuropsychobiology* 5:102–113.

Tanna VL and Winokur G. 1968. A Study of Association and Linkage of ABO Blood Types and Primary Affective Disorder. *Brit J Psychiatry* 114, 1175–1181.

Tanna VL, Winokur G, Elston RC and Go RCP. 1976. A Linkage Study of Depression Spectrum Disease: The Use of the Sib-Pair Method. *Neuropsychobiology* 2:52–62.

Targum SD, Gershon ES, Van Eerdewegh M and Rogentine N. 1979. Human Leukocyte Antigen System Not Closely Linked to or Associated with Bipolar Manic-Depressive Illness. *Biological Psychiatry* 14:615–636.

Targum SD and Schultz SC. 1982. Clinical Applications of Psychiatric Genetics. *Am J Orthopsychiat* 52:45–57.

Tarter RE, Hegedus AM and Gavaler JS. 1985. Hyperactivity in Sons of Alcoholics. *J Studies on Alcohol* 46:259–261.

Taylor MA and Abrams R. 1973. Manic States: A Genetic Study of Early and Late Onset Affective Disorders. *Arch Gen Psychiatry* 28:656–658.

Taylor MA and Abrams R. 1980a. Familial and Non-Familial Mania. *J Affect Disorders* 2:111–118.

Taylor MA and Abrams R. 1980b. Reassessing the Bipolar-Unipolar Dichotomy. *J Affect Disorders* 2:195–217.

Taylor MA and Abrams R. 1984. Mania and DSM-III Schizophreniform Disorder. *J Affect Disorders* 6:19–24.

Temple H, Dupont B and Shopsin B. 1975. Histocompatibility Studies in an Affectively Ill Jewish Population. In *Genetic Aspects of Affect Illness,* Mendlewicz J and Shopsin B, Eds. New York: Spectrum Publications, 45–53.

Thompson WD, Kidd JR, Weissman MM. 1979. A Procedure for the Efficient Collection and Processing of Pedigree Data Suitable for Genetic Analysis. *J Psychiatr Res* 15:291–303.

Thompson WD, Orvaschel H, Prusoff BA and Kidd KK. 1982. An Evaluation of the Family History Method for Ascertaining Psychiatric Disorders. *Arch Gen Psychiatry* 39:53–58.

Thomson G. 1981. A Review of Theoretical Aspects of HLA and Disease Associations. *Theoretical Pop Biology* 20:168–208.

Tienari P. 1963. Psychiatric Illness in Identical Twins. *Acta Psychiat Scand* 39:1–195

Torgersen S. 1983. Genetics of Neurosis: The Effects of Sampling Variation upon the Twin Concordance Ratio. *Brit J Psychiat* 142:126–132.

Torgersen S. 1985. Hereditary Differentiation of Anxiety and Affective Neuroses. *Brit J Psychiat* 146:350–534.

Torgersen S. 1986. Childhood and Family Characteristics in Panic and Generalized Anxiety Disorders. *Am J Psychiatry* 143:630–632.

Trzebiatowska-Trzeciak O. 1977. Genetic Analysis of Unipolar and Bipolar Endogenous Affective Psychoses. *Brit J Psychiat* 131:478–485.

Tsuang MT. 1975. Genetics of Affective Disorder. In *Psychobiology of Depression,* Mendels J, Ed. New York: Spectrum Publications, 85–100.

Tsuang MT. 1978. Genetic Counseling for Psychiatric Patients and Their Families. *Am J Psychiatry* 135:1465–1475.

Tsuang MT and Bray TD. 1975. *Diagnostic Manual for Use in Psychiatry (DMP).* University of Iowa College of Medicine, Department of Psychiatry, Iowa 500 Research Project.

Tsuang MT, Dempsey G, Dvoressky A and Struss A. 1977. A Family History Study of Schizoaffective Disorder. *Biological Psychiatry* 12:331–338.

Tsuang MT, Dempsey M and Rauscher F. 1976. A Study of Atypical Schizophrenia. *Arch Gen Psychiatry* 33:1157–1160.

Tsuang MT, Faraone SV and Fleming JA. 1985. Familial Transmission of Major Affective Disorders: Is There Evidence Supporting the Distinction between Unipolar and Bipolar Disorders? *Brit J Psychiat* 146:268–271.

Tsuang MT, Winokur G and Crowe RR. 1980. Morbidity Risks of Schizophrenia and Affective Disorders among First-Degree Relatives of Patients with Schizophrenia, Mania, Depression, and Surgical Conditions. *Brit J Psychiat* 137:497–504.

Tsuang MT, Woolson RF and Fleming JA. 1979. Long-Term Outcome of Major Psychoses: I. Schizophrenia and Affective Disorders Compared with Psychiatrically Symptom-Free Surgical Conditions. *Arch Gen Psychiatry* 36:1295–1301.

Tukey JW. 1977. *Exploratory Data Analysis.* Reading, Mass.: Addison-Wesley.

Turner WJ and King S. 1981. Two Genetically Distinct Forms of Bipolar Affective Disorder. *Biological Psychiatry* 16:417.

Turner WJ and King S. 1983. BPD2 An Autosomal Dominant Form of Bipolar Affective Disorder. *Biological Psychiatry* 18:63–87.

Uytdenhoef P, Linkowski P and Mendlewicz J. 1982. Biological Quantitative Methods in the Evaluation of Psychiatric Treatment: Some Biochemical Criteria. *Neuropsychobiology* 8:60–72.

Van Eerdewegh MM, Gershon ES and Van Eerdewegh PM. 1980. X-Chromosome Threshold Models of Bipolar Manic-Depressive Illness. *J Psychiat Res* 15:215–238.

Van Praag HM and DeHaan S. 1980. Central Serotonin Deficiency—A Factor Which Increases Depression Vulnerability? *Acta Psychiat Scand* 280:89–103.

Van Praag HM and Nijo L. 1984. About the Course of Schizoaffective Psychoses. *Comprehensive Psychiatry* 25:9–22.

Van Valkenburg C, Akiskal HS and Puzantian V. 1983. Depression Spectrum Disease or Character Spectrum Disorder? A Clinical Study of Major Depressives with Familial Alcoholism or Sociopathy. *Comprehensive Psychiatry* 24:589–595.

Vandenberg SG. 1967. Hereditary Factors in Normal Personality Traits (As Measured by Inventories). In *Recent Advances in Biological Psychiatry,* Wortis J, Ed. New York: Plenum Press, 65–104.

Vogel F. 1981. Neurobiological Approaches in Human Behavior Genetics. *Behavior Genetics* 11:87–102.

Vogel F and Motulsky AG. 1979. *Human Genetics: Problems and Approaches.* Berlin: Springer-Verlag.

Von Grieff H, McHugh PR and Stokes PE. 1975. The Familial History in Sixteen Males with Bipolar Manic-Depressive Illness. In *Genetic Research in Psychiatry,* Fieve RR, Rosenthal D and Brill H, Ed. Baltimore: Johns Hopkins, 233–239.

Von Knorring AL, Cloninger CR, Bohman M and Sigvardsson S. 1983. An Adoption Study of Depressive Disorders and Substance Abuse. *Arch Gen Psychiatry* 40:943–950.

Von Knorring L, Perris C, Oreland L, Eisemann M, Holmgren S and Perris H. 1985. Morbidity Risk for Psychiatric Disorders in Families of Probands with Affective Disorders Divided According to Levels of Platelet MAO Activity. *Psychiatry Research* 15:271–279.

Walsh BT. 1982. Endocrine Disturbances in Anorexia Nervosa and Depression. *Psychosomatic Medicine* 44:85–91.

Ward CH. 1962. The Psychiatric Nomenclature. *Arch Gen Psychiatry* 7:198–205.

Waters B, Marchenko I, Abrams N, Smiley D and Kalin D. 1983. Assortative Mating for Major Affective Disorder. *J Affect Disorders* 5:9–17.

Waters B, Thakar J and Lapierre Y. 1983. Erythrocyte Lithium Transport Variables as a Marker for Manic-Depressive Disorder. *Neuropsychobiology* 9:94–98.

Weinberg I and Lobstein J. 1936. Beitrag Zur Verervung Des Manisch-Depressiven Irreseins. *Psychiat en Neurol* 1:337.

Weinshilboum RM. 1979. Serum Dopamine B-Hydroxylase. *Pharmacological Reviews* 30:13–166.

Weissman MM and Boyd JH. 1984. The Epidemiology of Affective Disorders. In *Neurobiology of Mood Disorders,* Post RM and Ballenger JC, Eds. Baltimore: Williams & Wilkins.

Weissman MM, Gershon ES, Kidd KK, Prusoff BA, Leckman JF, Dibble E, Hamovit J, Thompson WD, Pauls DL and Guroff JJ. 1984. Psychiatric Disorders in the Relatives of Probands with Affective Disorders: The Yale-NIMH Collaborative Family Study. *Arch Gen Psychiatry* 41:13–21.

Weissman MM, Kidd KK and Prusoff BA. 1982. Variability in the Rates of Affective Disorders in the Relatives of Severe and Mild Major Non-Bipolar Depressives and Normals. *Arch Gen Psychiatry* 39:1397–1403.

Weissman MM, Merikangas KR, Wickramaratne P, Kidd KK, Prusoff BA, Leckman JF and Pauls DL. 1986. Understanding the Clinical Heterogeneity of Major Depression Using Family Data. *Arch Gen Psychiatry* 43:430–434.

Weissman MM and Myers JK. 1978. Affective Disorders in a US Urban Community: The Use of Research Diagnostic Criteria in an Epidemiological Survey. *Arch Gen Psychiatry* 35:1304–1311.

Weitkamp LR, Pardue LH and Huntzinger RS. 1980. Genetic Marker Studies in a Family with Unipolar Depression. *Arch Gen Psychiatry* 37:1187–1192.

Weitkamp LR, Stancer HC, Persad E, Flood C and Guttormsen S. 1981. Depressive Disorders and HLA: A Gene on Chromosome 6 That Can Affect Behavior. *New England J Medicine* 305:1301–1306.

Welner A, Croughan J, Fishman R and Robins E. 1977. The Group of Schizoaffective and Related Psychoses: A Follow-Up Study. *Comprehensive Psychiatry* 18:413–422.

Welner A, Welner Z and Fishman R. 1979. The Group of Schizoaffective and Related Psychoses: IV. A Family Study. *Comprehensive Psychiatry* 20:21–26.

Wender PH, Kety SS, Rosenthal D, Schulsinger F, Ortmann J and Lunde I. 1986. Psychiatric Disorders in the Biological and Adoptive Families and Adopted Individuals with Affective Disorders. *Arch Gen Psychiatry* 43:923–929.

Wentzel J, Roberts DF and Whalley LJ. 1982. HLA in Manic-Depressive Psychosis. *Psychological Medicine* 12:275–278.

Whalley LJ, Roberts DF, Wentzel J and Watson KC. 1981. Antinuclear Antibodies and Histocompatibility Antigens in Patients on Long-Term Lithium Therapy. *J Affect Disorders* 3:123–130.

Whitlock FA. 1982. *Symptomatic Affective Disorders*. New York: Academic Press.

Wierzbicki M. 1986. Similarity of Monozygotic and Dizygotic Twins in Level and Lability of Subclinically Depressed Mood. *J Clinical Psychology* 42(4):577–585.

Wilson AF, Elston RC, Siervogel RM and Tran LD. 1988. Linkage of a Gene Regulating Dopamine-B-Hydroxylase Activity and the ABO Blood Group Locus. *Am J Hum Genet* 42:160–166.

Wilson AF, Elston RC, Siervogel RM, Weinshilboum R and Ward LJ. 1984. Linkage Relationships between a Major Gene for Catecho-O-methyltransferase Activity and 25 Polymorphic Marker Systems. *Am J Med Genet* 19:525–532.

Winokur G. 1970. Genetic Findings and Methodological Considerations in Manic-Depressive Disease. *Brit J Psychiatry* 117:267–274.

Winokur G. 1973. The Types of Affective Disorders. *J Nerv and Mental Disease* 156:82–96.

Winokur G. 1978. Mania and Depression: Family Studies and Genetics in Relation to Treatment. In *Psychopharmacology: A Generation of Progress,* Lipton M, Dimascio A and Kilam K, Eds. New York: Raven.

Winokur G. 1979a. A Family History (Genetic) Study of Pure Depressive Disease. In *Genetic Aspects of Affective Illness,* Mendlewicz J and Shopsin B, Eds. New York: Spectrum, 27–33.

Winokur G. 1979b. Familial (Genetic) Subtypes of Pure Depressive Disease. *Am J Psychiatry* 136:911–913.

Winokur G, Cadoret R, Baker M and Dorzab J. 1975. Depression Spectrum Disease Versus Pure Depressive Disease: Some Further Data. *Brit J Psychiat* 127:75–77.

Winokur G, Cadoret R, Dorzab J and Baker M. 1971. Depressive Disease: A Genetic Study. *Arch Gen Psychiatry* 24:135–144.

Winokur G and Clayton P. 1967. Family History Studies: I. Two Types of Affective Disorders Separated According to Genetic and Clinical Factors. In *Recent Advances in Biological Psychiatry,* Wortis CJ, Ed. New York: Plenum Press.

Winokur G, Clayton PJ and Reich T. 1969. *Manic Depressive Disease.* St. Louis: Mosby.

Winokur G and Crowe RR. 1983. Bipolar Illness: The Sex-Polarity Effect in Affectively Ill Family Members. *Arch Gen Psychiatry* 40:57–58.

Winokur A, March V and Mendels J. 1980. Primary Affective Disorder in Relatives of Patients with Anorexia Nervosa. *Am J Psychiatry* 137:695–698.

Winokur G, Morrison J, Clancy J and Crowe R. 1972. The Iowa 500: II. A Blind Family History Comparison of Mania, Depression, and Schizophrenia. *Arch Gen Psychiatry* 27:462–464.

Winokur G, Morrison J, Clancy J and Crowe R. 1973. The Iowa 500: Familial and Clinical Findings Favor Two Kinds of Depressive Illness. *Comprehensive Psychiatry* 14:99–106.

Winokur G and Pitts FN, Jr. 1965. Affective Disorders: VI. A Family History Study of Prevalences, Sex Differences and Possible Genetic Factors. *J Psychiat Res* 3:113.

Winokur G and Tanna VL. 1969. Possible Role of X-Linked Dominant Factor in Manic Depressive Disease. *Diseases of the Nervous System* 30:89–94.

Winter H, Herschel M, Propping P, Friedl W and Vogel F. 1978. A Twin Study on Three Enzymes (DBH, COMT, MAO) of Catecholamine Metabolism: Correlations with MMPI. *Psychopharmacology* 57:63–69.

Wood D, Othmer S, Reich T, Viesselman J and Rutt C. 1977. Primary and Secondary Affective Disorder: I. Past Social History and Current Episodes in 92 Depressed Inpatients. *Comprehensive Psychiatry* 18:201–210.

Woodruff RA, Murphy GE and Herjanic M. 1967. The Natural History of Affective Disorders: I. Symptoms of 72 Patients at the Time of Index Hospital Admission. *J Psychiat Res* 5:255–263.

World Health Organization. 1973. *The International Pilot Study of Schizophrenia.* Geneva: WHO.

World Health Organization. 1979. *Schizophrenia: An International Follow-Up Study.* New York: Wiley.

Wright AF, Crichton DN, Loudon JB, Morten JEN and Steel CM. 1984.

B-Adrenoceptor Binding Defects in Cell Lines from Families with Manic-Depressive Disorder. *Ann Hum Genet* 48:201–214.

Yadalam KG, Jain AK and Simpsom GM. 1985. Mania in Two Sisters with Similar Cerebellar Disturbance. *Am J Psychiatry* 142:1067–1069.

Young JRP, Fenton GW and Lader MH. 1971. The Inheritance of Neurotic Traits: A Twin Study of the Middlesex Hospital Questionnaire. *Brit J Psychiat* 119:393–398.

Zerbin-Rudin E. 1969. Zur Genetik der Depressiven Erkrankungen. In *Das Depressive Syndrom,* Hippius H and Selbach H, Eds. Berlin: Urban and Schwarzenberg, 37–56.

Zerbin-Rudin E. 1982. Genetics of Affective Psychoses. In *Handbook of Biological Psychiatry: III. Brain Mechanisms and Abnormal Behavior-Genetics and Neuroendocrinology,* Van Praag HM, Lader MH, Rafaelson OJ and Sacher EJ, Eds. New York: Marcel Dekker, 35–58.

Zerbin-Rudin E. 1986. Schizoaffective and Other Atypical Psychoses: The Genetical Aspect. In *Schizoaffective Psychoses,* Marneros A and Tsuang MT, Eds. Berlin: Springer-Verlag, 225–231.

Zimmerman M, Coryell W and Pfohl BM. 1985. Importance of Diagnostic Thresholds in Familial Classification: Dexamethasone Suppression Test and Familial Subtypes of Depression. *Arch Gen Psychiatry* 42:300–304.

Zimmerman M, Coryell W, Pfohl B and Stangl D. 1986. The Validity of Four Definitions of Endogenous Depression. *Arch Gen Psychiatry* 43:234–244.

Zis AP and Goodwin FK. 1982. The Amine Hypothesis. In *Handbook of Affective Disorders,* Paykel ES, Ed. Guilford Press, 175–190.

Zvolsky P, Dostal T, Vinarova E, Soucek K. 1973. Genealogic Study of Patients Suffering from Primary Affective Disorder and Treated with Lithium. *Activitas Nervosa Superior* 15:90–154.

Zvolsky P, Vinarova E, Dostal T et al. 1974. Family History of Manic-Depressive and Endogenous Depressive Patients and Clinical Effect of Treatment with Lithium. *Activitas Nervosa Superior (Praha),* 16:194–195.

Index